OSWAL – GURUKUL

MOST LIKELY

ICSE QUESTION BANK

Computer Applications

CLASS X

By

PANEL OF AUTHORS

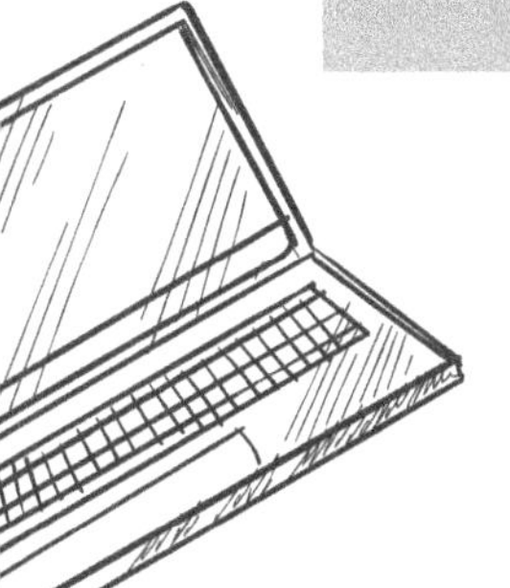

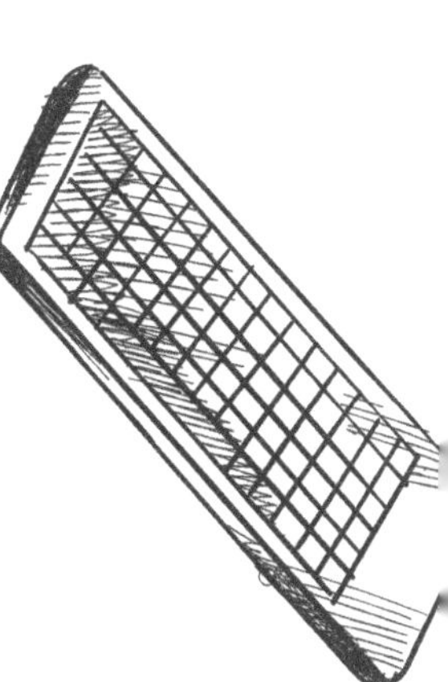

EDITION : 2022

ISBN : 978-93-92563-87-4

PRICE : ₹ 299.00

PRINTED AT :

PUBLISHED BY

OSWAL PUBLISHERS

Head Office : 1/12, Sahitya Kunj, M.G. Road, Agra – 282 002

Phone   : (0562) 2527771-4

Whatsapp : +91 74550 77222

E-mail   : info@oswalpublishers.in

Website   : www.oswalpublishers.com

The cover of this book has been designed using resources from Freepik.com

PREFACE

It is a matter of immense pride for us to present our 'MOST LIKELY ICSE QUESTION BANK' series, especially prepared for students appearing for Board examinations in the oncoming year.

This book is a perfect capsule for building self-confidence during exam. preparation. Based on chunking strategy, the 'Categorywise–Chapterwise' format with its exhaustive set of questions allow the students to cover every category in a chapterwise manner.

Covering easy categories first boosts student's self-esteem and the ascending score braces them to take up challenging categories without fear. This prepares the student to see the exam paper as achievable at all times.

With its simple language and style, it is a one-stop solution for smart study. We are confident that the book will enable the candidates to develop a better understanding of the curriculum and help them organize their learning process. This book shall definitely prove to be a fruitful tool for the students and encourage them towards scholastic excellence.

Constructive suggestions for further improvement of the book are always welcome.

Note: Questions marked with '*****' are frequently asked in previous years board examinations.

—Publisher

HOW TO SAVE WATER AT HOME

Turn off the tap when you have wet the tooth-brush or while applying soap to the dishes.

Take short showers. Prefer bucket-bath over shower one.

Soak your dishes first in warm water before cleaning them in running water. This will make the dirt come out much faster.

Leaky faucets can waste upto 20 gallons of water. Keep a close eye on them. Turn them off tightly.

Use broom instead of pipes to clean sidewalks or driveways.

Try watering plants during the early part of the day. Avoid watering them when it is too sunny or windy.

For harvesting rainwater use barrels or drums at the rooftop.

Avoid unnecessary throwing or splashing of water. Drink it to the last drop.

Wash your car manually instead of using a pipe.

Be conscious of the leaky washbasins/sinks.

Make use the waste water for cleaning floors.

Collected rainwater can be used for plants as it is rich in minerals.

CONTENTS

Note: Questions marked with '*****' are frequently asked in previous years board examinations.

SUGGESTIONS FOR STUDENTS

1. Follow the concepts given in the scope of the syllabus.

2. Clarify the concepts and practise them both, on the paper and on the computer.

3. Solve a lot of problems based on all the concepts.

4. Learn the syntax and working of every construct properly, with suitable examples.

5. Comprehend the key terms/definitions and then learn.

6. Practise Library class and its various functions. Check its output on the computer to understand their working.

7. Develop the habit to do dry run of a program, which you write. This will help in better understanding of concepts and aid in solving questions.

8. Apply simple logic in programs to get desired output.

9. Complete the assignments and cross check on the computer for their proper working. Get the assignments checked by your teacher.

10. Solve previous years' ICSE question papers to understand the types of questions asked and how to attempt an ICSE question paper.

11. Check output-based questions on the computer.

12. Design your own questions for string functions, math functions, loops - for, while, do while, etc.

13. Check for the logic for different variety of numbers-based questions and develop a logic for the same.

14. Do not resort to rote learning this subject but understand and practise the concepts learnt regularly.

15. Follow a proper study schedule when preparing for the examination.

16. After writing the program, dry run it with different inputs.

17. Write variable description /Mnemonic codes for every program.

18. Read the questions carefully and write the answers according to their requirements.

19. Explain programs using Mnemonic variables and comments.

20. Utilize the reading time to clearly understand the nature of the question.

Word of Advice

Chapter 1. Revision of Class IX Syllabus

Topics Found difficult By Students
- ➢ Use of Math.max() and Math.abs().
- ➢ Variable declaration with initial value.
- ➢ Type casting
- ➢ Program for printing the series (0, 7, 26, 63...).
- ➢ Dividing the four-digit number into two halves.
- ➢ Principles and features.
- ➢ Bits and Bytes.
- ➢ Name of different tokens.
- ➢ Conversion of data type.
- ➢ Continue statement.
- ➢ Declaration of instance variables and their initialisation.
- ➢ Generation of UNICODE characters.
- ➢ Library functions - its appropriate use.
- ➢ Menu driven program with pattern printing.
- ➢ Identifying the return data type of the library functions-print( ) and println( )
- ➢ Confusion in the use of print() and println() functions.
- ➢ Conversion of if-else –if to switch-case
- ➢ Output questions.
- ➢ Compare To() function and its working.
- ➢ Syntax of switch-case and array declaration and initialization.
- ➢ Pattern printing using nested loop.
- ➢ Using the key terms in definitions while writing the differences.
- ➢ Output of Math.floor() of negative values.
- ➢ Post increment and shorthand assignment operator.
- ➢ Data types and their sizes
- ➢ Calculation of bill amount and surcharge
- ➢ Output of program code using nested loop
- ➢ Classification of operators
- ➢ Concatenation of strings and spaces using '+' operator
- ➢ Output of program code using nested loop
- ➢ print()/println()
- ➢ next()/next Line()

1. Most of the students wrote the features of Java instead of principles of Object-oriented Programming.
2. Some students wrote operator in place of operand.
3. Many students did not write the storage capacities of data types in bytes correctly. Some students wrote the answers in bits and the unit was written in bytes or vice versa. Some of them wrote the incorrect memory size.
4. Most of the students were unable to differentiate tokens confidently. Many students, instead of keyword wrote access specified/access visibility.
5. Many students wrote character or char instead of character literal/constant.
6. Most of the students got confused between assignment operator and equality/relational operator and wrote the answer as equal to assignment operator.

7. Many students wrote the literal meaning of { } as braces / parenthesis / curly braces.

8. Many students got confused between bidirectional and multiple branching statements. Some students gave appropriate examples but could not explain in detail.

9. For the given question:

    String P = "20", Q ="19";

    int a = Integer.parseInt(P);

    int b = Integer.valueOf(Q);

    System.out.println(a+""+b);

    Some students added and showed the result as 39, some wrote 20 & 19 in two different lines or used '- ' in between 20 and 19 and wrote 19 20 some of them wrote 20 19 within double quotes.

10. Some students, instead of writing the name of different errors i.e syntax, logical and runtime error mentioned the examples of syntax errors only.

11. Many students were unsure about the concept of absolute representation mathematically. Some students used the mathematical operators as x instead of multiplication symbol (*) in the expression.

12. Some students simply converted the ternary operator statement to if...else.

13. For the given question:

    int i;

    for(i=5 ; i>=1 ;i--)

    {

       if(i%2 ==1)

    continue;

    System.out.print(i+ " ")

    }

    Some students gave the output as 4, 2, 1 instead of 4, 2. Several candidates did not have a clear idea of the number of times loop was repeated, when asked about the times loop will execute and wrote the output as 2 instead of 5. Some candidates were not clear about the difference between print () and println( ) and wrote the output as 4 2. A few students were unclear about Math.sqrt and Math.pow functions. Some students wrote syntax of Math. pow () as Math.pow (ax, 5) instead of a*Math. Pow(x, 5).

14. For the Evaluation the expression: IF THE VALUE OF X=2, Y=3 AND Z=1.V=X+ --Z+ Y++ +Y some students were unsure about post and pre-increment or decrement and change of self -value and so miscalculated the value of v. v=2+ - -1+3+4 = 10; v=2+0+3+3 =8; v=2+0+4+4=10.

15. Some students were unable to develop menu driven programs using switch case, some of them wrote two separate programs instead of one menu driven program, some do not have knowledge of type conversion, and some did not accept choice in the menu.

16. Some students wrote Initial and final values of looping statements incorrect. Some of them used twenty-six different print statements to display the Unicode characters and Missed out break statement. In the switch statement, students wrote s in capital terminated with a semicolon i.e. Switch (ch).

17. Many students wrote pattern without nested for loop and used five printing statements for displaying the pattern, some of them used print statement in place of println () statement.

18. Many students wrote the definition of encapsulation, instead the definition of abstraction. Some students did not write important keywords like hiding the background details or showing the essential details.

19. Many students did not put the parenthesis in the denominator. Some students were not familiar with the syntax of sqrt function.

20. Many students seemed to be unaware of the meaning of y+=. Most students made errors while evaluating prefix and post fix operators.

21. In many answer scripts, addition of the initial value of the variable to the evaluated value of the expression was incorrect. Some students added the decremented value to the evaluated value of the expression.

22. For the given question:

    Give the output of the following:

    (i) Math.floor (-4.7)

    (ii) Math.ceil(3.4) + Math.pow(2, 3)

    (i) Many students did not write the negative sign in the answer. Many students did not write the answer in decimals. Some students, instead of writing the answer as -5•0, wrote it as - 4 or - 4•0 or 4•0.

    (ii) Most students wrote 12 as the answer instead of 12•0.

23. Most students were not clear of the use of \n. The common errors made by the students were: Incredible "\n" world, "Incredible" + "\n" + "world".

24. For the given question :
    Convert the following if else if construct into switch case
    if(var==1)
    System.out.println("good");
    else if(var==2)
    System.out.println("better");
    else if(var==3)
    System.out.println("best");
    else
    System.out.println("invalid");
    The common errors made by majority of the students were:
    a. Case 1: if (var==1) or var==1.
    b. Switch var( ); or switch was missing.
    c. Break and default statements were missing.

25. The common errors made by most of the students were:
    a. if(bill>10000)? bill*10.0/100: bill*5.0/100.
    b. The assignment part of the statement was not being written.
    c. 'discount =' - not being written.

26. Most of the students were unable to identify the final limit of the loop. Some students wrote error in the condition of the loop.

27. Some common errors made by the students Output in most cases was written inside the loop and the break and flag statements were not   written.
    a. "Not a pronic number" was not printed,
    b. In the if condition, instead of (i*((i+1)==num), (i*i+1==num) was written.
    c. In the if statement, instead of the relational operator (==), assignment operator (=) was used.
    d. Mentioning that else statement inside the loop results in printing both the statements "Pronic Number" and also "Not a pronic number".

28. In many cases, students were unable to include important keywords like 'super class', 'sub class', 'base class' or 'derived class' etc., while explaining the term 'inheritance'. A few students just mentioned 'sharing properties' or wrote examples without any explanation.

29. Some students confused relational operator with logical operator.

30. Majority of students wrote the size of data types in terms of bits instead of bytes.

31. Some students were unaware about the purpose of %(modulus) operator and wrote that it is a percentage symbol.

32. Some students wrote the first character of the keyword import in uppercase.

33. Many students wrote examples of primitive data type instead of reference data type.

34. Some students were not clear about the concept of loop and use of break within the loop.

35. ASCII codes were not known by the students. The type conversion from char to int was also not clear to the students.

36. Some students did not have any idea of post and pre-increment or decrement operators, change of self -value was not very clear, as a result they miscalculated the value of 'x' as 6 or 5.

37. Some students who were confused with the multiple initialization in the question and wrote improper for loop.

38. The concept of nested loop was not clear to many students. In some cases, horizontal output was given instead of vertical.

39. Some students got confused with the Scanner class functions read () and read Line () with print (), println () and gave vague answers.

40. For the given question:
    Write a program to accept a number and check and display whether it is a spy number or not. (A number is spy if the sum of its digits equals the product of its digits.)
    Example: consider the number 1124, Sum of the digits = 1 + 1 + 2 + 4 = 8
    Product of the digits = 1 × 1 × 2 × 4 = 8

Common errors observed in most of the students were:

a. Used the value given as example in the question instead of accepting the value from the user.

b. Variable used to store sum and product were not initialized or both were initialized to 0.

c. Assignment operator (=) was used to compare two integer values instead of comparison operator(==).

d. Confusion in use of division and modulus operator.

41. For the given question:

Using

switch

statement

'

write a menu driven program

for the following:

(i) To find and display the sum of the series given below:

$$S = x^1 - x^2 + x^3 - x^4 + x^5 \ldots\ldots\ldots\ldots\ldots\ldots - x^{20}$$

(where x = 2)

(ii) To display the following series:

  1 11 111 1111 11111

For an incorrect option, an appropriate error message should be displayed.

A number of students misunderstood the question and wrote two separate programs. Some of the commonly made mistakes were:

(i) Value of variable 'x' was accepted instead of assigning.

(ii) Printed the second series directly using print () statement.

In some cases, break statement was missing and the first letter of default statement was in capital letter.

Chapter 2. Class as the Basis of all Computation

Topics Found difficult By Students
- ➤ Object creation.
- ➤ Keyword for class variable.
- ➤ Creation of object and method call.
- ➤ Output questions.
- ➤ Invoking functions with object
- ➤ Objects and instance of a class

1. The concept of object and class was not clear to many students. In some cases, the reason was not clear and vague answers were given.

Chapter 3. User - defined Methods

Topics Found difficult By Students
- ➤ Variable declaration with initial value.
- ➤ Return type of different functions.
- ➤ Declaration of instance variables and their initialisation.
- ➤ Output questions.
- ➤ Return a value from a user-defined function.
- ➤ How to convert first character of a word to uppercase after space.
- ➤ Calculation of bill amount and surcharge

1. Some students were confused between actual and formal parameters. A few students repeated the same words of the question.

2. Some students did errors **in void series (int x, int n) – To display the sum of the series given: x1 + x2 + x3 + ... xn terms,** instead of declaring the instance variables as global variables, declared and initialized in the constructor.

3. Most students were not clear about the concept of default constructor.

4. Some students initialised with some values instead of with default values.

5. Several students were able to write the if statements correctly but were unable to calculate the amount as cost - dis.

6. A number of students used different function names other than those specified in the question.

7. Several students, instead of accepting data by using methods of Scanner class, used a function with arguments.

8. A large number of students did not use the variable names as per the question. In some answer scripts, syntax of object creation and function calling statements were incorrect.

9. A few students accepted the data in the main function and passed as arguments to the input () function.

10. A few students, instead of directly calculating discount, calculated it as a slab.

11. The concept of overloading was not clear to some students.

12. The common errors made by them are they used Different functions with different names; Single function was used to define all the three logics.

13. Different function name, i.e., other than series () was used.

14. Instead of print statement students used return statement in the first function the variable sum was not declared.

15. Sum of the series was not found, only each term of the series was printed.

16. Several students did not declare the variable sum as double. Many students did not declare it at all.

17. Some students in the for loop, instead of i=2, wrote i=1. Some students wrote Output statement inside for loop.

18. A few students did not calculate the sum of the series.

19. Many students could not write the prototype of the function given in the question.

20. For the given question:

Design a class RailwayTicket with following description :

Instance variables/data members :

String name	:	**To store the name of the customer**
String coach	:	**To store the type of coach customer wants to travel**
long mobno	:	**To store customer's mobile number**
int amt	:	**To store basic amount of ticket**
int totalamt	:	**To store the amount to be paid after updating the original amount**

Member methods :

void accept() – **To take input for name, coach, mobile number and amount.**

void update() – **To update the amount as per the coach selected (extra amount to be added in the amount as follows)**

Type of Coaches	Amount
First_AC	700
Second_AC	500
Third_AC	250
Sleeper	None

void display() – **To display all details of a customer such as name, coach, total amount and mobile number.**

Write a main method to create an object of the class and call the above member methods.

Various types of errors were committed in this question by many students, namely:

a. Used a different class name other than the one given in the question.

b. Variable declaration was done at many places i.e. immediately after class and also inside accept()

c. Function names and variable names were different from the ones asked in the question.

d. The 'totalamt' which was to be calculated was accepted from the user.

e. Update() function.

f. Syntax error while writing input statement e.g. nextInt() - which letter to be written in capital.

g. While comparing types of coaches, words were not written within double quotes.

h. Calculation of extra amount.

i. Syntax errors in the object creation and function call statement.

21. For the given question:

Design a class to overload a function volume() as follows:

(i) double volume (double R) – with radius (R) as an argument, returns the volume of sphere using the formula.

   $V = 4/3 \times 22/7 \times R3$

(ii) double volume (double H, double R) – with height(H) and radius(R) as the arguments, returns the volume of a cylinder using the formula.

   $V = 22/7 \times R2 \times H$

(iii) double volume (double L, double B, double H) – with length(L), breadth(B) and Height(H) as the arguments, returns the volume of a cuboid using the formula.

   $V = L \times B \times H$

Few general mistakes were observed in all the three functions:

a. Declaration of the variable V, was missing.

b. Void was used in the prototype, but return statement was used in the body of the function.

c. Double was used in the prototype, but System.out.println() was used in the body of the function and 'return' statement was missing.

d. Void with System.out.println() was used. Though it shows no error, the combination is not as per the requirement in the question.

e. In the keyword return R was capital.

f. In the formula, instead of R*R*R, R3 was written.

g. Function name was not as per the question.

h. Function overloading concept was not followed.

i. Three different functions with different names were used.

22. Few students were not aware of 'pass by value' and 'pass by reference' concepts.

23. For the given question:

Define a class Electric Bill with the following specifications:

class : ElectricBill

Instance variables / data member:

String n – to store the name of the customer

int units – to store the number of units consumed

double bill – to store the amount to be paid

Member methods:

void accept( ) – to accept the name of the customer and number of units consumed

void calculate( ) – to calculate the bill as per the following tariff:

Number of units	Rate per unit
First 100 units	Rs.2.00
Next 200 units	Rs.3.00
Above 300 units	Rs.5.00

A surcharge of 2.5% charged if the number of units consumed is above 300 units.

void print ( ) -   To print the details as follows:

        Name of the customer: ....

        Number of units consumed: ....

        Bill amount: ....

Write a main method to create an object of the class and call the above member methods.

Various types of errors were committed in this question by many students, namely:

a. Used a different class name other than the one given in the question.

b. A single function was used instead of the ones asked for in the question.

c. Instance variables were not declared in the proper place.

d. Calculation of bill amount for units above 300 was incorrect.

e. Surcharge calculation was not done properly.

f. Syntax errors in the object creation and function call statement.

24. Common mistakes observed were:

a. Few students used separate programs or two functions with different names.

b. Functions were called without passing required arguments and accepted values as inputs inside the function body.

c. Counter variable was not declared and initialized as 0. In some cases, counter was not incremented.

d. Conversion of string into lowercase was not done.

e. Single quotes were missing in character literals a,e,i,o,u .

f. String function charAt() was used without a String object.

Chapter 4. Constructor

Topics Found difficult By Students
➤ Constructor concept.
➤ Output questions.

1. Some students wrote that constructor is used to construct objects, or it is used to make the program easier.
2. Some students were unable to write the difference between constructor and function correctly.

Chapter 5. Library Classes

Topics Found difficult By Students
➤ Type casting
➤ Conversion of data type.
➤ Library functions - its appropriate use.
➤ Output questions.
➤ Converting numeric string into an integer value.

1. Many students were not clear about the difference between the data type and wrapper classes. Some students wrote the data type and result in Uppercase.
2. Students were unable to understand the implicit conversion.
3. Many students identified the data type but while writing the answer committed errors. They wrote the term character/ Character instead of char.
4. Several students were not aware of string concatenation using '+' operator .

Chapter 6. Encapsulation

1. Some students were unable to write the return type in a method header/prototype.
2. Most students wrote very general answers for public members as they can be seen by everyone or shown to or used by everyone or public premises. For private member, some wrote they cannot be seen by everyone or only user can see or use, or everything is not shown or private premises.

Chapter 7. Arrays

> *Topics Found difficult By Students*
> - Loops for sorting elements in an array.
> - Sorting technique (inner loop condition).
> - Arrays used with commercial / calculation-based programs.
> - Output questions.
> - Syntax of switch-case and array declaration and initialization.
> - Sorting strings
> - Index of an array

1. Some students wrote two full programs instead of the difference between the linear search and the binary search technique. Some students wrote the difference between bubble sort and selection sort.

2. Majority of the students made an error in the counting of array index. Several students were unclear about array subscripts. Some students stated the array index counting from 1 instead of from 0. A few students wrote the answer in capital letter.

3. Majority of the students got confused with length and length () method. Many students found the length of the last element i.e. Big Data instead of finding the length of the array.

4. Some of the common mistakes were observed by the students i.e. Array was not created properly and input was written without using a loop or String input been taken.

5. In sorting part, outer loop was written as - for (int i=1;i<=15;i++) inner loop - for(int j=0 ; j<=15 ; j++).

6. Syntax of the method to input value into array being incorrect a[ ] =sc.next() or nextint();.

7. Some students wrote the types of searching and sorting instead of writing their differences. Few students used the same words as given in the question i.e. searching means to search something and sorting means sorting data.

8. For the given question:

   Write a menu driven program to display the pattern as per user's choice.

Pattern 1	Pattern 2
ABCDE	B
ABCD	LL
ABC	UUU
AB	EEEE
A	

   For an incorrect option, an appropriate error message should be displayed.

   Most students attempted well barring a few exceptions who showed following mistakes :

   a. Menu was not displayed.

   b. Input for choice was not taken.

   c. Pattern printing was done using multiple print statements.

   d. Nested loop logic was not used.

   e. To start with new line,println( ) was missing,.

   f. - ASCII value was used to print ABCDE but was not converted properly. (Loop value started   with 65 and was checked for <= 69, but conversion to character was incorrect).

   g. Two separate classes were written instead of one.

   h. In the statements, switch and default. first character s and d were in capital letters.

9. For the given question:

   Write a program to accept name and total marks of N number of students in two single subscript array name [ ] and totalmarks [ ].

   Calculate and print:

   (i) The average of the total marks obtained by N number of students.

       [average = (sum of total marks of all the students)/N]

(ii) Deviation of each student's total marks with the average.

[deviation = total marks of a student – average]

Only a few students could not attempt it correctly due to following miscues:

a. Value of N (size of the array) was taken after arrays, name and total marks were created.

b. While accepting the values into the array, the index number was missing. Instead of name[i], students wrote name[]= sc.next().

c. All operations i.e. input, calculating an average and deviation was done in one Loop.

d. The average of the total marks obtained by N number of students was calculated inside for loop.

e. Deviation of each student's total marks with average marks was not Displayed, rather it was printed outside for loop.

10. For the given question:

Write a program to input integer elements into an array of size 20 and perform the following operations:

(i) Display largest number from the array.

(ii) Display smallest number from the array.

(iii) Display sum of all the elements of the array.

Few general mistakes were observed:

a. Syntax error in declaring or creating an array.

b. Array elements were not accepted from the user but assigned.

c. Initialization of the variables max, min, and sum were not done properly. Some students initialized the variables within the loop.

d. Loop was not formed correctly.

   (for i=0;i<=20;i++)

11. For the given question:

Write a program to input forty words in an array. Arrange these words in descending order of alphabets, using selection sort technique. Print the sorted array.

Common mistakes observed were:

a. Integer array was declared instead of String array.

b. Most students made Syntax error in declaration of an array.

c. Declaration of temporary variable as an integer type instead of String type.

d. Some students gave incorrect limits for inner and outer loops.

e. Compare To() method was not used.

f. Used other methods of sorting instead of Selection sort.

g. Array elements were sorted in ascending order in place of descending order.

h. Printing of sorted elements was not done.

Chapter 8. String Handling

Topics Found difficult By Students

➢ Extraction of character using substring ().

➢ Extraction of word.

➢ Sorting technique (inner loop condition).

➢ Library functions - its appropriate use.

➢ Output questions.

➢ Compare To() function and its working.

➢ String and Character functions.

➢ How to convert first character of a word to uppercase after space.

➢ Sorting strings

➢ Sorting techniques

➢ Usage of library function, substring () and Math.min()

1. Some students were not clear about the working of substring (). A few students got confused with both print statements and so jumbled up the outputs

2. For the given question:

   Write a program to input a sentence and convert it into uppercase and count and display the total number of words starting with a letter 'A'.

   Example:

   Sample Input: ADVANCEMENT AND APPLICATION OF INFORMATION TECHNOLOGY ARE EVER CHANGING.

   Sample Output: Total number of words starting with letter 'A' = 4.

   Some students wrote variety of logic in the program. The common errors observed in this program were:

   a. Not added a space before or after the string.

   b. Extracting the part of the string was not done correctly.

   c. Instead of checking for A, a character was accepted and checked for that character.

   d. Instead of nextLine(), next() was written.

   e. In the for loop, index started from 1 instead of 0. For (int i=1; i<=s.length();i++).

   f. Counter variable was not initialised to 0.

   g. The counter variable was initialised inside for loop.

   h. Output statement was written inside for loop to display count.

   i. Next character after space was taken as ch+1.

   j. String functions were called/invoked without String Variable/object.

3. Most students were not clear about the difference between Character class functions and String functions. Most of the students were not aware that, is UpperCase() happens to be a Character class function.

4. The concept of string and usage of string functions were not clear to many students.

5. Many students wrote return type as String, instead of writing Boolean.

6. Many students wrote return type as float or integer. Some students mentioned data types with the first letter in uppercase.

7. In few answer scripts only the first occurrence of E was converted.

8. Some students, instead of writing false as the answer, wrote 5>6. Some students were unclear whether the position of second argument was included in the output or not. Some students extracted the character at third index also.

9. For the given question:

   Write a program in Java to accept a string in lower case and change the first letter of every word to upper case. Display the new string.

   Sample input: we are in cyber world

   Sample output: We Are In Cyber World

   Some of the commonly made mistakes were:

   a. Not taking care of the index of charAt() or substring() function.

   b. Incorrect initial and final values of the for loop- forr(int i=1; i<=l;i++).

   c. Accessing first character after space was done by writing (ch+1).

   d. Converting the first character after space was done as:

   ch.toUpperCase() or (ch+1).toUpperCase()

   e. Displaying output without space between the words.

   f. Getting an incorrect output as only the first character was converted and displayed.

Chapter at a Glance | Set 1 |

- Java is a general purpose, object oriented programming language developed by Sun Micro systems of USA in 1991.

  we can develop two types of Java programs :
  (i) Stand alone applications.
  (ii) Web applets.
- **Stand alone applications** are programs written in Java to carry out certain tasks on a stand alone local computer. In fact, Java can be used to develop programs of all kinds of applications, which earlier, were developed using languages like C and C++.

  Java programs involves 2 steps :
  (i) Compiling source code into byte code using javac compiler.
  (ii) Executing the byte code program using java interpreter.
- **Applets** are small Java programs developed for internet applications. An applet located on a distant computer (server)can be down loaded via internet and executed on a local computer (client) using a Java-enable web browser.
- Blue J. is a development environment to write and compile Java programs. It is developed by Monash University, Australia, in Java by Blue J requires JDK 1.3 or above (Java dovelopment kit), it is window based or band software.
- **Working in Blue J**

  To start Blue J clicked at Start ➢ programs ➢ Blue J.

  To write a Java program, one need to follow the given steps :
  (i) Create a Blue J project.
  (ii) Add a new class to the project.
  (iii) Edit a class code.
  (iv) Compile the source code.
  (v) Now save the code.

  Execution in Blue J is usually done by creating an object first and then invoking any of object's (public) methods.
- **Key Features :**
  (i) Output from the console window can be saved as a text file.
  (ii) Source code from the class can be printed.

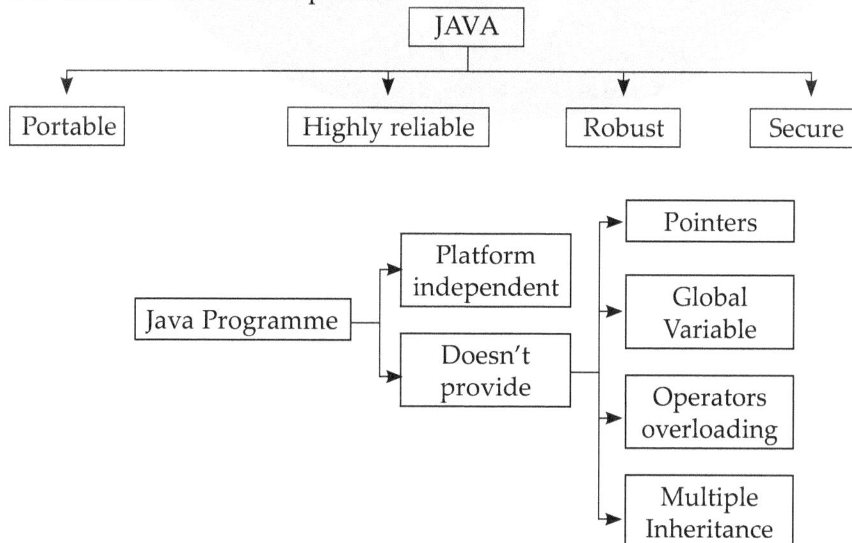

➤ **Java Statements**

The statements in Java are like sentences in natural language. A statement is an executable combination of token ending with a semicolons (;) mark. Statements are usually executed in sequence in order in which they appear.

Chapter 2. Class as the Basis of all Computation

➤ Object oriented programming is an approach that provides, a way of modularizing programs by creating partitioned memory area for both data and functions, that can be used as templates for creating copies of such modules on demand.

➤ **What is Class**

A class represents a set of common properties and behaviours shared by all objects.

➤ **Classes as Abstractions for Sets of Objects**

(i)   A class is a named software representation for an abstraction.

(ii) An object is a distinct instance of a given class that is structurally identical to all instances of that class.

(iii) Software code in OOP is written to define classes, instantiate objects, and manipulate these objects.

➤ **Class as Object Factory**

An object factory is a producer of objects. It accepts some information about how to create an object, such as values depicting its state and then returns an instance of that object.

Class is an object maker or object factory as it contains all the statements needed to create an object, its attributes as well as the statements to describe the operations that the object will be able to perform. By utilizing this and by providing initial values depicting an object's state, new objects can be created from the class as and when required.

➤ **Object :**

An object is a software bundle of variables and related methods.

The object can have state and behavior, which is expressed by the variables and methods within that object.

➤ It consists of 2 parts :

(i)   Data structure, referred to as attributes.

(ii) Processes that may correctly change data structure, referred to as functions or methods.

➤ **Example :** A person object have the following attributes :

(i)   First name

(ii) Last name

(iii) Age

(iv) Weight.

➤ **Messages :** Software objects interact and communicate with each other by sending messages to each other.

➤ **Characteristics of Objects**

The real world objects share two characteristics, state and behavior :

(i)   **State :** An object can be in many states. The state is also called as attribute or properties of object.

(ii) **Behavior :** The capability of an object to do something is its behavior.

(iii) **Identity :** The name associated with an object helps in identifying the object.

➤ **OOPs Principles**

There are four OOP's principles which are as follows :

(i)   **Encapsulation :** It is the mechanism that binds code and the data it manipulates together.

(ii) **Inheritance :** This is the process of creating new classes called derived classes from existing classes called super classes.

(iii) **Polymorphism :** The ability to take more than one form is called polymorphism for example a method can perform different-different operations with different type or no. of arguments. It allows two or more classes to respond to the same method in different ways.

(iv) **Abstraction :** The concept of giving only required information without showing internal and implementation detail, is called abstraction.

➢ **Variable**
   (i)   A variable is a memory location to store any data or constant.
   (ii) The declaration of a variable generally takes the following form type variablename;
➢ **Constants**
   A constant is a fixed value which can not be change during the execution of program.
➢ **Constants are of the following type :**
   Integer constant　　: 12, 2000, – 10 etc.
   Real constant　　　: 0.00012, – 2.8707, 29.287, – 0.28
   Character constants : 'A', '–', '", '.'
   String constants　　: "RAM", "A/49, Kamla Nagar, Agra
   　　　　　　　　　　　"12 28"
   boolean constant　　: true, false.
➢ **Concept of Data Type**
   Java like any other language provides ways and facilitates to handle different types of data by providing data types.
➢ Data types are means to identify the type of data and associated operators of handling it.
➢ Java data types are of two types :
   (i)   Primitive data type.
   (ii) Derived data type.
➢ **Primitive Data Type**
   Primitive data types are also called basic data types. These are inbuilt data types available in Java. These data types are used to define other derived data types.
➢ Java support the following four types of primitive data types :
   (i)   **Numeric Integral Types :** The data types that are used to store numeric values falls under this sub-category.

Type	Size	Minimum Value	Maximum Value
byte	One byte	—128	127
short	Two bytes	—32,768	32,767
int	Four bytes	—2,147,483,648	2,147,483,647
long	Eight bytes	—9,223,372,036,854,775,808	9,223,372,036,854,775,807

   (ii) **Fractional Numeric Type :** These data types can store fractional numbers i.e., numbers having decimal points.

Type	Size	Minimum Value	Maximum Value
float	4 bytes	3.4e—038	3.4e + 038
double	8 bytes	1.7e—308	1.7e + 308

   (iii) **Character Type :** It is used to store characters.

Type	Size	Minimum Value	Maximum Value
char	16 bits (2 bytes)	Single character	0 to 65.536

   (iv) Boolean Type : It is used to represent a single True/False value.

Type	Size	Minimum Value	Maximum Value
boolean	8 bits (used only 1 bit)	Logical or boolean values	True or False

➢ **Derived data types :** These data types also called compound or user defined data types. These are defined or derived by primitive data type.
➢ Classes, Arrays and Interfaces are examples of derived data type.
➢ **Class as a Composite Type**
   The data types that are based on fundamental or primitive data types are known as composite data types. Since these data types are created by users these are also known as user-defined data types.
➢ **Java provides the following operators :**
   (i)   Arithmetic operators : These operators perform arithmetical operations.

(ii) Relational operator : These operators are used to compare the values.

(iii) Logical operators : They perform logical operations.

(iv) Assignment operators : They assign one value to another.

(v) Shift operators : They performs bit manipulation on data by shifting the bits of its first cperald right or left. (>>, <<, >>>)

(vi) Bitwise operators : These operators work with integral types i.e., byte, short; int and log type. (&, !, ↑, –)

(vii)Conditional or ternary operaators : It stores value depending open conditions.

      condition ? Value 1 : Value 2 :

➢ Other operators (P:, [ ], –, (Parameters), (type), new, instance of).

(i) Arithmetic Operators :

Operators	Description	Example
+	Addition	a + b
–	Subtraction	a – b
×	Multipication	a × b
/	Division	a / b
%	Modulus	a % b

(ii) Relational Operators :

Operators	Description	Example
= =	check for equality	a = = b
! =	not equal to	a ! = b
<	less than	a < b
>	greater than	a > b
< =	less than or equal to	a < = b
> =	greater than or equal to	a > = b

(iii) Logical Operators :

Operators	Description	Example
&&	And	opr 1 && opr 2
||	Or	opr 1 || opr 2
!	Not	! opr 1

(iv) Assignment Operators :

Operators	Description	Example
=	equal to	$a = 7$
+ =	add to the variable	$a + = 5$ means $a = a + 5$
– =	subtract from variable	$a – = 5$ means $a = a – 5$
× =	multiply to variable	$a × = 2$ means $a = a × 2$
/ =	divide into variable	$a / = 2$ means $a = a/2$
% =	Modulus by variable	$a \% = 2$ means $a = a \% 5$

➢ **Operation on Primitive Data types**

Primitive data type operations deal only with value i.e., actual read value (rvalue). That is, they store the read value directly in them.

➢ **Expressions**

An expression in Java is any valid combination of operators, constants and variables i.e., a legal combination of Java tokens.

The expressions in Java can be of any type :

(i) Arithmetic expression.

(ii) Relational expression.

(iii) Compound expressions, etc.

➢ Arithmetic expressions can be of the following types :

(i) Pure integer expressions, and

(ii) Pure real expressions.

(iii) Mixed expression.

➤ In pure expressions, all the operands are of same type and in mixed expressions the operands are of mixed type i.e., mixture of real and integer expressions.

Chapter 3. User - defined Methods

➤ **Function**

Function can be defined as a named unit of a group of program statements. This unit can be invoked from other parts of the program.

➤ **Function Definition :** The general form of a function definition is as given below :

[access-specifier] [modifier] return-type function-name (parameter list)
{

    body of the function

}

➤ **Function Prototype :** A function prototype is the first line of the function definition that tells the program about the type of the value returned by the function and the number and type of arguments to be passed into function.

➤ **Function Signature :** A function signature basically refers to the number and types of arguments. Function signature and return type makes a function prototype.

➤ **Actual and Formal Parameters**

The parameters that appear in function definition are called formal parameters.

The parameters that appear in function call statement are called actual parameters.

➤ **Arguments to functions**

Arguments to function can be of the following types :

(i)   Primitive data types i.e., char, byte, short, int, long, float, double boolean

(ii) Reference data types i.e., objects or arrays.

➤ **A function is invoked in two manners :** Call by value and call by reference, these are also called as pass by value and pass by reference.

➤ **Pass by Value :** The pass by value method copies the values of actual parameters into the formal parameters, *i.e.,* the function makes its own copy of agrument values and use them, thus original argument values does not changes. In Java all primitive data types are passed by value.

➤ **Pass by Reference :** In this method a reference of arguments are passed to function parameters, no another copy of arguments is created by function. So the changes made on parameters of function, will directly affect the original arguments passed. In java all objects, arrays and other derived data types are passed by reference method.

➤ **Returning from a function**

Returning from a function not only terminates the function's execution but also passes the control back to the calling function.

Generally, a return statement is used to terminate a function whether or not it returns a value.

The return statement is useful in two ways :

(i)   An immediate exit from the function is caused as soon as a return statement is encountered and the control passes back to the function caller.

(ii) It is used to return a value to the calling function.

➤ **Pure and Impure functions**

A pure function is the one that takes objects and/or primitives as arguments but does not modify the objects. The return value of a pure function is either a primitive or a new object created inside the method.

An impure function changes/modifies the state of a received object.

➤ **Function Overloading**

A function name having several definitions in the same scope that are differentiable by the number or types of their arguments, is said to be an overloaded function.

Function overloading not only implements polymorphism but also reduces number of comparisons in a program and thereby makes the program run faster.

Chapter 4. Constructor

➢ **Constructor**

Constructor is a special member function with the same name as its class name, and it is used to initialize the objects of that class with a legal initial value. Constructor has no return type, not even void. Constructor is called automatically when an object of the class is declared.

Defining a constructor : Generally a constructor should be defined under the public section of a class, so that its objects can be created in any function.

➢ Following code fragment defines a constructor

```
class X { int i;
            Public int, j, k;
            Public x ( )
            {
            i = 0;
            j = 0;
            k = 0;    // constructor
            }
            :         // other members
            };
```

➢ **Type of Constructors**

The constructor functions in Java can be of two types. These are :

(i) **Non-Parameterized or Default Constructor :** A constructor that accepts no parameter is called the non-parameterized or default constructors.

    e.g.,   X 01 = new X();

    will create the object 01 of type X by invoking the default constructor.

(ii) **Parameterized Constructor :** A constructor that takes arguments are called parameterized constructor. The parameterized constructors allow us initialize the various data elements of different objects with different values when they are created :

    e.g.,   ABC obj1 = new ABC (13, 11.4, 'P')

➢ This statement will create an object obj 1 of type ABC and invoke the constructor of ABC to initialize obj1 with values 13, 11.4, and 'P'.

Chapter 5. Library Classes

➢ **Simple Input**

Input is any information that is needed by your program to complete its execution. There are many forms that program input may take, such as character input or mouse click, audio input or graphic input or file input etc. System-in refers to an input stream managed by the system class that implements the standard input stream.

➢ **Simple Output**

Output is any information that the program must convey to the user. System.out refers to an output stream managed by the system class that implements the standard output stream. System.out is an instance of the Print Stream class defined in the Java.io package.

➢ **IO Streams**

A source of input data is called an input stream and the output data is called output stream.

Streams can either be byte oriented that reads bytes of data or binary data. Or the streams can be character oriented that use a character encoding scheme to read characters :

➢ **Wrapper Classes**

Wrapper classes wrap the value of a primitive type in an object.

Java has the following wrapper classes-Boolean, byte, integer, float, character, short, long and double.

➢ **String**

In Java, string is a sequence of characters or a group of character once initialized then its contents cannot be modified.

➢ **Creating Strings :** Strings in Java are created by declaring object of string class and initialising it with a string literal e.g., string name = "I am a student";

➢ **Packages**

Packages are containers for classes that are used to keep the class name space compartmentalized.

Java packages are classified into two types :

(i)   Java API package and (ii) User defined package.

The general form of the package statement is:

    package pkg;

e.g., package mypackage

➢ **Import Statement**

The import statement is used to import a specific class or interface into the current file.

e.g., import graphics . circle;

The import statement must be at the beginning of a file before any class or interface definitions and makes the class or interface available for use by the classes and interfaces defined in that file.

➢ **Types of Program Error**

A part of the compiler's job is to analyze the program code for "Correctness". There can be different types of incorretness that can occur in a Java Program.

➢ From the point of view of time/phase of error detection, error – types as :

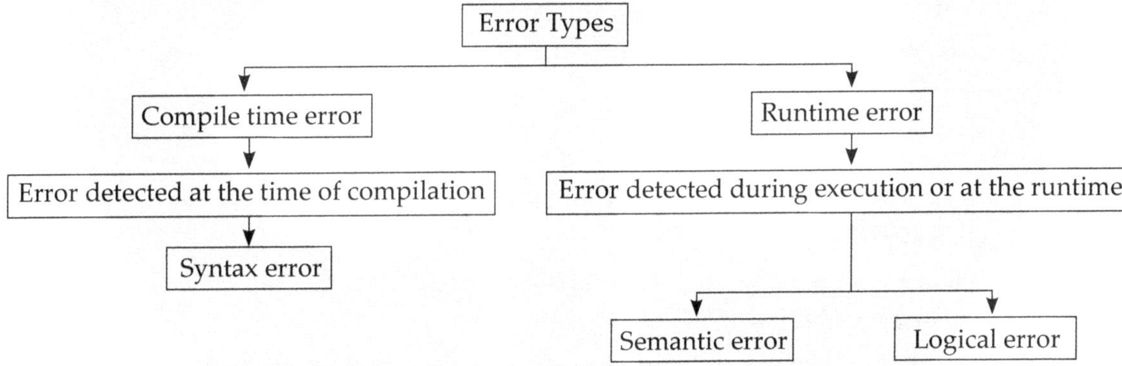

➢ A bunch of bytes stored on some storage device is called file.

➢ Various features supported by Java for file processing are as follows.

➢ **Java Streams**

A stream in Java is a path alongwith data flows. It has a source and a destination which may be physical devices or programs or other streams in the same program. There are two types of stream classes in Java :

(i)   **Byte Stream classes :** Used for Byte oriented input/output. These can be categorized into two-inputstream class and outputstream class.

(ii) **Character Stream Classes :** Character stream classes used for character oriented input/output. These can be also be categorized as-reader classes and writer classes.

➢ **Operations on Files**

➢ With files, one can perform various operations e.g.,

(i)   Obtaining input from a file (File Input)

(ii) Writing output to a file (File Output).

➢ To perform output on text files, following steps are performed :

(i)   Create FileWriter stream for a file to be written onto.

(ii) Connect it to Buffered Writer.

(iii) Connect BufferedWriter to PrintWriter.

(iv) Write text on file using print ()/println().

(v) Once through, close the streams using close ().

➢ To perform input on text files, following steps are performed :

(i)   Create Filereader Stream for a file to be read.

(ii) Connect it to BufferedReader.

(iii) Read text from file using readLine().

(iv) Once through close the file streams close().

➢ To perform output on binary files, following steps are performed :

(i)   Create a FileOutputStream and link it with the file.

(ii) Connect it to DataOutputStream.

(iii) Write data on the file using any of the write() functions.

(iv) Once through close the streams.

➢ To perform input on binary files, following steps are performed :

(i)   Create FileInputStream and link it with file.

(ii) Connect it to a DataInputStream.

(iii) Read data using any of the read () functions.

➢ **String Tokenizer**

A string tokenizer can identify and parse (seggregate) tokens in a string. String Tokenizer class is found in Java.util Package.

String Tokenizer class also provides two methods that are immediately used for processing strings : (i) String Tokenizer method, (ii) Next Token.

➢ **Stream Tokenizer**

A stream tokenizer can identify and parse tokens in a stream, allowing the tokens to be read one at a time.

Chapter 6. Encapsulation

➢ Wrapping up of data and methods into a single unit is called Encapsulation.

➢ **Visibility Modifiers**

Java accomplishes encapsulation through appropriate use of visibility modifiers. These are :

➢ **Public :** It means that anyone can call this method.

➢ **Private :** Means that only the methods in the same class are permitted to use this methods.

➢ **Protected :** Means that methods in this class and methods in any subclasses may use this method.

➢ **Scope and Visibility Rules**

The program part(s) in which a particular piece of code or a data value (e.g., variable) can be accessed is known as the piece-of-code's or variable's scope.

Visibility is a related term, which refers to whether one can use a variable from a given place in the program.

Scope and Visibility Rules

	Scope	Visibility	Purpose
Public classes and variables	public	visible to all classes	Methods and variables of interest to users of the class.
protected classes and variables	protected	visible to classes outside the package that inherit the class, also to all classes in the package.	Methods and variables of interests to third parties who may extend your class.
classes and variables declared with nothing	default	visible to all classes of the package.	Methods and variables involved in cross-class communication within the package.

Private classes and variables	private	visible only within in the classes, not by inheritors, not by other classes in the package.	Variables and methods that should not or would not be changed by someone extending the class. Proper functioning of the class depends on them working precisely as written.
Variables declared inside method bodies or other blocks	local	visible only the block of the method in which the variables were declared.	Temporary working variables.

Chapter 7. Arrays

➢ An array is a collection of data of the same type that are referenced by a common name.

➢ **Types of Arrays**

Arrays are of different types :

(i)   One dimensional arrays.

(ii) Multi-dimensional arrays.

➢ **Declaring Arrays :** Following statements declare an array marks of type int and which can hold 50 elements :

    int marks [ ] = new int [50]; or

    int [ ] marks = new int [50];

➢ **Using Arrays :** An array element may be used in any place where an ordinary variable of the same type may be used.

➢ **Searching in 1-D Arrays**

➢ There are two common search techniques to search for an element in an array. These are as :

(i)   **Linear Search :** In linear search, each element of the array is compared with the given item to be searched for, one by one.

(ii) **Binary Search :** Binary search searches for the given item in a sorted array. The search segment reduces to half at every successive stage.

➢ **Sorting**

Sorting of an array means arranging the array elements in a specified order i.e., either ascending or descending order. The two types of sorting techniques are :

(i)   **Selection Sort :** In selection sort, the smallest key from the remaining unsorted array is searched for and put in the sorted array. This process repeats until the entire array is sorted.

(ii) **Bubble Sort :** In bubble sort, the adjoining values are compared and exchanged if they are not in proper order. This process is repeated until the entire array is sorted.

Chapter 8. String Handling

➢ Statements are the instructions given to the computer to perform any kind of action. The flow of control in a program can be in three ways :

(i)   The sequence construct : Statements gets executed sequentially in this type of construct.

(ii) The selection construct : It means the execution of statement(s) depending upon a condition test.

(iii) The iteration construct : It means repetition of a set-of-statements depending upon condition-test.

➢ **Types of Selection Statements**

Java provides two types of selection statements : If and switch

(i)   The if-else statement tests an expression and depending upon its truth value one of the two sets-of-action is executed. The if-else statement can be nested also :

(ii) The conditional operator ? Can be used as an alternative to if-else.

(iii) Switch statement tests a value against a set of integer or character constants. A switch statement can be nested also.

➢ **Iteration Statements**

The statements that allow a set of instructions to be performed repeatedly are iteration statements. These are also called loops or looping statement.

Java provides three loops :

(i) **The while loop :** It evaluates a test expression before allowing entry into the loop. Its basic format is :

initialisation;

while (test condition)

{

body of the loop

}

A while loop can also be infinite loop, if its loop control variable is not updated within its body. It can also be empty loop, if it contains just a null statement in its body.

(ii) **The do-while loop :** This loop is executed at least once always as it evaluates the test expression at the end of the loop. Its basic form is as :

do

{

body of the loop

} While (testcondition);

(iii) **The for loop :** It is another entry controlled loop that provides a more concise loop control structure. The general form of for loop is :

for (initialisation; test condition; step.)

{

Body of the loop

}

➢ **Jump Statements**

The statements that facilitates the unconditional transfer of program control from one part to another are called jump statements.

Java provides three jump statements :

(i) The return Statement is used to return from a function.

(ii) The break statement can appear in any of the loops and causes the termination of the loop and then the control passes over the statement following the loop containing break.

(iii) The continue statement abandons the current iteration of the loop by skipping over the rest of the statements in the loop body.

❏

Chapter 1. Revision of Class IX Syllabus

1. Name the keyword that :
   (i)   Informs that an error has occurred in an input/output operation.
   (ii) Distinguishes between instance variables and class variables.

Ans. (i)   throws IOException   (ii)   static

2. Write one difference between '/' and '%' operator.

Ans. '/' operator returns the quotient of the two operands when divided while '%' operator returns the remainder of the two operands.

3. Mention two different styles of expressing a comment in a program.

Ans. (i)   // Single line comment   (ii)   /* Multiple Line Comment */

4. What is the wrapping of data and methods in a single unit called ?

Ans. Wrapping of data and methods in a single unit is called Encapsulation.

5. How many types of programs can be developed in Java ?

OR

How many types of Java programs are there ?

Ans. There are two types of programs in Java:
   1.   Stand alone applications and   2.   web applets.

6. Where are the stand alone applications written ?

Ans. Stand alone applications are written in local stand alone computers.

7. State the number of bytes occupied by char and int data types.

Ans. char occupies 2 bytes and int occupies 4 bytes.

8. How do objects interact with one another ?

Ans. Objects interact with each other by message passing.

9. Mention the combination of both data and the functions that operate on that data under a single unit.

Ans. Encapsulation is the combination of both data and the functions that operate on the data under a single unit known as Class.

10. What is an identifiable entity with some characteristics and behaviour?

Ans. Object is an identifiable entity with some characteristics and behaviour.

11. What is the property that allows two or more classes to respond to the same message in different ways?

Ans. Polymorphism is the property that allows two or more classes to respond to the same message in different ways.

12. What is the process by which one object acquires the properties of another object?

Ans. The process by which one object acquires the properties of another object is called inheritance.

13. What is the process of representing essential features without including the background details or explanations?

Ans. Abstraction is the process of representing essential features without including the background details or explanations.

14. What is inheritance?

Ans. Inheritance is the ability of an object of one class to acquire the properties of another (parent) class.

15. Mention a class member representing some behaviour of an object.

Ans. A method is a member function that represents some behaviour of an object.

16. Mention another name for member variables.

Ans. Instance variables.

17. What is JDK?

Ans. JDK is a Java development kit that comes with a collection of tools that are used for developing and running Java programs.

18. How can we start working in BlueJ?

Ans. To start BlueJ on Windows 10 click at start > BlueJ > BlueJ.

19. What is JVM?

Ans. JVM is a virtual processor which interprets and converts bytecode into machine executable code.

20. State the Java concept that is implemented through:

    (i)   a superclass and a subclass.

    (ii)   the act of representing essential features without including the background details.

Ans. (i)   Inheritance.   (ii) Abstraction.

21. Define encapsulation.

Ans. Encapsulation : The wrapping up of data and methods into a single unit called class is known as encapsulation.

22. Name any two OOP's principles.

Ans. (i)   Encapsulation.   (ii) Polymorphism.

23. Define abstraction ?

Ans. Abstraction refers to the act of representing essential features without including the background details or explanations.

24. Name the package that contains Scanner class.

Ans. java.util

25. What is the escape sequence used as a new line character ?

Ans. '\n'

26. A set of valid characters that a language can recognize.

Ans. Valid characters recognized by a language consists of Alphabets (A-Z, a-z), Numerals (0-9) and special characters (?, @, }, % etc.)

27. Word carrying special meaning and purpose for the complier.

Ans. Keyword.

28. User defined names for different parts of program.

Ans. Identifiers.

29. Data items that never change their value during a program run.

Ans. Literals or contants.

30. The region of program within which a variable is accessible.

Ans. Scope.

31. Smallest individual unit in a program.

Ans. Token.

32. Keyword that turns a variable declaration into a constant declaration.

Ans. Final.

33. Variables which are created once for the entire class and are shared by all the objects.

Ans. Static or class variables.

34. A symbolic name for a computer memory location.

Ans. Variable.

35. Character set used in Java are called.

Ans. Unicode.

36. What is a literal?

OR

What are constants ?

Ans. Literal/Constants in Java refer to fixed values that do not change during the execution of a program.

37. Name the extension used to name java files ?

Ans. Extension used to name java files is java.

38. Arrange following data types in ascending order of their sizes : double, int, char, boolean short.

Ans. Boolean, char, short, int, double.

39. What is the scope of a variable ?

Ans. The scope of a variable means the block of the code, in which the variable can be accessed.

40. State the number of bytes occupied by char and int data types.

Ans. Char occupies 2 bytes and int occupies 4 bytes.

41. Objects of operations are referred as.

Ans. Operands.

42. Operators used in mathematical expressions.

Ans. Arithmetic operators.

43. The operator used after the variable as n++.

Ans. Post increment operator.

44. The operator used before the variable as ++n

Ans. Pre increment operator.

45. Conditional operator is also called.

Ans. Ternary operator.

46. What changes the precedence of the operations ?

Ans. Parantheses.

47. Name the type of error (syntax, runtime or logical error) in each case given below:

    (i)   Division by a variable that contains a value of zero.

    (ii) Multiplication operator used when the operation should be division.

    (iii) Missing semicolon

Ans. (i)   Runtime error.   (ii) Logical error   (iii) Syntax error.

48. What is the use of ! (Not) operator ?

Ans. The logical Not operater ! is used to negate the result of an expression. This is a unary operator.

Expression	Result
ture	false
false	true

49. Write following expressions in shorthand form:

    (i)   a = a * 6   (ii) b = b + 10;

Ans. (i)   a *= 6;   (ii) b += 10;

50. The increment operator increases the value of a variable by how much ?

Ans. The increment operator increases the value of a variable by 1.

51. What will be the value of x = ((1/0.0) – (1/– 0.0))?

Ans. Infinity.

52. Which of the following are valid comments ?

    (i)   /* comment */   (ii) /* comment   (iii) // comment   (iv) */ comment */

Ans. (i)   /*comment */ and   (iii) //comment are valid comments.

53. Operators with higher precedence are evaluated before operators with relatively lower precedence. Arrange the operators given below in order of higher precedence to lower precedence.

    (i)   &&   (ii) %   (iii) >=   (iv) ++

Ans. ++, %, >= , &&

54. Name the operators listed below:

    (i)   <   (ii) ++   (iii) &&   (iv) ? :

Ans. (i)   < is a Relational / Comparison operator.

     (ii)   ++ is a Unary increment operator.

     (iii) && is a Logical AND operator.

     (iv)   ? : is a Conditional / Ternary operator.

55. What is a decrement operator ? Explain with an example.

Ans. The operator '– –' is called the decrement operator. It can be used in pre-decrement or post- decrement form. It decreses the value of the variable by 1.

For example:

i – –;

– –a;

56. Write the exception thrown by the read() method of InputStream class ?

Ans. IOException.

57. Name a statement which is not a legal programming construct.

Ans. Jumping statement.

58. Which clause is optional in switch case ?

Ans. Default.

59. What is the rule of nested statements ?

Ans. Inner statements should end before outer statements.

60. If statement can also be alternatively represented through.

Ans. Ternary operator.

61. While is a conditional or looping statement.

Ans. Looping statement.

62. Absence of which statement causes a fall-through in a switch statement.

Ans. Break.

63. Name the data types used in switch case.

Ans. int, char.

64. Name two statements in java that support jumping.

Ans. Break and continue.

65. Name the iteration statements in Java.

Ans. For, while, do-while.

66. Name two decision making statements.

Ans. If and switch case.

67. What is an infinite loop ? Give an example.

Ans. The loop which executes endlessly without having any exit condition is called an infinite loop.

For example:

```
int i = 0;
while(1)
{
    i++;
    System.out.println(i);
}
```

68. Define Java byte code.*

Ans. It is a machine instruction for java processor chip called JVM.

69. What is an operator? Name any two types of operators used in Java.*

Ans. Operator is a symbol which specifies the type of operation to be performed on the operands.

Ex: Arithmetic Operator (+,-,*,/,%) or Relational operator(>,<,>=,<=, ==, !=) etc.

70. What is the use of import statement in Java?*

Ans. Import keyword is used to include predefined classes and functions in our program which are available in java.

import java.util.*; will include all the classes of util package in our program.

---

71. Write the output of the following statement:*

System.out.println("A picture is worth \t \"A thousand words.\" ");

Ans. A picture is worth " A thousand words."

72. Name any two basic principles of Object-oriented Programming.*

Ans. Encapsulation and Abstraction.

73. Write the memory capacity (storage size) of short and float data type in bytes.*

Ans. short requires 16 bits or two(2) bytes of storage whereas float requires 32 bits or four(4) bytes of storage.

74. What are the various types of errors in Java ?*

Ans. Compile time errors, Runtime errors and Logical errors.

Chapter 2. Class as the Basis of all Computation

1. Why is class known as an object factory ?

Ans. A number of objects can be created by using a class. Each object is referred to as an instance of the class. It contains the same attributes and methods which are defined inside the class. Therefore, a class is known as an object factory.

2. How can the state of an object be represented ?

Ans. The state of an object is represented through the values/attributes of its characteristics at a given point of time.

3. What does the values of member variables define ?

Ans. The values of member variables define the state of an object.

4. What is the region within which a variable/piece-of-code is accessible called ?

Ans. Scope of a variable.

5. What is a variable declared inside a method or block known as ?

Ans. A variable declared inside a method or block is called a local variable.

6. Define a variable's scope.

Ans. The program part(s) in which a particular piece-of-code or a data value (e.g., variable) can be accessed is known as the variable's scope.

7. How is the behaviour of an object represented?

Ans. The behaviour of an object is represented through methods or functions.

8. Why is an object called an instance of a class ?

Ans. Since an object contains all the necessary information (Data members and member functions) specified inside the class, therefore, it is known as the instance of a class.

9. What is a class variable which is available to the entire class known as ?

OR

Data or variables defined inside a class?

Ans. Class variable which is available to the entire class is known as an instance variable.

10. User defined type conversion is called.

Ans. Type casting.

11. Code contained within a class.

Ans. Methods.

12. State the two kinds of data types.

Ans. Primitive data types, Non-Primitive/Composite data types.

13. Give one example each of a primitive data type and a composite data type.

Ans. int, short are primitive data types and array, classes are the examples of composite data types.

14. Classify the following as primitive or non-primitive data types:

| (i)   char | (ii) arrays | (iii) int | (iv) classes |

Ans. primitive:

| (i)   char, | (iii) int non-primitive |
| (ii) arrays, | (iv) classes |

15. Name the primitive data type in Java that is:
    (i) a 64-bit integer and is used when you need a range of values wider than those provided by int.
    (ii) a single 16-bit Unicode character whose default value is '\u0000'.

Ans. (i) long   (ii) char

16. State one difference between the floating point literals float and double.

Ans. float occupies 4 bytes of storage whereas double occupies 8 bytes of storage.

17. Which of the following are primitive data types?*

| (i)   double | (ii) String | (iii) Char | (iv) Integer |

Ans. (i) double, char are primitive data types.

Chapter 3. User - Defined Methods

1. What are methods ?

Ans. A method defines the behaviour of a class. Each method consists of a set of instructions to perform a specific task.

2. Name the following:
    (i) A keyword used to call a package in the program.
    (ii) Any one reference data type.

Ans. (i) import   (ii) class/object

3. What is the role of the keyword void in declaring functions ?

Ans. Void means no data type. In function declaration it is used to indicate that the function will not return any value.

4. If a function contains several return statements, how many of them will be executed ?

Ans. Only one.

5. Which OOP principle implements function overriding ?

Ans. Polymorphism.

6. In Java, methods reside in...............

Ans. Classes.

7. Function not returning any value has return type as.

Ans. Void.

8. The number and type of arguments of a function are known as.

Ans. Function signature.

9. How many value can a function return ?

Ans. A function returns only one value.

10. Parameters appearing in function definition is known as.

Ans. Formal parameters.

11. The function call in which the data in actual parameters remain intact is known as.

Ans. Call by value.

12. The function call in which the data in actual parameters get changed is called.

Ans. Call by reference.

13. Many functions with the same name refers to.

OR

Functions sharing same name is called.

* Frequently asked previous years Board Exam Questions.

Ans. Function overloading.

14. Name the Java keyword that:
    (i)   indicates that a method has no return type.
    (ii) stores the address of the currently - calling object.

Ans. (i)   void   (ii) this

15. The default initial value of a boolean variable data type.

Ans. False

16. Write the function prototype for the function "sum" that takes an integer variable (x) as its argument and returns a value of float data type.

Ans. float sum(int x).

17. Write the prototype of a function check which takes an integer as an argument and returns a character.

Ans. Char check(int n)

18. What is meant by private visibility of a method ?

Ans. Private methods can be called only in the class in which they are defined. Outside that class they cannot be accessed.

19. State the types of functions ?

Ans. Types of functions are:
    (i)   Pure functions.   (ii) Impure functions.

20. How can a function call be invoked ?

Ans. Function call can be invoked by specifying its name followed by parameters enclosed in round brackets.

21. Write the prototype of the function that returns a double value and takes three double parameters x, y and z as its parameters.

Ans. double sample(double x, double y, double z);

22. Write the prototype of a static method named calculator that accepts two short type variables as its arguments and returns an integer value.

Ans. static int calculator(short x, short y);

23. Write the prototype of a function 'divide' that takes two integer values and returns the quotient of double type.

Ans. Double divide (int x, int y):

24. Write the prototype of its overloaded function that takes two double values as formal parameters and returns the quotient of double type.

Ans. double divide(double m, double n);

Chapter 4. Constructors

1. A member function having the same name as that of its class is called.

Ans. A member function having the same name as that of its class is called constructor.

2. Constructor that can take arguments is called.

OR

Constructors that can take arguments.

Ans. Constructor that can take arguments is called parameterized constructor.

3. A constructor that accepts no parameter is called.

Ans. A constructor that accepts no parameter is called default constructor.

4. Constructors can be used to perform.

Ans. Initialization.

5. A special function for automatic initialization of object during creation.

Ans. A special function for automatic initialization of object during creation is a constructor.

6. Two or more constructor function defined in a class.

Ans. Constructor overloading.

7. Keyword which refers to the current object.

Ans. This.

8. An anonymous short lived object.

Ans. Temporary object.

9. Two types of constructors.

Ans. Two types of constructors are parameterized and non-parameterized.

10. What does an explicit call to the constructor creates ?

Ans. Temporary Instances.

11. What is the main purpose of the default constructor provided by the compiler ?

Ans. It initializes the data members by null or zero value.

12. Mention the main purpose of using this keyword.

Ans. The this keyword is used to refer to the current calling object.

13. Which unit of the class gets called, when the object of the class is created ?

Ans. Constructor.

Chapter 5. Library Classes

1. Write the return data type of the following function.

    (i)   endsWith( )   (ii) log( )

Ans. (i)   boolean   (ii) double

2. What is the data type that the following library functions return ?

    (i)   isWhitespace(char ch)   (ii) Math.random()

Ans. (i)   boolean   (ii) double

3. What is the use of System.out.println command in a Java program ?

Ans. The command System.out.println is used to print the output on the computer screen followed by a new line.

4. Symbols that trigger some operations.

Ans. Operators.

5. Classes that correspond to each of the simple types.

Ans. Wrapper classes.

6. A package is a collection of.

Ans. Classes and interfaces.

7. Name the Package that should be imported in Java program for obtaining system date and time.

Ans. java.util.

8. Pre defined classes in the form of packages are called.

Ans. Java class libraries.

9. Command through which packages and classes are imported.

OR

A keyword, to use the classes defined in a package.

Ans. Import.

10. Class that wrap the value of a primitive type in an object.

Ans. Wrapper classes.

11. Give the name the package needed to import reading and writing functions.

Ans. java.io;

12. Wrapper classes in Java.

Ans. Boolean, Byte, Integer, Float, Character, Short, Double.

13. Name the package that contains wrapper classes.

Ans. java.lang

14. The property of java which provides a large number of classes grouped into different packages.

Ans. Java API.

15. What is meant by a package ? Name any two java Application Programming Interface packages.

Ans. Package is the collection of pre defined classes and interfaces having common functionality.

e.g. : java.io, java.lang

16. Name any two wrapper classes.

Ans. Integer, Double.

17. A package that is invoked by default.

Ans. java.lang;

18. What are static variables ?

Ans. Static variables are used when we want to have a variable common to all instances of a class.

19. A method that converts a string to a primitive integer data type.

Ans. Integer.parseInt( )

Chapter 6. Encapsulation

1. What is a visibility modifier ?

Ans. It is also called an access specifier. It is used to restrict the access of specific variables and methods from outside the class.

2. Define the term visibility.

Ans. Visibility is a related term which refers to whether one can access a given variable or method from a given scope of the program.

3. Define the term Local variable and Class variable.

Ans. Local variable : Variable declared inside a method or a block is known as Local variable.

Class variable : Class variable are the variables which are available to the entire class.

4. Name the keyword which :*

(i)   indicates that a method has no return type.

(ii) makes the variable as a class variable.

Ans. (i)   void

(ii) static

Chapter 7. Arrays

1. Legal subscripts in Java, for an array having N elements.

Ans. 0 to N – 1

2. Total size of array A having 25 elements of char type.

Ans. 50 bytes.

3. Total size of array [100] of int type is ?

Ans. 400 bytes.

4. The act of arranging the array elements in a specified order is known as.

Ans. Sorting.

5. Given array 12, 3, 8, 5. What will be the array like after two passes of selection sort ?

Ans. 3, 5, 8, 12.

6. Given an array 12, 3, 8, 5. What will be the array like after two passes of bubble sort ?

Ans. 3, 5, 8, 12.

7. An array 18, 13, 2, 9, 5 is 13, 2, 9, 18, 5 after three iteration of inner loop. Which sorting technique is applied on it ?

Very Short Questions

Ans. Bubble sort.

8. What is an array ?

Ans. An array is a collection of data of the same type that are referenced by a common name.

9. What do you understand by out-of-bound subscripts ?

Ans. The subscripts other than 0 to n – 1 for an array having n elements, are called out-of-bounds subscripts.

10. How can an array be declared ?

Ans. An array can be declared by specifying its base type, name and size.

For example:

int a[10];

11. Where are array elements stored ?

Ans. Array elements are stored in the contiguous memory locations of RAM.

12. Write the formula which determined the total bytes required to store a one-dimensional array.

Ans. Formula : Size of type * size of array.

13. Name the search or sort algorithm that:

    (i)   Makes several passes through the array, selecting the next smallest item in the array each time and placing it where it belongs in the array.

    (ii) At each stage, compares the sought key value with the key value of the middle element of the array.

Ans. (i) Selection sort.   (ii) Binary search.

14. Name the keyword that:

    (i)   is used for allocating memory to an array.

    (ii) causes the control to transfer back to the method call.

Ans. (i) new keyword.   (ii) return statement.

15. What do you mean by 'sorting' ?

Ans. Sorting of an array means arranging the array elements in a specified order.

16. Consider the following list of numbers and show the arranged list after the fifth iteration of bubble sort in ascending order.

2, 3, 9, 1, 0, 8, 4.

Ans. 0, 1, 2, 3, 4, 8, 9.

17. Which element is num[9] of the array num ?

Ans. Tenth element.

18. If, array[] = {1, 9, 8, 5, 2};

    (i)   What is array.length() ?   (ii) What is array[2] ?

Ans. (i)   5   (ii) 8

19. Declare a 2-d array of size 2 × 3 to store only characters.

Ans. char ch[][] = new ch[2][3];

20. Create an integer array of size 3 × 2 and initialise it with values between 1 to 9.

Ans. int a[][] = {{6, 1}, {2, 5}, {3, 7}};

Chapter 8. String Handling

1. A method that returns a copy of the invoking string from which any leading and trailing whitespace has been removed.

Ans. trim().

Chapter 1. Revision of Class IX Syllabus

1. Name two jump statements and their use.

Ans. (i) Break statement is used to terminate the execution of the current block or loop or switch statement.

(ii) Continue statement is used to skip over a set of statements and forces the next iteration of a loop. It can only be used with loops.

2. State one similarity and one difference between while and for loop.

Ans. Similarities:

Both are pre tested and entry

controlled loop.

Dissimilarities :

In for loop initialization, condition and iteration statements are placed together but in while loop all three statements are need to be written separately.

3. What is meant by an infinite loop ? Give an example.

Ans. An infinite loop is a loop that never terminates. It can be created by skipping the condition.

e.g., int i;

for (i=1;; i++)

System.out.println("Endless loop");

This loop will run forever as there is no condition under which it will terminate.

4. State one similarity and one difference between while and do while loop.

Ans. **Similarity :** While and do while loops are used to repeat a block of statements as long as the user wants.

Difference : While loop starts executing the block of statements only if the condition of the loop is true whereas, do while tests the condition at the end of the loop so the statement executes at least once even if the condition is false.

5. State the comparisons of if and ternary operator.

Ans. (i) Compared to if-else sequence ternary operator (? :) offers a more clean and compact code.

(ii) Conditional operator (? :) produces an expression and hence a single value can be assigned or incorporated into a larger expression, whereas if statement can have multiple statements, multiple assignments and expressions.

(iii) When ternary operator is used in its nested form, it becomes complex and difficult.

6. What process would loops include ?

Ans. (i) Initialization of a counter.

(ii) Execution of the statements in the loop.

(iii) Test of special condition for execution of the loop.

(iv) Incrementing/Decrementing the counter.

7. What is the role of continue statement in a program ?

Ans. Continue as the name implies causes the loop to be continued with the next iteration after skipping the remaining statements below it.

8. What is an exception ?

Ans. It is the anomalous (unexpected) situation which occurs during the program execution.

9. Specify the three modes through which programs can be executed ?

Ans. Three modes through which statements in a program may be executed are sequentially, selectively or iteratively.

10. What is the function of jump statement ?

Ans. Jump statement transfers control to another part of the program.

11. What is an infinite loop ? Write an infinite loop statement using the while loop.

Ans. Non terminating loop is called infinite loop.

For example :

```
int i;
i = 1;
while(i > 0)
{
    System.out.println("Non Terminating loop");
}
```

12. What is the use of fall through in switch statement. Explain with example ?

Ans. When switch statement is used to execute a set of statements based on more than one condition, being true, without the break statement. This is known as fall through.

For example :

```
char ch = 'a';
switch(ch)
{
    case 'a' :
    case 'e' :
    case 'i' :
    case 'o' :
    case 'u' : System.out.println("Character is a Vowel"); break;
    default : System.out.println("Character is a Consonant");
}
```

13. What does a class encapsulate ?

Ans. A class encapsulates the data members and the member functions. Data members represent state of an object and member function represents behaviour of an object.

14. What does the token 'keyword' refer to, in the context of Java ? Give an example for keyword.

Ans. Keywords are reserve words which convey a special meaning to the java compiler.

For example : void, if, break, else, continue etc.

15. Mention any two attributes required for class declaration.

Ans. Two attributes required for class declaration are:

    (i)   Data members.   (ii)   Member functions.

16. What is the use of exception handling in Java ?

Ans. Sometimes exceptional conditions in traditional environments often arise in situations such as "division by zero" or "file not found". Such kind of situations are handled by the exception handling mechanism in Java.

17. Define the term bytecode.

Ans. Bytecode is a machine instruction for a java processor compiler called JVM. It is independent of any platform and can run in any environment.

18. What is the use of the keyword 'this' ?

Ans. 'this' keyword is used to point to the current object of the class. It is also used to differentiate between an instance variable and a local variable.

19. Java is known to be a platform neutral language, why ?

Ans. Java language is not tied to any particular hardware or operating system. Program developed in Java can be executed anywhere on any system.

20. Write any four features of Java language ?

Ans. (i)   Java is platform independent.   (ii)   It is portable.

(iii) It is highly reliable. (iv) It is an object oriented language

21. What do you know about BlueJ ?

Ans. BlueJ is a Java development environment. It is an IDE (Integrated Development Environment) which includes an editor, compiler, debugger, virtual machine and terminal. It offers an easy way to run Java programs and view documentation.

22. What are the different tools of BlueJ ?

Ans. BlueJ includes the following tools in it:

(i) An editor, which can use to write the programs.

(ii) A debugger, which helps to find problems in code.

(iii) A compiler, which compiles the code.

(iv) A terminal, which lets us see outputs.

(v) JVM, a virtual machine to execute the Java program.

23. How can objects be created in BlueJ ?

Ans. To create an object of a class, firstly compile the class and then follow these steps:

(i) Right click on the class icon and from the shortcut menu select new <classname>

(ii) Now create object dialog will appear here, specify the name for new object and click OK.

(iii) Once you click OK in create object dialog, BlueJ will create an object with that name and show its icon in the object bench.

24. What are objects ? How are they created from a class ?

Ans. An object is an identifiable entity with some characteristics and behaviour.

To create an object of a class in BlueJ:

(i) Compile the class and Right click on the class and from the shortcut menu select new <classname>.

(ii) Create object, a dialog box will appear, here specify the name for the new object to be created and click OK.

25. How are objects implemented in software terms ?

Ans. The object is implemented in software terms as follows:

(i) Characteristics or attributes are implemented through member variables or data members of the object.

(ii) Behaviour is implemented through member functions called methods.

(iii) It is given a unique name to give it an identity.

26. Explain the term encapsulation with example.

Ans. The wrapping up of data and methods into a single unit (called class) is known as encapsulation. For example an engine of a car or any vehicle contains many small parts which enable the entire machinery system to work. It has small parts and its functionalities combined as a system.

27. What do you mean by abstraction ? How are abstraction and encapsulation related to each other ?

Ans. Abstraction means hiding. It is the act of representing essential features and hiding the background details.

Encapsulation is the way of combining both data and the functions that operate on the data under a single unit. Encapsulation is the way of implementing abstraction.

28. How do objects encapsulate state and behaviour ?

Ans. State and behaviour of objects are interweaved, they are said to encapsulate state and behaviour for instance, a car object has characteristics like number of wheels, seats, make etc. and behaviours like move, stop, blow horn etc. Now all these things are combined together in the form of 'car'. We cannot segregate them. Thus, we can say that objects encapsulate their 'state' and 'behaviour'. As their state and behaviour are inter linked, they cannot exist separately.

29. Explain inheritance.

Ans. Inheritance is the process of creating a new class from an existing class. These existing classes are called super class or base class, and new classes derived from them are called derived or subclasses. This concept provides extendibility and reusability of code.

30. What role does polymorphism play as a Java feature ?

Ans. It means the ability to take more than one form. Through polymorphism, the same message is delivered to objects of different class and each object responds differently based on its class.

Polymorphism plays an important role in allowing objects having different internal structures to share the same external interface.

31. What are the features of Java ?

Ans. (i) **Simple :** Java is easy to learn and understand.

(ii) **Object Oriented :** Java is a fully object oriented language. It has all the OOP's features like encapsulation, abstraction, inheritance etc.

(iii) **Platform independent :** Java code is compiled into a platform independent intermediate code called the bytecode, which can be executed on any platform.

(iv) **Multithreaded :** With multi-threaded feature of java, programs can be written to perform many tasks simultaneously.

(v) **High performance :** Java is compiled into bytecode which is highly optimised by the java compiler to execute fast.

32. What is an Exception ? Name two Exception handling blocks.

Ans. Exception is an unexpected situation which occurs during the execution of a program. It can be handled using try, catch and finally statement block.

33. What does the class consists of ?

Ans. A class consists of:

(i) **Data members or instance variables :** It contains information necessary to represent the property of an object.

(ii) **Methods :** It performs operations on the data members of the class.

34. Mention the levels of scope and visibility offered by Java.

Ans. (i) Data declared at the class level can be used by all methods in that class.

(ii) Data declared within a method can be used only in that method. Data declared within a method is called local data.

(iii) Variables that are declared in a block i.e., local variables are available to every method inside of that block.

(iv) Variables declared in interior blocks are not visible outside of that block. Variables declared in exterior blocks are visible to the interior blocks.

35. Give the rules for naming variables in Java.

Ans. (i)   The valid characters in variable names are, A to Z, a to z, 0 to 9, _, $.

(ii) Variable name cannot start with digits.

(iii) Any keyword cannot work as a variable name.

(iv) Variable names are also case-sensitive.

(v) Variable names can be of unlimited length.

36. Why are methods in java declared static ?

Ans. In Java language, when a method of a class needs to be referenced without the help of their objects, they are declared as static. They are called with reference to their class name only.

37. What are nested classes ?

Ans. It is possible to define a class within another class, such classes are known as nested classes. A nested class has access to the members, including private members of the class in which it is nested. However, the enclosing class does not have access to the members of the nested class.

38. Define a variable.

Ans. The variable is the basic unit of storage in Java program, used to store data into memory. A variable is defined as the combination of an identifier, a type, and an optional initialization. A variable name can be chosen by the programmer in a meaningful way so as to reflect what it represents in a program.

39. Give an example to show declaration of variables having different data types.

Ans. Short a;

int b = 10;

float average = 74.9;

char name = 'x';

40. What does declaration of variable mean to computer ?

Ans. Declaration of variable does three things:

(i)   It tells the compiler what the variable name is.

(ii) It specifies what type of data the variable will hold.

(iii) The place of declaration decides the scope of the variable.

41. Identify the statements listed below as assignment, increment, method invocation or object creation statements.

(i)   System.out.println("Java");

(ii) costPrice = 457.70;

(iii) Car hybrid = new Car();

(iv) petrolPrice++;

Ans. System.out.println("Java");   is a method invocation statement

costPrice = 457.50;   is an assignment statement.

Car hybrid = new Car();   is an object creation statement.

petrolPrice++;   is an increment statement.

42. What is the use of a ternary operator? Give its syntax.

Ans. Ternary operator is an operator that operates on three operands. It is also known as a conditional operator. It is used as an alternative of if else statement.

Syntax : variable = condition ? true value : false value;

e.g., : max = a > b ? a : b;

Here, max will get the value of a if it is greater than b, otherwise it will get the value of b.

43. What do you mean by binary, unary and ternary operator.

Ans. Unary operator are those which operate on a single operand

Example :

++, − −, !, etc.

a++;

− − a;

! (a == 10)

− a

Binary operators are those which operate on two

operands. Example +, −, / ,*, ==, <... etc.

Ternary operator is the operator which operates on three operands. The only ternary operator is (?:).

44. What are logical operators ?

Ans. Logical operator combines the result of two or more expressions.

The result of a logical operator is true or false.

Symbol	Description
&&	AND
||	OR
!	NOT

45. What is the function of Bitwise operator ?

Ans. Bitwise operator can be applied to the integer types long, int, short and byte. The operators act upon the individual bits of the operands. They work on integer data only.

Some of the Bitwise operators are:

~   Bitwise complement

&   Bitwise AND

^   Bitwise XOR

| Bitwise OR etc.

46. What is a compound statement ? Give an example.

Ans. Compound statements are those, which contain one or more statements inside it.

Examples of compound statements are loops, methods, if(), switch() etc.

47. Explain associativity property of an operator.

Ans. Operators in Java have precedence associated with them. This precedence is used to determine how an expression involving more than one operator is evaluated. The operator at higher level of precedence are evaluated first. The operators of the same precedence are evaluated either from left to right or from right to left depending on the level.

48. What changes are introduced during the final assignment of one type of variable to another type ?

Ans. (i)   Float into int causes truncation of the fractional part.

(ii)   Double to float causes rounding of digits.

(iii) Long into int causes dropping of the excess order bits.

49. Define precedence of operators.

Ans. Java allows the following order of precedence to the operators in priority from top to bottom in different rows. The operators present on the same row indicate the same order of preference and can be executed first by placing them within parenthesis.

. (DOT) operator, [] for arrays, () parenthesis

$++, --,+, -, !, \sim$	: increment, decrement, unary plus, unary minus, NOT, bitwise NOT respectively.
$*, /, \%$	: Multiplication, division and modulus
$+, -$	: Addition and subtraction
$<<, >>, >>>$	: Shift operators
$<, >, <=, > === , ! =$	: Relational (comparison) operators
$\&$	: AND
$\wedge$	: XOR
$\mid$	: OR
$\&\&$	: Logical AND
$\mid\mid$	: Logical OR
$? :$	: Conditional operator
$=, + =, - =, * =, / =, \% =, \wedge =,$ $\& =, \mid =, << =, >> =, >>> =$	: Assignment operators

50. What are relational operators, give examples ?

Ans. Relational operators are used to compare values between two operands.

e.g., : if x = 10 then, x < 20 is true.

There are six relational operators used in Java :

Operators	Meaning
<	Less than
<=	Less than or equal to
>	Greater than
>=	Greater than or equal to
==	Equal to
!=	Not equal to

51. What is the purpose of the new operator ?

Ans. New operator is used to dynamically (at Run-time) create an object and assign initial values to it. It allocates required memory space for the object in RAM.

Syntax : <Class_Name> Object_Name = new <Class_Name>();

Eg. : student s = new student();

52. What is Buffering ?

Ans. A Buffer is a temporary storage used to hold data until enough has been collected that it is worth transferring. Buffering can be used for both input and output.

53. Write a Java expression for the following:*

$$\sqrt{b^2 - 4ac}$$

Ans. Math.sqrt(b*b – 4*a*c)

54. Evaluate the following if the value of $x = 7, y = 5$*

$x + = x++ + x+ ++ y$

Ans. $x = 28, y = 6$

55. Give the output of the following program segment and mention how many times the loop will execute:*

```
int k;
for (k = 5 ; k < = 20; k + = 7)
if (k% 6==0)
continue;
System.out.println (k);
```

Ans. Loop will execute 3 times output 19.

56. Rewrite the following program segment using logical operators:*

```
if (x > 5)
if (x > y)
System.out.println (x+y);
```

Ans.
```
if(x > 5 && x > y)
System.out.println(x + y);
```

57. Convert the following if else if construct into switch case:*

```
if (ch== 'c' || ch=='C')
System.out.print("COMPUTER");
else if (ch== 'h' || ch=='H')
System.out.print("HINDI");
else
System.out.print("PHYSICAL EDUCATION");
```

Ans.
```
switch(ch)
{
case 'c' :
case 'C' : System.out.print( " COMPUTER " ) ;
break;
case 'h' :
case 'H' : System.out.print( " HINDI" ) ;
break;
default: System.out.print("PHYSICAL EDUCATION" ) ;
}
```

58. Give the output of the following:*

    (i)   Math.pow (36,0.5) + Math.cbrt (125)

    (ii)   Math.ceil (4.2) + Math.floor (7.9)

Ans. (i)   6.0 + 5.0 = 11.0

      (ii)   5.0 + 7.0 = 12.0

59. Rewrite the following using ternary operator:*

if(n1>n2)

r = true;

else

r = false;

Ans. r = n1 > n2 ? true : false ;

60. Write a difference between unary and binary operator.*

Ans.

Unary Operator	Binary Operator
1. The operator that acts on a single operand is called a unary operator.	The operator that acts on two operands is called a binary operator.
2. E.g., ++,--	E.g., +, –, *, /

61. Identify and name the following tokens :*

(i)   public   (ii) 'a'   (iii) ==   (iv) { }

Ans. (i)   public — Keyword.   (iii) == — Operator.

(ii) 'a' — Character Literal.   (iv) { } — Separator.

62. Differentiate between if else if and switch-case statements.*

Ans.

if else if	switch case
1. It can work with all relational operators.	It can only test for equality.
2. It can work with any data type.	It can only work with byte, short, char and int primitive data types.

63. Write a Java expression for the following :*

$|x^2 + 2xy|$

Ans. Math.abs(x * x + 2 * x * y)

64. Evaluate the following expression if the value of x = 2, y = 3 and z = 1.*

v = x + --z + y++ + y

Ans. 9

65. What is meant by a package ? Give an example.*

Ans. A package is a collection of inter-related classes and interfaces having common functionality. e.g., java.io, java.util, java.lang, etc.

Chapter 2. Class as the Basis of all Computation

1. Why a class is known as composite data type ?

Ans. A class is made from a collection of primitive data types, therefore, it is known as a composite data type.

```
Ex : class Student
{
    int rno;
    String name;
    double marks;
}
```

2. Assign the value of pie (i.e., 3.142) to a variable with requisite data type.

Ans. double pie = 3.142;

or

final double pie = 3.142;

3. Define all data types available in java and their sizes also.

Ans.

Type	Size
byte	1 byte
int	4 byte
short	2 byte
long	8 byte
float	4 byte
double	8 byte
character	2 byte
boolean	1 byte

4. Define class ? Give example of class and object.

Ans. A class may be thought of as a 'data type', classes are user-defined data types and behave like the built in types of a programming language. If furniture has been defined as a class, then sofa will be its object. Sofa belongs to the class 'Furniture'.

5. Define Instance variable. Give an example of the same.

Ans. Instance Variable : Variables defined inside the class are called instance variables. Instance variables are defined to represent state.

```
public class student
{
    public int RollNo;
    public String name;
}
```

In above class Roll No. and name are instance variables.

6. How are objects created ?

Ans. An object is essentially a block of memory that contains space to store all the instance variables.

Creating an object is also referred to as instantiating an object.

Objects in Java are created using new operator. The new operator creates an object of the specified class and overturns a reference to that object.

Example :

Object : rect1

Declaring Object

Rectangle rect1;

Instantiate

rect1 = new rectangle();

7. What are member variables ? State their access modifiers.

Ans. Member variables are also known as instance variables. These member variables are used to store value in the class. It may be public, private, protected or with no access modifiers where private , protected and members with no access modifiers remain hidden from outside world and thereby support data-hiding.

8. Explain public, private and protected variables.

Ans. Public variables can be accessed inside as well as outside the class. Private variables can be accessed only inside the class in which it is defined. Protected variables can be accessed in the class in which it is defined as well as in its derived classes.

9. Give an example showing declaration of instance variables.

Ans.
```
class Rectangle
{
    int length;
```

Short Questions

        int width;
    }

The class rectangle contains two integer type instance variables. It is allowed to declare them in one line as well. For example: int length, width;

These variables are only declared and therefore no storage space has been created in the memory. Instance variables are also known as member variables

10. What do you understand by the term data abstraction ? Explain with an example.

Ans. Abstraction refers to the act of representing essential features of a class without including its background details or explanations. For example switch board. We only press certain switches according to our requirement without knowing what is happening inside and how it is happening.

11. What is inheritance and how is it useful in Java ?

Ans. Inheritance is a process by which a class called derived class inherits the properties of another class called base class. The greatest advantage of inheritance is the code reusability. Classes can be written, compiled and saved. New classes can be derived from existing classes adding additional features in it. This saves time and effort.

12. Explain the term object using an example.

Ans. Object is a basic entity in OOPs. Object may be a person, place or any other real-world entity that is to be programmed. Each object contains data & functions to manipulate data.

E.g. : A student object may contain roll number, name and class as data members and input and display as member functions as below :

Roll No.

Name

Class

Section

Input()

Display()

13. State the Java concept that is implemented through:

    (i)   A superclass and a subclass.

    (ii) The act of communication among objects of a class.

Ans. (i)   Inheritance.   (ii) Message Passing.

14. Encapsulation is one of the major properties of OOP. How is it implemented in software terms ?

Ans. Encapsulation is implemented by making a class and defining instance variables and methods in it. Methods follow a set of instructions by accessing data and working on it.

15. How is abstraction related to the user's perspective?

Ans. An abstraction is a named collection of attributes and behaviour relevant to modeling a given entity for some particular purpose. An object is used by its properties and functionalities without knowing in what way it is working. For example : a car is an object , one uses its features like steering, breaks, accelerators etc without knowing its background details and explanations.

16. What is the need of a class in Java ?

Ans. A class is the fundamental building block of a pure object oriented programming language, Java. Class combines data representation and methods for manipulating that data into one unit. Classes in Java are needed to represent a real-world entity having its properties and functions.

Classes provide convenient methods for packing together a group of logical related data items and functions that work on them. In Java, the data items are called instance variables and the functions are called methods.

17. What is the relationship between objects and classes ?

Ans. An object is an instance of a class. A class is a template or blue print for an object.

18. Write the method to define a class.

Ans. A class is declared by using the keyword 'class'. The general form of a class definition is shown below :

class < class name >

```
{
     data type - instance variable 1;
     data type - instance variable 2;
     type method name 1 (parameter list)
     {
         body of method
     }
}
```

19. List the variables from those given below that are composite data types :

   (i)   static int x;   (iii) obj.display();   (v) String str;

   (ii) arr [i] = 10;   (iv) private char chr;

Ans. (ii) arr is an array, (iii) obj is an object and (v) str is an object of String class therefore all three are composite data types.

20. What are the types of casting shown by the following examples ?

   (i)   double x = 15.2

       int y = (int)x;

   (ii) int x = 12;

       long y = x;

Ans. (i)   Explicit type casting   (ii) Implicit type casting

21. Consider the following class :

```
public class myClass
{
     public static int x = 3, y = 4;
     public int a = 2, b = 3;
}
```

   (i)   Name the variables for which each object of the class will have its own distinct copy.

   (ii) Name the variables that are common to all objects of the class.

Ans. (i) a, b since they are instance variables.   (ii) x, y since they are class variables.

22. What is this keyword ? What is its significance ?

Ans. The member functions of every object have access to a sort of magic keyword named 'this', which refers to the object itself. Thus, any member function can find out the reference of the object of which it is a member.

The this keyword represents an object that invokes a member function. It stores the address of the object that is invoking a member function and it is an implicit argument to the member function being invoked.

The this keyword is useful in returning the object (reference) of which the function is called.

23. Why an object is called an instance of a class ?

Ans. As an object encapsulates state and behaviour present inside the class therefore, we can say object is an instance of a class.

24. What is the use of the keyword import ?

Ans. Import keyword is used to provide access to classes stored inside a package in our program.

   e.g., : import java.io.*; will provide all the classes stored inside package io, which can be used in our program.

25. How new operator is used ?

Ans. For dynamic (Run-time) initialization of an object of a class the new operator is used. The object allocates required memory to the variable in RAM.

Syntax : <Class_Name> Object_Name = new <Class_Name>();

   e.g., : student s = new student();

26. What do you mean by a temporary instance of a class ? What is its use ? How is it created ?

Ans. A temporary instance of a class means an anonymous object of the same class which is short-lived. Its benefit is when an object is required only for a very short time, we need not reserve memory for it for a long time. A temporary object for the same purpose can be created which remains in the memory as long as the statement defining it is getting executed, after the statement, this object is automatically destroyed and the memory is released. Therefore, memory remains occupied only for the time when it is needed.

A temporary instance is created by an explicit call to the constructor. For instance, the following statement creates a temporary instance of type time and invokes print() member function of class time for it.

new time().print();

27. Write a difference between class and an object.*

Ans. Class is a set of objects that shares common characteristics and behaviour whereas object is an instance of a class.

Chapter 3. User - Defined Methods

1. When there are multiple definitions with the same function name, what makes them different from each other ?

Ans. Function Signature makes them significantly different from each other. Function signature includes number of arguments, its type and order of data types.

2. What are the two ways of invoking functions ?

Ans. Functions can be invoked in two ways :

    (i)   Call by value.   (ii)   Call by reference.

3. Define an impure function.

Ans. The functions which change the state of objects are called impure functions.

```
Eg. :
class text
{
int Qty;
int Price;
public void set(int q, int s)
{
Qty = q; Price = s;
}
    int getamt()
    {
        return Qty * Price;
    }
}
```

In the above class, the set function is an impure function because it changed the integer variable's values but, getamt function is not an impure function.

4. What is a function ? Why do we use functions while program handling ?

Ans. A function is a named unit of a group of program statements. This unit can be invoked from other parts of the program.

The most important reason to use functions is to make program handling easier as only a small part of the program is dealt with at a time, thereby avoiding ambiguity. Another reason to use functions is to reduce the program size.

5. Write the advantages of using functions in programs ?

OR

Write two advantages of using functions in a program.

Ans. Advantages of using functions in programs are :

    (i)   Functions lessen the complexity of programs.

    (ii) Function hides the implementation details.

    (iii) Function enhances reusability of code.

6. What are static members ?

Ans. The members that are declared with the keyword static are called static members. These members are associated with the class itself rather than individual objects, the static variables and static methods are often referred to as class variables and methods in order to distinguish them from their counter parts, such as, instance variables and instance methods.

7. State the restrictions of static methods.

Ans. (i)   They can only call other static methods.

    (ii) They can only access static data.

    (iii) They cannot refer to this or super in any way.

8. Give an example to show the methods print() and println().

Ans. class demo

```
{
    public static void main(String args [ ])
    {
        System.out.print("Hello");
        System.out.println("How are");
        System.out.print("you");
    }
}
```

    Output :

        Hello How are you.

9. Why are methods added within class ?

Ans. A class usually consists of two things – instance variables and methods. Most of the time methods are used to access the instance variables defined by the class. This prevents the data stored in instance variables to be accidently modified while using in a program. Also it hides the implementation details to the outside world *i.e.,* abstraction.

10. Mention the importance of return statement.

Ans. Return statement works like jump statement. The return statement is used to explicitly return from any method. It passes program control back to its caller. The return statement can also return a value to its calling functions so this is also used to send data to the caller.

    This statement has two forms :

    (a) Return;   (b) Return value.

11. State the important things that are required to remember about returning values?

Ans. The two types of important things to remember about returning values are:

    (i)   The type of data returned by a method must be compatible with the return type specified by the method.

    (ii) There can be multiple return statements in a method.

12. What is the use of void before function name ?

OR

    What is the role of keyword void in declaring functions ?

Ans. void data type specifies an empty set of values and it is used as the return type for functions that do not return a value. Thus, a function that does not return a value is declared as follows : void < functions name > (parameter list)

```
{
    //body of function
}
```

13. What is the use of function overloading ?

Ans. Function overloading implements polymorphism. This means, it is possible to define two or more methods with the same name in the same class. It also reduces the number of comparisons in a program thereby making the program run faster.

14. Why do you think function overloading must be a part of an object oriented language ?

Ans. Function overloading must be a part of an object oriented language as it is the feature that implements polymorphism in an object oriented language. That is the ability of an object to behave differently in different circumstances. Also with the function overloading, the programmer is relieved from the burden of choosing the right function for a given set of values. This important responsibility is carried out by the compiler when the program is compiled.

15. What is the use of 'this' keyword ?

Ans. 'this' keyword can only be used inside a method. this is a reference variable which refers to the current object, for which the method is called for. This reference can be treated like any other object reference. The 'this' keyword is used only for those special cases in which you need to explicitly use the reference to the current object.

16. State the method that :

    (i)   Converts a string to a primitive float data type.

    (ii) Determines if the specified character is an uppercase character.

Ans. Float.parseFl

oat();

Character.is

Uppercase();

17. State the data type and value of res after the following is executed :

char ch = 't'

res = Character.toUpperCase(ch);

Ans. Data type of res is char and value of res = 'T'.

18. Give the prototype of a function search which receives a sentence "sentnc" and a word "wrd" and returns 1 or 0 ?

Ans. int search(String sentnc, String wrd);

19. Give the prototype of a function check which receives a character (ch) and an integer (n) and returns true or false.

Ans. Boolean check(char ch, int n);

20. What are Java methods/functions ? Give its syntax with example.

Ans. A method/function is a set of java statements referred under a common name. It performs a certain task or operation. It can be parameterized or non-parameterized.

Syntax for method declaration :

<modifier><return type> <method_name>([parameter list]);

Here the parameter list is optional. For example :

```
public int sum(int a, int b)
{
    int c;
    c = a + b;
    return(c);
}
```

21. What are the restrictions of static methods ?

Ans. The following are the restrictions of static methods :

    (i)   They can only call other static methods.

    (ii) They can only access static data.

    (iii) They cannot refer to this or super keywords in anyway.

22. How are packages implemented ? Give an example.

Ans. A package is implemented by the keyword 'package'.

Package<package name>;

For example :

package test1;

public class testclass

```
{
    public void testmethod1()
    {
    System.out.println("method1 of testclass");
    }
    public static void main(String args[])
    {
    testclass c1 = new testclass();
    c1.testmethod1();
    }
}
```

23. (i) What is call by value ?

(ii) How are the following passed ?

(1) Primitive types.

(2) Reference types

Ans. (i) Call by value is the process of passing a copy of values of arguments to the method parameters.

All primitive data types like int, double, char etc., are passed by value.

(ii) (1) Primitive data types are passed by value.

(2) All reference types (Objects of classes) are passed by reference.

24. State a difference between call by value and call by reference.*

Ans.

Call By Value	Call By Reference
1. In this, local copy of parameters are created and whatever changes are made inside the function get reflected in the local copies while the original copy remains unaffected.	In this, no local copy of parameters are created therefore whatever changes are made inside the function get reflected in the original copies.
2. In this primitive data types are passed.	In this non-primitive data types are passed.

Chapter 4. Constructors

1. What is a constructor ? When is it invoked ?

Ans. Constructor is a member function used to create and initialize the object with legal set of values.

It is automatically invoked at the time of object creation.

2. Why do we need a constructor as a class member ?

Ans. Constructor is used to set the initial state of an object. It is executed automatically at the time of object creation. So, if we want to initialise an object's instance variable as soon as it is created into the memory. We need to define constructor in the class.

3. Explain instance variable. Give an example.

Ans. The attributes of an object are represented by variables known as instance variables.

E.g., consider an object account, the instance variables for account can be :

---

* Frequently asked previous years Board Exam Questions.

balance

accountType

clientName

4. Define constructors ?

Ans. A constructor is a member function of a class that is automatically called, when the object is created of that class. It has the same name as that of the class name and its primary job is to initialize the object to a legal value for the class.

5. Why do we need a constructor as a class member ?

Ans. Constructor is used to set the initial state of an object. It is executed automatically at the time of object creation. So if we want to initialize an object's instance variable as soon as it is created into memory, we have to define a constructor for the class.

6. Write two characteristics of a constructor.

Ans. (i)   Constructors have the same name as that of the class.

(ii)   They do not return any value, not even void.

7. Only a function that has access to the constructor can use the objects of this class. Comment on this statement.

Ans. Since, every time an object is created, it is automatically initialized by the constructor of the class.

Therefore, it is very much necessary for the function using an object that it must have access to the constructor of that class so that the object being defined could be properly constructed. Thus, a function not having access to the constructor of a class cannot use objects of that class.

8. Give an example showing the definition of a constructor.

Ans.
```
public class Res
{
        private int marks;
        private double per;
        private int tot;
        public Res()// constructor function.
        {
            marks = 227;
            per = 37.8;
            tot = 0;
        }
}
```

9. Explain parameterized constructors.

Ans. If we want to initialize objects with our desired values, we can use parameters with constructors and initialize the data members based on the arguments passed to it also like any other method. Constructors that can take arguments are called parameterized constructors.

10. Given an example of constructor passing data through parameters.

Ans.
```
public class Result
{
    private int per;
    private int tot;
    public Result(int R)
    {
    per = R;
    tot = 0;
    }
}
```

11. Mention some special characteristics of constructors.

Ans. The special characteristics of constructors are :

    (i)   Constructors should be declared in the public section of the class.

    (ii) They are invoked automatically when an object of the class is created.

    (iii) They do not have any return type and cannot return any values.

    (iv) Like any other function, they can accept arguments.

    (v) A class can have more than one constructor.

    (vi) Default constructors do not accept parameters.

    (vii) If no constructor is present in the class, the compiler provides a default constructor.

12. What is a default constructor?

Ans. Default constructor is the method of the class which will be automatically called at the time of object creation, when no argument is passed.

13. What is constructor overloading?*

Ans. Defining more than one constructors having same name but different signature is called constructor overloading.

```
class Overload
{
    String s;
    public Overload()
    {
        s="DPC Jhansi";
    }
    public Overload( String s1)
    {
        s=s1;
    }
}
```

Chapter 5. Library Classes

1. What is a wrapper class ? Give an example.

Ans. Wrapper classes are those classes which wraps predefined basic data type (int, double, char etc.). Some examples of wrapper classes are Integer, Double, Character, etc. These classes extends the features of basic data types.

2. What do you mean by type conversion ? How is implicit conversion different from explicit conversion ?

Ans. Conversion of one data type into another is called type conversion. It is of two types : Implicit : Automatic conversion of one data type into another that takes place without the user's intervention.

Explicit : Forced conversion of one data type into another that takes place in accordance with the user's requirements.

3. What conditions should be met in order to convert automatically one kind of data type to another ?

Ans. The required conditions are as follows :

    (i)   The two types are compatible.

    (ii) The destination type is larger than the source type.

4. State the values of n and ch.

    char c = 'A';

    int n = c + 1;

    char ch = (char) n;

Ans. n = 66;

    ch = 'B';

5. State the purpose and return data type of the following String functions :

    (i)   indexOf()   (ii) compareTo()

Ans. (i)   int indexOf(char ch) function is used to return the first occurrence of ch, if present in a string otherwise it returns –1. Its return type is int.

    (ii) int compareTo(String s) function is used to compare two strings lexicographically. Its return type is int. It returns positive value if the first string is greater, negative value if second string is greater and 0 (zero) if both are equal.

6. Name the class that is used for different mathematical functions. Give an example of a mathematical function.

Ans. Math class is used for mathematical functions.

Examples of mathematical functions :

abs(), sqrt(), pow(), etc.

```
class test
{
    public static void main(String[] args)
    {
        int x = – 10;
        int y = 9;
        System.out.println("Absolute value of x is" + Math.abs(x));
        System.out.println("Square root of y is" + Math.sqrt(y));
        System.out.println("Cube of y is" + Math.pow(y, 3));
    }
}
```

7. What is a wrapper class ? Give an example.

Ans. Wrapper classes are those classes which wrap predefined Basic data type (int, double, char etc.). Some examples of wrapper classes are integer, Double, character etc. These classes extends the features of basic data types.

8. What is a package ? Give an example.

Ans. A package is a container of related classes. A package allows to keep a name for a group of classes, in which you can store your classes without a concern that it will collide with some other class list.

Some inbuilt Java packages are listed below :

Java.lang : it collects the classes which are used by java compiler itself and these classes are imported automatically.

Java.io : input/output classes.

Java.net : classes for networking.

9. Give the purpose of the following functions, with example :

    (a) cbrt()   (b) ceil()   (c) floor()   (d) round()

Ans. (a) cbrt() : This function is used to return the cube root of a given numeric value or expression passed as an argument. It accepts an argument as a double data type and returns the result as a double data type.

    For example :

    double c, a = 125;

    c = Math.cbrt(a);

    System.out.println("cube root =" +c);

    Output : cube root = 5.0

    (b) ceil() : This function is used to return the double value which is greater than or equal to the passed argument and is equal to the nearest integer. It also accepts the argument as double type.

    For example :

```
double c, a = 125.9;
c = Math.ceil(a);
System.out.println(c);
Output : 126.0
```

(c) floor() : This function is used to return the double value which is less than or equal to the passed argument and is equal to the nearest integer. It also accepts the argument as double type.

For example :

```
double c, a = 125.9;
c = Math.floor(a);
System.out.println(c);
Output : 125.0
```

(d) round() : This function returns the value of the argument accepted as float type rounded to the nearest integer. The returned value is obtained by adding ½ to the passed value and then take the nearest integer which is less than or equal to that value.

For example :

```
int c;
float a = 125.6;
c = Math.round(a);
System.out.println(c);
Output : 126
```

10. What are wrapper classes ? Why are they used ?

Ans. A wrapper class is a class in which a primitive data type is wrapped into, that is, a primitive datatype is wrapped into an object by a wrapper class. They are used to provide more features to the existing primitive datatypes.

11. What are the different wrapper classes present in Java ?

Ans. The following are the list of wrapper classes with their primitive datatypes :

Primitive	Wrapper Class
boolean	Boolean
byte	Byte
char	Character
int	Integer
float	Float
double	Double
long	Long
short	Short

12. Define the following with example.

    (a) Autoboxing   (b) Unboxing

Ans. (a) The automatic conversion of a primitive datatype to its equaivalent wrapper object is known as autoboxing.

For example :

```
(i)    Integer i = 20;
(ii)   i = 10;
       Integer a = new Integer(i);
```

(b) The automatic conversion of wrapper class to its corrosponding primitive datatype is called Unboxing.

For example :

```
(i)    Integer i = new Integer(5);
       int a = i;
(ii)   Character ch = 'x';
       char a = ch;
```

13. Name a method to convert a value to string ? Give example.

Ans. The method toString() is used to convert a primitive datatype to String.

For example :

String s = Float.toString(10.25);

14. What is autoboxing in Java? Give an example.*

Ans. Converting primitive types to corresponding wrapper class object is called Autoboxing.

For eg: int to Integer, double to Double type etc.

Chapter 6. Encapsulation

1. What do you mean by the term 'Encapsulation' ?

Ans. Wrapping data and methods into a single unit is called Encapsulation. This is a fundamental concept of OOPs. Encapsulation is the way to implement abstraction. Encapsulating related methods and variables into a neat software bundle (class) is a simple yet powerful idea that provides two benefits to software developers : Modularity and data hiding.

   (i)   Modularity means source code for an object which can be written independently of the source code of another object.

   (ii)   Data hiding refers to preventing an object from being directly accessed from outside the class.

2. What will be the visibility of :

   (i)   A public class.　　　　　　(iii) A default class.

   (ii)   A protected class.　　　　　(iv) A private class.

Ans. The visibility of :

   (i)   Public Class : Visible to all classes.

   (ii)   Protected Class : Visible to classes inside or outside the package that inherit the class.

   (iii) Default Class : Visible to all classes of the same package.

   (iv)   Private Class : Visible only within the class in which it is defined.

3. How are private members of a class different from public members ?

Ans. (i)   Private members of a class are the most restricted members of a class whereas public members of a class are the least restricted members of a class.

   (ii)   Private members are accessible in their own class whereas public members are accessible in all parts of a java program.

4. Give the functions of keywords used with main() method :

   (i)   Public　　　　　　　　(ii)   Static　　　　　　　　(iii) Void.

Ans. (i)   **Public :** The keyword public is an access specifier that declares the main method as unprotected and therefore making it accessible to all other classes.

   (ii)   **Static :** It declares the method as one that belongs to the entire class and not a part of any particular object of the class.

   (iii) **Void :** The modifier void states that the main method does not return any value.

5. What is meant by private visibility of a method ?

Ans. Private methods can be used in the class in which they are defined. Outside that class they cannot be accessed.

Chapter 7. Arrays

1. Write statements to show how finding the length of a character array char[] differs from finding the length of a String object str.

Ans. For array, length is a property so we use char.length to get the length of a char array and for a string object, length is a function so we use str.length().

2. Write a statement each to perform the following task on a string :
   (i)   Find and display the position of the last space in a string s.
   (ii)   Convert a number stored in a string variable x to double data type.

Ans. (i)   int index, pos;

```
index = s.lastIndexOf(' ');
pos = index + 1;
System.out.println("Position is" + pos);
```

   (ii)   double a = Double.parseDouble(x);

3. What is an array ? Write a statement to declare an integer array of 10 elements.

Ans. An array is a group of indexed data items of the same type that are referred to by a common name.

```
int[] n = new int [10];
```

4. What is selection sort ?

Ans. In selection sort the smallest (or largest depending upon the desired order) key from the remaining unsorted array is searched for and put in the sorted array. The process repeats untill the entire array is sorted.

5. What is Bubble sort ?

Ans. In bubble sort, the adjoining values are compared and exchanged if they are not in proper order. This process is repeated until the entire array is sorted.

6. State the conditions under which binary search is applicable.

Ans. For binary search (i) The list must be sorted, (ii) Lower bound and upper bound and the sort order of the list must be known.

7. What is the use of Arrays ?

Ans. (i)   Arrays are used to store same type of elements in contagious memory locations.
   (ii)   In the place of defining many variables to store the same type of data, we can define an array, so we can give a single name to more than one location, this will make a program precise and program length short.
   (iii)   Different values of arrays can be easily accessed by using index numbers.
   (iv)   By using arrays we can process a large amount of data using loops.

8. State the total size in bytes, of the arrays a[4] of **char** data type and p[4] of float data type.

Ans. a[4] will occupy 2 * 4 = 8 Bytes.

   p[4] will occupy 4 * 4 = 16 Bytes.

9. How many types of arrays are there ? How are they declared ?

Ans. Arrays are of two types :
   (i)   Single dimensional array.
   (ii)   Multi-dimensional array.

   Their declarations are as follows :
   (i)   Single dimensional array declaration :

```
int a[] = new int[5];
```

   (ii)   Double dimensional array declaration :

```
int a[][] = new int[3][5];
```

10. What is the difference between the linear search and the binary search technique ?*

Ans.

Linear Search	Binary Search
1. It can work with both sorted and unsorted arrays.	It can only work with sorted arrays.
2. It takes more number of comparisons.	It takes less number of comparisons.

11. String x[] = {"Artificial intelligence", "IOT", "Machine learning", "Big data"};*

   Give the output of the following statements :

(i)   System.out.println(x[3]);

(ii) System.out.println(x.length);

Ans. (i)   Big Data

(ii) 4

Chapter 8. String Handling

1. What are strings ?

Ans. A sequence of characters are known as string. In java there is an inbuilt class present, named String. All strings should be given in double quotes sign. (" ")

A string can be declared as :

String s = "hello";

Here, s is the string variable having "hello" assigned to it .

2. Write a statement for each of the following :

(i)   Store a number 275 as a String.

(ii) Convert the string to a numeric value.

(iii) Add it to the existing total of 1000 to update the total.

Ans. (i)   String k;

      k = "275";

(ii) int n = Integer.parseInt(k);

(iii) int total = 1000;

      total = total + n;

3. How can string be created by two methods ?

Ans. String can be created by two methods :

(i)   From string literal :

      e.g. : String str = "Welcome";

(ii) Using new keyword :

      e.g. : char.str[] = {'w', 'e', 'I, 'c',

      'o', 'm', 'e'}; String str1 = new

      String(str);

      System.out.println(str1);

4. How can strings be modified ?

Ans. String objects are immutable, whenever you want to modify a string, you must either copy a string into a string buffer or use one of the string methods, which will construct a new copy of the modified string.

5. What is the method substring() used for ?

Ans. Method substring() is used to extract a substring from a string. It has two forms:

(i)   String substring(int start index)

(ii) String substring(int start index, int end index).

6. State the difference between length and length() in Java.*

Ans. Length is a variable used with arrays to find its size whereas length() is a function used with Strings to determine the no. of characters present in it.

If arr[] = {1,2,3,4,5} then arr.length will return 5.

If s="JAVA" the s.length() will return 4.

7. Write the output for the following:*

String s1 = "Life is Beautiful";

```
System.out.println ("Earth" + s1.substring(4));
System.out.println( s1.endsWith("L") );
```

Ans. Earth is Beautiful

false

8. What is the data type returned by the following library methods?*
   (i)   isWhitespace()
   (ii) compareToIgnoreCase()

Ans. (i)   boolean

(ii) int

9. Write the return data type of the following functions :*
   (i)   startsWith( )
   (ii) random( )

Ans. (i)   boolean

(ii) double

10. Write the output for the following :*

```
String s1 = "phoenix"; String s2 = "island";
System.out.println(s1.substring(0).concat
(s2.substring(2) ) );
System.out.println(s2.toUpperCase());
```

Ans. phoenixland

ISLAND

Short Questions

Chapter 1. Revision of Class IX Syllabus

1. WAP to calculate the area of a circle showing the declaration of variables and methods ?

Ans.
```java
class circle
{
        float radius; float P = 3.14f;
        void getData(float x, float y)
            {
                    radius = x; P = y;
            }
        float circArea()
            {
                    float area = P * radius * radius;
                    return(area);
            }
}
public class circArea
{
public static void main(String [] args)
{
        float area1, area2;
        circle circ1 = new circle();
        circle circ2 = new circle();
        circ1.radius = 17.5f;
        circ1.P = 3.14f;
        area1 = circ1.radius * circ1.radius * circ1.P;
        circ2.getData(15.5f, 3.14f);
        area2 = circ2.circArea();
        System.out.println("Area 1 = " + area1);
        System.out.println("Area 2 = " + area2);
}
}
```
Output :
Area1 = 961.25
Area2 = 754.385

2. Define a class salary described as below :

Data Members : Name, Address, Phone, Subject Specialization, Monthly Salary, Income Tax.

Member methods :

(i) To accept the details of a teacher including the monthly salary.

(ii) To display the details of the teacher.

(iii) To compute the annual Income Tax as 5% of the annual salary above ₹ 1,75,000.

Write a main method to create an object of a class and call the above member method.

Ans.
```java
public class salary
{
    String Name, Address, Phone, subspec;
    int msalary;
    double itax;
    public void accept(String n, String ad, String ph, String s, int ms)
    {
        Name = n;
        Address = ad;
        Phone = ph;
        subspec = s;
        msalary = ms;
    }
    public void display()
    {
        System.out.println("Name" + Name + "\n Address" + Address + "\n Phone  No." + Phone + "\n
        Subject Specification " + subspec + "\n monthly salary" + msalary + "\n Income Tax" + itax);
    }
    public void compute()
    {
        long Asalary = msalary * 12; if(Asalary > 175000)
        itax = 5/100 * (Asalary - 175000);
        else
        itax = 0;
    }
    public static void main(String [] args)
    {
        salary s = new salary();
        s.accept("Rahul", "New Agra", "285956", "computer science", 1200);
        s.compute();
        s.display();
    }
}
```

3. There is a special two-digit number which is such that when the sum of its digits is added to the product of its digits, the result is equal to the original two-digit number.

   Example : Consider the number 59. Sum of digits = 5 + 9 = 14

   Product of its digits = 5 × 9 = 45

   Sum of the sum of digits and product of digits = 14 + 45 = 59

   Write a program to accept a two-digit number.

   Add the sum of its digits to the product of its digits.

   If the value is equal to the number input, output the message "Special 2-digit number" otherwise, output the message "Not a special 2-digit number".

Ans.
```java
import java.io.*;
class Special
{
    int n, a, b, s, p;
    void display()
    {
```

```java
BufferedReader br = new BufferedReader(new InputStreamReader(System.in));
System.out.println("Enter a two digit no.");
N = Integer.parseInt(br.readLine());
a = n/10;
b = n % 10;
s = a + b;
p = a * b;
if(s + p == n)
{
    System.out.println("Special 2-digit number");
}
else
{
    System.out.println("Not a Special 2-digit number");
}
    }
}
```

4. Write a program to input a number and check and print whether it is a Pronic number or not. (Pronic number is the number which is the product of two consecutive integers)

Example :

$12 = 3 \times 4$

$20 = 4 \times 5$

$42 = 6 \times 7$

Ans.
```java
import java.util.*;//importing package
class Pronic
{
        int n, i = 1, p = 0;
        void display()
        {
            Scanner sc = new Scanner(System.in);
            System.out.println("Enter a number");
            n = sc.nextInt();
            int flag = 0;
            for(i = 0; i < n; i++)
            {
                if(i * (i + 1) == n)
            {
                flag = 1;
                break;
            }
            }
        if(flag == 1)
            System.out.println("It is a pronic number");
        else
            System.out.println("It is not a pronic number");
        }
}
```

Name	Type	Description
n	int	To store a number.
i	int	Loop variable.
p	int	To store product.
flag	int	Flag variable.

5. Write a program to input a number and print whether the number is a special number or not. (A number is said to be a special number, if the sum of the factorial of the digits of the number is same as the original number).

Example : 145 is a special number, because 1! + 4! + 5! = 1 + 24 + 120 = 145

(Where ! stands for factorial of the number and the factorial value of a number is the product of all integers from 1 to that number, example 5! = 1 * 2 * 3 * 4 * 5 = 120).

Ans.
```java
import java.io.*;
class Special
{
    int s = 0, n, r, f, i, t;
    void check()throws IOException
    {
        BufferedReader br = new BufferedReader(new InputStreamReader(System.in));
        System.out.println("Enter a no.");
        N = Integer.parseInt(br.readLine());
        t = n;
        while(n > 0)
        {
            r = n % 10;
            f = 1;
            for(i = 1; i <= r; i++)
            {
            f = f * i;
            }
            s = s + f;
            n = n / 10;
        }
        if(s == t)
        {
            System.out.println("Special no.");
        }
        else
        {
            System.out.println("Not a Special no.");
        }
    }
}
```

6. Write a program to read 2 numbers and calculate their sum, differences, product and modulus?

Ans.
```java
public class res
{
    public static void main(String[] args)
    {
```

```java
        int a = 10, b = 6;
        System.out.println("Sum is " + (a + b));
        System.out.println("Difference is " + (a - b));
        System.out.println("Product is " + (a * b));
        System.out.println("Remainder is " + (a % b));
    }
}
```

7. WAP to input 2 numbers and print the largest number using relational operators.

Ans.
```java
public  class check
{
    public static void main(String args[])
    {
        int a, b;
        a = Integer.parseInt(args[0]);
        b = Integer.parseInt(args[1]);
        if(a > b)
        System.out.println(a);
        else
        System.out.println(b);
    }
}
```

8. WAP to input a number, increment it 2 times using the increment operator and print the final result.

Ans.
```java
import java.util.*;
public class inc
{
    public static void main(String[] args)
    {
        int a;
        Scanner sc = new Scanner(System.in);
        System.out.println("Enter a number");
        a = sc.nextInt();
        ++a;
        ++a;
        System.out.println(a);
    }
}
```

9. Write a program that output the results of the following evaluations based on the number entered by the user.

  (i)   natural logarithms of the number.

  (ii) absolute value of the number.

  (iii) square root of the number.

  (iv) random numbers between 0 and 1.

Ans.
```java
import java.io.*;
public class test
{
    public static void main(String args[]) throws IOException
    {
```

```
int n;
BufferedReader b = new BufferedReader(new InputStreamReader(System.in));
System.out.println("Enter A Number");
n = Integer.parseInt(b.readLine());
System.out.println("Log of number is " + Math.log(n));
System.out.println("Absolute value of number is " + Math.abs(n));
System.out.println("Square root is " + Math.sqrt(n));
System.out.println("Random Numbers are : ");
for(int i = 1; i <= 10; i++)
{
System.out.println(Math.random());
}
}
}
```

10. Write a program to accept a word and convert it into lowercase if it is in uppercase, and display the new word by replacing only the vowels with the character following it. Example :

Sample Input : computer Sample Output : cpmpvtfr.

Ans.
```
import java.io.*;
class Change
{
    String s, s1 = "";
    int i, l; char ch;
    void change()
    {
        BufferedReader br = new BufferedReader(new InputStreamReader(System.in));
        System.out.println("Enter a string");
        s = br.readLine();
        s = s.toLowerCase(); l = s.length();
        for(i = 0; i < l; i++)
        {
            ch = s.charAt(i);
            if(ch == 'a' || ch == 'e' || ch == 'i' || ch == 'o' || ch == 'u')
            {
                ch = (char)(ch + 1);
            }
            s1 = s1 + ch;
        }
        System.out.println(" New Word is " + s1);
    }
}
```

11. Define a method named checkprime() to return true when the given number is prime otherwise return false.

Ans.
```
public class test
{
    boolean checkprime(int x)
    {
        boolean p = true;
        for(int n = 2; n < x; n++)
```

```
        {
            if(x % n == 0)
            {
                p = false; break;
            }
        }
        return p;
    }
    public static void main(String args[])
    {
        int t = 10; boolean R;
        test T = new test();
        R = T.checkprime(t);
        :
        :
        }
    }
```

12. Define a class with a function to return the sum of the digits of a number.

Ans.
```
class test
    {
        int sum(int n)
        {
            int s = 0;
            int x;
            while(n != 0)
            {
                x = n % 10;
                s = s + x;
                n = n/10;
            }
            return s;
        }
    :
    :
    }
```

13. Write a program to bubble sort the following set of values in ascending order :

5, 3, 8, 4, 9, 2, 1, 12, 98, 16 :

output :   1
             2
             3
             4
             5
             8
             9
             12
             16
             98

Ans.
```java
public class test
{
    public static void BubbleSort()
    {
        int a[] = {5, 3, 8, 4, 9, 2, 1, 12, 98, 16};
        int l = a.length - 1; for(int i = 0; i < l; i++)
        {
            for(int j = 0; j < l - i; j++)
            {
                if(a[j] > a[j + 1])
                {
                    int t = a[j];
                    a[j] = a[j + 1];
                    a[j + 1] = t;
                }
            }
        }
        System.out.println("Sorted Array is ");
        for(int i = 0; i <= l; i ++)
        {
            System.out.println(a[i]);
        }
    }
    public static void main(String args[])
    {
        BubbleSort();
    }
}
```

14. WAP to read an integer using Data Input Stream and print whether it is odd or even.

Ans.
```java
import java.io.*;
{
    public static void main(String args[])
    {
        DataInputStream in = new DataInputStream(System.in);
        int n = 0;
        System.out.println("Enter a digit");
        n = in.readInt();
        if(n % 2 == 0)
        {
            System.out. println("you entered an even number");
        }
        else
        {
            System.out.println("you entered an odd number");
        }
    }
}
```

15. Write a program Display following series :

   (i) 1, 3, 5, 7, 9, 11.........21   (ii) 20, 16, 12, 8............0   (iii) $1^2 + 2^2 + 3^3 + 4^2.........10^2$.

Ans. (i)

```java
public class series 1
{
    public static void main(String args[])
    {
        int x;
        for(x = 1; x <= 21; x = x + 2)
        {
            System.out.println(x);
        }
    }
}
```

(ii)

```java
public class series 2
{
    public static void main(String args[])
    {
        int x = 20;
        for(x = 20; x >= 0; x = x - 4)
        {
            System.out.println(x);
        }
    }
}
```

(iii)

```java
public class series 3
{
    public static void main(String args[])
    {
        int x , y, s = 0;
        for(x = 1, x <= 10; x++)
        {
            y = x * x;
            s = s + y;
        }
        System.out.println(s);
    }
}
```

16. Write a program to calculate and print the sum of odd numbers and the sum of even numbers for the first n natural numbers.

The integer n is to be entered by the user.

Ans.

```java
class test
{
    public static void sum(int n)
    {
        int s1, s2;
        s1 = s2 = 0;
        for(int I = 1; I <= n; I++)
        {
```

```
    if(I % 2 == 0)
    s1 = s1 + I;
    else
    s2 = s2 + I;
    }
    System.out.println("Sum of even numbers"+s1);
    System.out.println("Sum of odd numbers"+s2);
    }
}
```

17. Write a program to input a number and display its factorial.

Ans.
```
import java.io.*;
public class test
{
    public static void main(String args[]) throws IOException
    {
        int num, fact = 1;
        BufferedReader br = new BufferedReader(new InputStreamReader(System.in));
        System.out.println("Enter a number");
        String n = br.readLine();
        num = Integer.parseInt(n);
        for(int x =1; x <= num; x++)
        {
            fact = fact * x;
        }
        System.out.println("factorial is " + fact);
    }
}
```

18. Write a program to input a number and check it for prime or not prime.

Ans.
```
import java.io.*;
public class test
{
    public static void main(String args[]) throws IOException
    {
        int num;
        BufferedReader br = new BufferedReader(new InputStreamReader(System.in));
        System.out.println("Enter a number");
        num = Integer.parseInt(br.readLine());
        int prime = 1;
        for(int x = 2; x < num; x++)
        {
        if(num % x == 0)
        {
        prime = 0;
        break;
        }
        }
        if(prime ==1)
        System.out.println("number is prime");
```

```
            else
                System.out.println("number is not prime");
        }
    }
```

19. Write a program to display the sum of the following series :

s = a/1 + a/2 + a/3………… + a/n. where a = 2 and n = 10.

Ans.
```
public class test
{
    public static void main(String args[])
    {
        int a = 2, n = 10;
        double sum = 0, y;
        for(int x = 1; x <= n; x++)
        {
            y = (double) a/x;
            sum = sum + y;
        }
        System.out.println(sum);
    }
}
```

20. Write a program to display the sum of the first 10 even numbers using for() loop; also repeat this process by using while() and do while() loop.

Ans. (a)
```
public class test1
{
    public static void main(String args[])
    {
        int x, sum = 0;
        for(x = 2; x <= 20; x += 2)
        {
            sum = sum + x;
        }
        System.out.println(sum);
    }
}
```

(b)
```
public class test2
{
    public static void main(String args[])
    {
        int x = 2, sum = 0;
        while(x <= 20)
        {
            sum = sum + x;
            x = x + 2;
        }
        System.out.println(sum);
    }
}
```

(c) public class test3
```
{
    public static void main(String args[])
    {
        int x = 2, sum = 0;
        do
        {
            sum = sum + x;
            x += 2;
        }
        while(x <= 20);
    System.out.println(sum);
    }
}
```

21. (i) Write a program to read 2 numbers and print the smallest number using if.

(ii) Repeat the above program using if else.

Ans. (i) public class small
```
{
    public static void main(String args[]) throws IOException
    {
        int a, b;
        BufferedReader br = new BufferedReader(new InputStreamReader(System.in));
        System. out. println("Enter the 1st number");
        a = Integer.parseInt(br.readLine());
        System.out.println("Enter the 2nd number");
        b = Integer.parseInt(br.readLine());
        if(a < b)
        System.out.println(a);
        if (b < a)
        System.out.println(b);
    }
}
```

(ii) public class small
```
{
    public static void main(String args[]) throws IOException
    {
        int a, b;
        BufferedReader br = new BufferedReader(new InputStreamReader(System.in));
        System.out.println("Enter the 1st number");
        a = Integer.parseInt(br.readLine());
        System.out.println("Enter the 2nd number");
        b = Integer.parseInt(br.readLine());
        if(a < b)
        {
            System.out.println(a);
        }
        else
```

```
                {
                    System.out.println(b);
                }
            }
        }
```

22. Write a program to read marks in 3 subjects of a student, calculate average, and print it with a message.

Ans.
```
import java.io.*;
public class av
{
    public static void main(String args[]) throws IOException
    {
        float a, b, c, tot = 0, av = 0;
        BufferedReader br = new BufferedReader(new InputStreamReader(System.in));
        System.out.println("Enter the marks in 1st subject");
        a = Float.parseFloat(br.readLine());
        System.out.println("Enter the marks in 2nd subject");
        b = Float. parseFloat(br.readLine());
        System.out.println("Enter the marks in 3rd subject");
        c = Float.parseFloat(br.readLine());
        tot = a + b + c;
        av = tot/3;
        if(av < 50)
        {
        System.out.println("Work hard");
        }
        else
        {
        System.out.println ("good");
        }
    }
}
```

23. Write a program to display the following output :

```
5 5 5 5 5
5 4 4 4 4
5 4 3 3 3
5 4 3 2 2
5 4 3 2 1.
```

Ans.
```
import java.io.*;
public class test
{
    public static void main(String args[])
    {
        int x = 5, y = 5;
        for(int a = 5; a >= 1; a--)
        {
            for(int b = 5; b >= a; b--)
            {
                System.out.print(b);
```

```java
        }
        for(int c = 1; c <= y - 1; c++)
        {
            System.out.print(y);
        }
            y--;
        System.out.println();
        }
    }
}
```

24. Input a number and find the sum of all its digits.

Ans.
```java
import java.io.*;
public class test
{
    public static void main(String args[]) throws IOException
    {
        int num;
        BufferedReader br = new BufferedReader(new InputStreamReader(System.in));
        String n = br.readLine();
        num = Integer.parseInt(n);
        int R, s = 0;
        while(num != 0)
        {
            R = num % 10;
            s = s + R;
            num = num/10;
        }
        System.out.print("sum of digits is" + s);
    }
}
```

25. Input a number and count the number of digits.

Ans.
```java
import java.io.*;
public class digitcount
{
    public static void main(String args[]) throws IOException
    {
        int num;
        BufferedReader br = new BufferedReader(new InputStreamReader(System.in));
        System.out.println("Enter a number");
        String n = br.readLine();
        num = Integer.parseInt(n);
        int R, s = 0;
        int cnt = 0;
        while(num != 0)
        {
            R = num % 10;
            cnt++;
            num = num/10;
```

```
        }
            System.out.print("number of digits are" + cnt);
        }
    }
```

26. Display the following outputs using nested loops :

(a)	(b)	(c)	(d)	(e)
$ $ $ $ $	1	1	1	5 4 3 2 1
$ $ $ $ $	1 1	2 2	1 2	5 4 3 2
$ $ $ $ $	1 1 1	3 3 3	1 2 3	5 4 3
$ $ $ $ $	1 1 1 1	4 4 4 4	1 2 3 4	5 4
$ $ $ $ $	1 1 1 1 1	5 5 5 5 5	1 2 3 4 5	5

Ans. (a)
```java
import java.io.*;
public class sample1
{
    public static void main(String args[])
    {
        int x, y;
        for(x = 1; x < 5; x++)
        {
            for(y = 1; y <= 5; y++)
            {
                System.out.print("$");
            }
            System.out.println();
        }
    }
}
```

(b)
```java
import java.io.*;
public class sample2
{
    public static void main(String args[])
    {
        int x, y;
        for(x = 1; x < 5; x++)
        {
            for(y =1; y <= x; y++)
            {
                System.out.print("1");
            }
            System.out.println();
        }
    }
}
```

(c)
```java
import java.io.*;
public class sample3
{
    public static void main(String args[])
    {
```

```java
        int x, y;
        for(int x = 1; x <= 5; x++)
        {
                for(int y = i; y <= x; y++)
                {
                        System.out.print(x);
                }
            System.out.println();
                }
                }
        }
```

(d)
```java
    import java.io.*;
    public class sample4
    {
                public static void main(String args[])
                {
                    for(int x = 1; x <= 5; x++)
                    {
                                for(int y = 1; y <= x; y++)
                                {
                                    System.out.print(y);
                                }
                            System.out.println();
                        }
                    }
            }
```

(e)
```java
    import java.io.*;
    public class sample5
    {
        public static void main(String args[])
        {
        int x, y;
            for (x = 1; x < 5; x++)
            {
                for(y = 5; y >= x; y--)
            {
            System.out.print("y");
            }
        System.out.println();
            }
    }
    }
```

27. Write a program to display the following output :

```
*
* * *
* * * * *
* * * * * * *
* * * * * * * * *
```

```java
Ans. import java.io.*;
     public class sample6
     {
         public static void main(String args[])
         {
         int x, s;
         int k = 1;
             for(x = 1; x <= 5; x++)
             {
                 for( s = 1; s <= x * 2 - 1; s++)
                 {
                     System.out.print(" * ");
                 }
             System.out.println();
             }
         }
     }
```

28. Write a program which finds whether a given year is a leap year or not.

```java
Ans. .import java.io.*;
     public class sample7
     {
         public static void main(String args[]) throws IOException
         {
             int yr;
             BufferedReader br = new BufferedReader(new InputStreamReader(System.in));
             String s = br.readLine();
             yr = Integer.parseInt(s);
             if((yr % 4 == 0 && yr % 100 != 0) || (yr % 400 == 0))
             System.out.println("This year is leap year");
             else
             System.out.println("This is not a leep year");
         }
     }
```

29. Input a number and if the given number is even then give its square otherwise display its 3 multiples.

```java
Ans. import java.io.*;
     public class sample8
     {
         public static void main(String args[]) throws IOException
         {
             BufferedReader br = new BufferedReader(new InputStreamReader(System.in));
             String s = br.readLine();
             int n = Integer.parseInt(s);
             if(n % 2 == 0)
             System.out.print("square is " + n * n);
             else
             System.out.print("multiples are" + n * 1 + "\n" + n * 2 + "\n" + n * 3);
         }
     }
```

30. Input a student's marks in 4 subjects and calculate the average and find the grade according to the following catagries :

avg >= 60-First Division,

avg >= 45-2nd Division,

avg >= 33-3rd division otherwise fail.

Ans.
```java
import java.io.*;
public class sample9
{
    public static void main(String args[]) throws IOException
    {
        int M1, M2, M3, M4, T;
        BufferedReader br = new BufferedReader(new InputStreamReader(System.in));
        M1 = Integer.parseInt(br.readLine());
        M2 = Integer.parseInt(br.readLine());
        M3 = Integer.parseInt(br.readLine());
        M4 = Integer.parseInt(br.readLine());
        T = M1 + M2 + M3 + M4;
        double av = T/4;
        if(av >= 60)
        System.out.print("First Division");
        else if(av >= 45)
        System.out.print("Second Division");
        else if(av >= 33)
        System.out.print("Third Division");
        else
        System.out.print("failed");
    }
}
```

31. Store 3 numbers and display the greatest number using nested if();

Ans.
```java
import java.io.*;
public class sample9
{
    public static void main(String args[])
    {
        int n1 = 10, n2 = 20, n3 = 90, gr;
        if(n1 > n2)
        {
            if(n1 > n3)
            {
                gr = n1;
            }
            else
            {
                gr = n3;
            }
        }
        else
        {
```

```
            if(n2 > n3)
            {
                gr = n2;
            }
            else
            {
                gr = n3;
            }
        }
        System.out.print("greatest no. is" + gr);
    }
}
```

32. Repeat the above program using logical operator (&&).

Ans.
```
import java.io.*;
public class sample10
{
    public static void main(String args[])
    {
        int n1 = 10, n2 = 12, n3 = 9, gr;
        if(n1 > n2 && n1 > n3)
        gr = n1;
        if(n2 > n1 && n2 > n3)
        gr = n2;
        else
        gr = n3;
        System.out.print(gr);
    }
}
```

33. Using a switch statement, write a menu driven program to convert a given temperature from Fahrenheit to Celsius and vice versa. For an incorrect choice, an appropriate error message should be displayed.

(HINT : C =5/9× (F – 32) and F = 1.8 × (C + 32))

Ans.
```
import java.io.*;
public class test
{
    public static void main(String args[]) throws IOException
    {
        double F, c;
        BufferedReader br = new BufferedReader(new InputStreamReader(System.in));
        System.out.println(" 1. Celsius to Fahrenheit");
        System.out.println("2. Fahrenheit to Celcius");
        System.out.println("Enter your choice");
        int ch = Integer.parseInt(br.readLine());
        System.out.println("Enter temperature");
        int tm = Integer.parseInt(br.readLine());
        switch(ch)
        {
            case 1 :
            F = 1.8 * tm + 32;
```

```
            System.out.println("Temperature in Fahrenheit is" + F);
            break;
            case 2 :
            c = 5/9.0 * (tm - 32);
            System.out.println("Temperature in Celsius" + c);
            break;
            default :
            System.out.println("Invalid choice");
        }
    }
}
```

34. Input character through keyboard. Until we enter '*' Display total number of vowels and frequency of each vowel separately.

Ans.
```
import java.io.*;
public class sample11
{
        public static void main(String args[]) throws IOException
        {
        char ch='1';
        int a, e, i, o, u, v;
        a = e = i = o = u = v = 0;
        BufferedReader br = new BufferedReader(new InputStreamReader(System.in));
            while(ch != '*')
            {
            ch = (char)br.read();
            switch(ch)
            {
                case 'A' :
                case 'a' :
                a++;
                break;
                case 'e':
                case 'E':
                e++;
                break;
                case 'i' :
                case 'I' :
                i++;
                break;
                case 'o' :
                case 'O' :
                o++;
                break;
                case 'u':
                case 'U':
                u++;
                break;
            }
```

```java
        }
v = a + e + i + o + u;
System.out.println("frequency of a is" + a);
System.out.println("frequency of e is" + e);
System.out.println("frequency of i is" + i);
System.out.println("frequency of o is" + o);
System.out.println("frequency of u is" + u);
System.out.println("total volwels are" + v);
        }
    }
```

35. Write a program to display the sum of the following series :

11 + 22 + 33 + 44 +......... 1010;

Ans.
```java
import java.io.*;
public class sample12
{
        public static void main(String args[])
        {
        long sum = 0;
        long p;
        for(int x = 1; x < 10; x++)
        {
        p = (long)Math.pow(x,x);
        sum += p;
        }
    System.out.print(sum);
        }
    }
```

36. Write a program to display the first 10 fibonacci numbers.

Ans.
```java
import java.io.*;
public class sample13
{
        public static void main(String args[])
        {
            int cnt = 2;
            int a, b, c;
            a = 0;
            b = 1;
            System.out.println(a);
            System.out.println(b);
            while(cnt <= 10)
            {
                c = a + b;
                System.out.print(c);
                a = b;
                b = c;
                cnt++;
            }
        }
    }
```

37. Input a number and display its multiplication table.

Ans.
```java
import java.io.*;
public class sample14
{
        public static void main(String args[]) throws IOException
        {
            int n, t;
            BufferedReader br = new BufferedReader(new InputStreamReader(System.in));
            String s = br.readLine();
            n = Integer.parseInt(s);
            for(int k = 1; k <= 10; k++)
            {
                t = k * n;
                System.out.println(n + "*" + k + "=" + t);
            }
        }
}
```

38. Input a number and check whether it is an armstrong number or not (A number is armstrong if it is equal to the sum of the cubes of its digits).

Ans.
```java
import java.io.*;
public class sample15
{
        public static void main(String args[]) throws IOException
        {
            String s;
            int t;
            BufferedReader br = new BufferedReader(new InputStreamReader(System.in));
            s = br.readLine();
            int n = Integer.parseInt(s);
            t = n;
            int R, C, sum = 0;
                do
                {
                    R = n % 10;
                    c = R * R * R;
                    sum = sum + c;
                    n = n/10;
                }
                while(n != 0);
            if(t == sum)
            System.out.println("The number is an Armstrong number");
            else
            System.out.println("The number is not an Armstrong number);
        }
}
```

39. Design a class RailwayTicket with following description :

Instance variables/data members :

String name : To store the name of the customer

String coach : To store the type of coach customer wants to travel

long mobno : To store customer's mobile number

int amt : To store basic amount of ticket

int totalamt : To store the amount to be paid after updating the original amount

Member methods :

void accept() – To take input for name, coach, mobile number and amount.

void update() – To update the amount as per the coach selected

(extra amount to be added in the amount as follows)

Type of Coaches Amount

First_AC 700

Second_AC 500

Third_AC 250

Sleeper None

void display() – To display all details of a customer such as name, coach, total amount and moible number.

Write a main method to create an object of the class and call the above member methods.

Ans.
```java
import java.util.*;//importing package
public class RailwayTicket
{
    String name, coach;
    long mobno;
    int amt, totalamt;
    void accept()
    {
        Scanner sc = new Scanner(System.in);
        System.out.println("Enter the Details");
        name = sc.nextLine();
        coach = sc.nextLine();
        mobno = sc.nextLong();
        amt = sc.nextInt();
    }
    void update()
    {
        if(coach.equalsIgnoreCase ("First_AC"))
        {
            totalamt = amt + 700;
        }
        else if(coach.equalsIgnoreCase("Second_AC"))
        {
            totalamt = amt + 500;
        }
        else if(coach.equalsIgnoreCase("Third_AC"))
        {
            totalamt = amt + 250;
        }
        else
        {
            totalamt = amt;
        }
```

```
    }
    void display()
    {
        System.out.println("Name : " + name);
        System.out.println("Coach : " + coach);
        System.out.println("Mobile no. : "+ mobno);
        System.out.println("Amt : " + amt);
        System.out.println("Total Amt :" + totalamt);
    }
    public static void main(String args[])
    {
        RailwayTicket ob = new RailwayTicket();
        ob.accept();//function call
        ob.update();
        ob.display();
    }
}
```

Name	Type	Description
name	String	To store the name of the customer.
coach	String	To store name of coach.
mobno	long	To store customer's mobile number.
amt, totalamt	int	To store amount and total amount.

40. The LCM of two numbers can be found as follows :

If the larger number is also a multiple of the smaller number, it is the LCM of the two numbers, otherwise the next multiple of the larger number can be found and it can be checked, if it is a multiple of the smaller number. This process can be continued till the LCM is found.

Write a program to find the LCM of two numbers.

Ans.
```
import java.io.*;
public class LCM
{
    public static void main(String args[]) throws IOException
    {
        int n1, n2;
        int h, t;
        String s;
        BufferedReader br = new BufferedReader(new InputStreamReader(System.in));
        s = br.readLine();
        System.out.println("Enter two numbers");
        n1 = Integer.parseInt(s);
        s = br.readLine();
        n2 = Integer.parseInt(s);
        if(n1 < n2)
        {
                t = n2;
                n2 = n1;
                n1 = t;
        }
```

```
                h = 1;
                while(n1 % n2 != 0)
                {
                n1 = n1 * h;
                h++;
                }
                System.out.println("The LCM is = " + n1);
                }
        }
```

41. A cloth showroom has announced the following festival discounts on the purchase of items, based on the total cost of the items purchased :

TOTAL COST DISCOUNT (IN PERCENTAGE)

Less than or equal to ₹ 2000 5%

₹ 2001 to ₹ 5000 25%

₹ 5001 to ₹ 10000 35%

Above ₹ 10000 50%

Write a program to input the total cost and to compute and display the amount to be paid by the customer after availing the discount.

Ans.
```java
import java.io.*;
public class test
{
        public static void calc(double cost)
        {
                double d;
                if(cost <= 2000)
                d = 5.00/100 * cost;
                else if(cost > 2000 && cost <= 5000)
                d = 25.00/100 * cost;
                else if(cost > 5000 && cost <= 10000)
                d = 35.00/100 * cost;
                else
                d = 50.00/100 * cost;
                System.out.println("total amount is" + (cost - d));
        }
}
```

42. Write a program to read a positive integer from the console and find out whether it is an automorphic or not. (Automorphic numbers are those which are found on the extreme right side of their square).

e.g., 52 = 25

62 = 36

252 = 625

Hence, 5, 6, 25 are automorphic numbers.

Ans.
```java
import java.io.*;
public class Automorphic
{
        public static void main(String args []) throws IOException
        {
                int num, s;
                int i, j, m, n, f;
```

```java
int [] a = new int [10];
int [] b = new int [5];
BufferedReader input = new BufferedReader(new InputStreamReader(System.in));
System.out.println("Enter Number = ");
String x = input.readLine();
num = Integer.parseInt(x);
s = num * num;
i = 0;
j = 0;
f = 0;
while(num != 0)
{
    b[i] = num % 10;
    num /= 10;
    ++i;
}
while(s != 0)
{
    a[j] = s % 10;
    s /= 10;
    ++ j;
}
for(n = 0, m = 0; n < i; n++, m++)
{
    if(a[m] != b[n])
    f = 1;
}
if(f == 0)
    System.out.println("Number is Automorphic");
else
    System.out.println("Number is not Automorphic");
    }
}
```

43. Using the switch statement, write a menu driven program to calculate the maturity amount of a Bank Deposit.

The user is given the following options :

1. Term Deposit.

2. Recurring Deposit.

For option (i) accept principal (P), rate of interest (r) and time period in years (n).

Calculate and output the maturity amount (A) receivable using the formula:

$$A = P\left[1+\frac{r}{100}\right]^n$$

For option (ii) accept Monthly Installment (P), rate of interest (r) and time period in months (n). Calculate and output the maturity amount (A) receivable using the formula:

$$A = P \times n + P \times \frac{n(n+1)}{2} \times \frac{r}{100} \times \frac{1}{12}$$

For an incorrect option, an appropriate error message should be displayed.

Ans.
```java
import java.io.*;
class Bank
{
    double p, r, n, A;
    int ch;
    void display()
    {
    BufferedReader br = new BufferedReader(new InputStreamReader(System.in));
    System.out.println("1. Term Deposit");
    System.out.println("2. Recurring Deposit");
    System.out.println("Enter your choice");
    ch = Integer.parseInt(br.readLine());
    switch(ch)
    {
        case 1 : System.out.println("Enter principal, rate and time in years");
                p = Double.parseDouble(br.readLine());
                r = Double.parseDouble(br.readLine());
                n = Double.parseDouble(br.readLine());
                A = p * Math.pow(1 + r/100, n);
                break;
        case 2 : System.out.println("Enter monthly installment, rate and time in months");
                p = Double.parseDouble(br.readLine());
                r = Double.parseDouble(br.readLine());
                n = Double.parseDouble(br.readLine());
                A = (p * n) + (p * n * (n + 1)/2 * r/100 * 1.0/12);
                break;
        default : A = 0;
                System.out.println("Wrong Choice");
                break;
    }
    System.out.println("Maturity Amount" + A);
    }
}
```

44. Using the switch statement, write a menu driven program :

(i) To check and display whether a number input by the user is a composite number or not (A number is said to be a composite, if it has one or more than one factor excluding 1 and the number itself).

Example : 4, 6, 8, 9 ...

(ii) To find the smallest digit of an integer that is input.

Sample input : 6524

Sample output : Smallest digit is 2

For an incorrect choice, an appropriate error message should be displayed.

Ans.
```java
import java.io.*;
class Menu
{
    int n, ch, i, c = 0, d, min=0;
    void display()
    {
        BufferedReader br = new BufferedReader(new InputStreamReader(System.in));
```

```java
System.out.println("1. Composite");
System.out.println("2. Minimum Digit");
System.out.println("Enter Your Choice");
ch = Integer.parseInt(br.readLine());
System.out.println("Enter a number");
n = Integer.parseInt(br.readLine());
switch(ch)
{
    case 1 :
    for(i = 1; i <= n; i++)
    {
        if(n % i == 0)
        {
        c++;
        }
    }
    if(c != 2)
    {
        System.out.println(n + " is composite no.");
    }
    else
    {
        System.out.println(n + " is not a composite no.");
    }
    break;
    case 2 :
    while(n > 0)
    {
        d = n%10;
        min=d;
        if(d < min)
        {
            min = d;
        }
        n = n/10;
    }
    System.out.println("Smallest Digit is : " + min);
    break;
    default: System.out.println("Wrong Choice");
}
}
}
```

45. Write a menu driven program to display the pattern as per user's choice.

Pattern 1	Pattern 2
ABCDE	B
ABCD	LL
ABC	UUU

AB	EEEE
A	

For an incorrect option, an appropriate error message should be displayed.

Ans.
```java
import java.util.*;
class series
{
    public static void main(String arg[])
    {
        Scanner sc = new Scanner(System.in);
        System.out.println("1 for Pattern 1 and 2 for Pattern 2");
        System.out.println("enter the choice");
        int ch = sc.nextInt();
        switch(ch)
        {
            case 1 : String s = "ABCDE";
            for(int i = s.length(); i > 0; i--)
            {
                System.out.println(s.substring(0, i));
            }
            break;
            case 2 : String s1 = "BLUE";
            for(int i = 0; i < s1.length(); i++)
            {
                for(int j = 0; j <= i; j++)
                {
                    System.out.print(s1.charAt(i));
                }
                System.out.println();
            }
            break;
            default : System.out.println("invalid choice");
        }
    }
}
```

Name	Type	Description
ch	int	To store the choice.
i, j	int	For loop variables.
s	String	To store the string.
s1	String	To store the string.

46. The International Standard Book Number (ISBN) is a unique numeric book identifier which is printed on every book. The ISBN is based upon a 10-digit code. The ISBN is legal if :

$1 \times digit1 + 2 \times digit2 + 3 \times digit3 + 4 \times digit4 + 5 \times digit5 + 6 \times digit6 + 7 \times digit7 + 8 \times digit8 + 9 \times digit9 + 10 \times digit10$ is divisible by 11.

Example : For an ISBN 1401601499

Sum $= 1 \times 1 + 2 \times 4 + 3 \times 0 + 4 \times 1 + 5 \times 6 + 6 \times 0 + 7 \times 1 + 8 \times 4 + 9 \times 9 + 10 \times 9 = 253$ which is divisible by 11.

Write a program to :

(i) Input the ISBN code as a 10-digit integer.

(ii) If the ISBN is not a 10-digit integer, output the message, "Illegal ISBN" and terminate the program.

(iii) If the number is 10-digit, extract the digits of the number and compute the sum as explained above.

If the sum is divisible by 11, output the message, "Legal ISBN". If the sum is not divisible by 11, output the message, "Illegal ISBN".

Ans.
```java
import java.io.*;
class Number
{
    long n, t, rev = 10, d, s = 0;
    int c = 0, x = 1;
    void display()
    {
        BufferedReader br = new BufferedReader(new InputStreamReader(System.in));
        System.out.println("Enter a number");
        n = Long.parseLong(br.readLine());
        t = n;
        while(t > 0)
        {
            c++;
            t = t/10;
        }
        if(c != 10)
        {
            System.out.println("Illegal ISBN");
            System.exit(0);
        }
        else
        {
            while(n > 0)
            {
                d = n%10;
                s = s + d * rev;
                n = n/10;
                rev--;
            }
            if(s % 11 == 0)
            {
                System.out.println("Legal ISBN");
            }
            else
            {
                System.out.println("Illegal ISBN")
            }
        }
    }
}
```

47. Given below is a hypothetical table showing rates of Income Tax for male citizens below the age of 65 years :

Taxable Income (TI) (in ₹) Income Tax (in ₹)

Does not exceed ₹ 1,60,000

Is greater than ₹ 1,60,000 and less than or equal to ₹ 5,00,000

Nil

(TI - 1,60,000) × 10%

Is greater than ₹ 5,00,000 and less than or equal to ₹ 8,00,000 [(TI - 5,00,000) × 20%] + 34,000

Is greater than ₹ 8,00,000 [(TI - 8,00,000) × 30%] + 94,000

Write a program to input the age, gender (male or female) and Taxable Income of a person.

If the age is more than 65 years or the gender is female, display "wrong category".

If the age is less than or equal to 65 years and the gender is male, compute and display the Income Tax payable as per the table given above.

Ans.
```java
import java.io.*;
public class IncomeTax
{
    public static void main(String args[]) throws IOException
    {
        BufferedReader br = new BufferedReader(new InputStreamReader(System.in));
        int age;
        String gender;
        double T1, Itax = 0.0;
        System.out.println("Enter age, gender, taxable income");
        age = Integer.parseInt(br.readLine());
        gender = br.readLine();
        T1 = Double.parseDouble(br.readLine());
        if(age > 65 || gender.equalsIgnoreCase("female"))
        System.out.println("Wrong Category");
        else if(age <= 65 && gender.equalsIgnoreCase("male"))
        {
            if(T1 <= 160000)
            System.out.println ("Nil");
            else if(T1 <= 160000 && T1 <= 500000)
            Itax = (T1 - 160000) * 0.10;
            else if(T1 > 500000 && T1 <= 800000)
            Itax = (T1 - 160000) * 0.20 + 34000;
            else if(T1 > 800000)
            Itax = (T1 - 800000) * 0.30 + 940000;
        }
        System.out.println("IncomeTax" + Itax);
    }
}
```

48. Using the switch statement, write a menu driven program to :

(i) Generate and display the first 10 terms of the Fibonacci series 0, 1, 1, 2, 3, 5…

The first two Fibonacci numbers are 0 and 1, and each subsequent number is the sum of the previous two.

(ii) Find the sum of the digits of an integer that is input.

Sample Input : 15390

Sample Output : Sum of the digits = 18

For an incorrect choice, an appropriate error message should be displayed.

Ans.
```java
import java.io.*;
public class menu
{
    public static void main(String args[]) throws IOException
    {
        int ch, S = 0, n;
        BufferedReader br = new BufferedReader(new InputStreamReader(System.in));
        System.out.println("1. Fibonacci");
        System.out.println("2. Sum of Digits of Number");
        ch = Integer.parseInt(br.readLine());
        switch(ch)
        {
            case 1 :
                int f = 0, s = 1, t = 0;
            System.out.println(f + '\t' + s);
            for(int i = 1; i <= 8; i++)
            {
                t = f + s;
                System.out.println('\t' + t);
                f = s;
                s = t;
            }
            break;
            case 2 :
                System.out.println("Enter Number to get the sum of digits");
            n = Integer.parseInt(br.readLine());
            while(n != 0)
            {
                S = S + n % 10;
                n = n/10;
            }
            System.out.println("sum of the digits"+S);
            break;
            default : System.out.println("enter correct choice");
        }
    }
}
```

49. Write a menu driven program to perform the following : (Use switch - case statement)

(i) To print the series 0, 3, 8, 15, 24 ... n terms (value of 'n' is to be an input by the user).

(ii) To find the sum of the series given below :

$S = 1/2 + 3/4 + 5/6 + 7/8 ... 19/20$.

Ans.
```java
import java.io.*;
public class Menu
{
    int i, ch, n, x;
    double s = 0;
    void display()
    {
```

```java
BufferedReader br = new BufferedReader(new InputStreamReader(System.in));
System.out.println("Enter 1. To Print the Series");
System.out.println("Enter 2. To Print the Sum of Series");
System.out.println("Enter Your Choice");
ch = Integer.parseInt(br.readLine());
switch(ch)
{
    case 1 : System.out.println("Enter a number");
    n = Integer.parseInt(br.readLine());
    for(i = 1; i <= n; i++)
    {
        x = i * i - 1;
        System.out.print(x + ",");
    }
    break;
    case 2 : for(i = 1; i <= 19; i++)
    {
        s = s + i / (i + 1);
        i++;
    }
    System.out.print(s);
    break;
    default : System.out.println("Wrong Choice");
    break;
}
}
}
```

50. Shasha Travels Pvt. Ltd. gives the following discount to its customers :

Ticket amount	Discount
Above ₹ 70000	18%
₹ 55001 to ₹ 70000	16%
₹ 35001 to ₹ 55000	12%
₹ 25001 to ₹ 35000	10%
less than ₹ 25001	2%

Write a program to input the name and ticket amount for the customer and calculate the discount amount and net amount to be paid. Display the output in the following format for each customer :

Sl. No.	Name	Ticket charges	Discount	Net amount
1.	—	—	—	—

(Assume that there are 15 customers, first customer is given the serial no (Sl.No.) 1, next customer 2 .... and so on).

Ans.
```java
import java.io.*;
class Travels
{
    String name[] = new String[15];
    int tic[] = new int[15];
    int i;
    double dis, net;
```

```java
void calc()
{
BufferedReader br = new BufferedReader(new InputStreamReader(System.in));
for(i = 0; i < 15; i++)
{
System.out.println("Enter name and ticket amount");
name[i] = br.readLine();
tic[i] = Integer.parseInt(br.readLine());
}
System.out.println("SI. No.\t Name \tTicket Charges \t Discount \t Net Amount");
for(i = 0; i < 15; i++)
{
    if(tic[i] > 70000)
    {
        dis = 0.18 * tic[i];
    }
    else if(tic[i] >= 55001 && tic[i] <= 70000)
    {
        dis = 0.16 * tic[i];
    }
    else if(tic[i] >= 35001 && tic[i] <= 55000)
    {
        dis = 0.16 * tic[i];
    }
    else if(tic[i] >= 25001 && tic[i] <= 35000)
    {
        dis = 0.10 * tic[i];
    }
    else
    {
        dis = 0.02 * tic[i];
    }
    net = tic[i] - dis;
    System.out.println((i + 1) + "\t" +name[i] + "\t" + tic[i] + "\t" +
    dis + "\t" + net);
}
}
}
```

51. Write a menu driven program to accept a number and check and display whether it is a prime number or not OR an automorphic number or not. (Use switch-case statement).

   (i)   Prime number : A number is said to be a prime number if it is divisible only by 1 and itself and not by any other number.

        Example : 3, 5, 7, 11, 13 etc.

  (ii) Automorphic number : An automorphic number is the number which is contained in the last digit(s) of its square.

        Example : 25 is an automorphic number as its square is 625 and 25 is present as the last two digits.

Ans.
```java
import java.io.*;
class Menu
```

```java
    {
        int ch, n, i, c = 0, flag = 0, s;
        void check()
        {
            BufferedReader br = new BufferedReader(new InputStreamReader(System.in));
            System.out.println("1. Prime");
            System.out.println("2. Automorphic");
            System.out.println("Enter Your Choice");
            ch = Integer.parseInt(br.readLine());
            System.out.println("Enter a Number");
            n = Integer.parseInt(br.readLine());
            switch(ch)
            {
                case 1: for(i = 1; i <= n; i++)
                {
                    if(n % i == 0)
                    {
                        c++;
                    }
                }
                if(c == 2)
                {
                System.out.println("Prime no.");
                }
                else
                {
                System.out.println("Not a Prime no.");
                }
                break;
                case 2: s = n * n;
                while(n > 0)
                {
                    if(n % 10 != s % 10)
                    {
                        flag = 1;
                        break;
                    }
                    else
                    {
                        n = n / 10;
                        s = s / 10;
                    }
                }
                if(flag == 0)
                {
                    System.out.println("Automorphic no.");
                }
                else
```

```
        {
            System.out.println("Not an Automorphic no.");
        }
        break;
            default : System.out.println("Invalid Choice");
        break;
        }
    }
}
```

52. Write a program to accept a number and check and display whether it is a spy number or not.
    (A number is spy if the sum of its digits equals the product of its digits.)
    Example : consider the number 1124,
    Sum of the digits = 1 + 1 + 2 + 4 = 8
    Product of the digits = 1 × 1 × 2 × 4 = 8

Ans.
```java
import java.util.*;// importing package
class Spy
{
    int n, d, p = 1, s = 0;
    void display()
    {
        Scanner sc = new Scanner(System.in);
        System.out.println("Enter a no.");
        n = sc.nextInt();
        while(n > 0)
        {
            d = n % 10;
            s = s + d;
            p = p * d;
            n = n/10;
        } // while loop ending
        if(s == p)
        {
            System.out.println("It is a Spy number");
        }
        else
        {
            System.out.println("It is not a Spy number");
        }
    }
}
```

Name	Type	Description
n	int	To input a number
d	int	To store a digit
p	int	To store product of digits
s	int	To store sum of digits

53. Write a program to input a string in uppercase and print the frequency of each character.
    Example :

INPUT : COMPUTER HARDWARE

OUTPUT :

CHARACTERS	FREQUENCY
A	2
C	1
D	1
E	2
H	1
M	1
O	1
P	1
R	3
T	1
U	1
W	1

Ans.
```
import java.io.*;
class Frequency
{
    String s;
    int i, j, l, f;
    void display()
    {
        BufferedReader br = new BufferedReader(new InputStreamReader(System.in));
        System.out.println("Enter a string in upper case");
        s = br.readLine();
        l = s.length();
        for(i = 65; i <= 90; i++)
        {
            f = 0;
            for(j = 0; j < l; j++)
            {
                if(s.charAt(j) == i)
                {
                f++;
                }
            }
            if(f > 0)
            {
                System.out.println((char)i + "\t" + f);
            }
        }
    }
}
```

54. Write a menu driven class to accept a number from the user and check whether it is a palindrome or a Perfect number.

(i) Palindrome number :

   (a number is a Palindrome which when read in reverse order is same as read in the right order)

Example : 11, 101, 151 etc.

(ii) Perfect number :

(a number is called Perfect if it is equal to the sum of its factors other than the number itself.)

Example : 6 = 1 + 2 + 3.

Ans.

```java
import java.io.*;
public class number
{
    public static void main(String args[]) throws IOException
    {
        int n,p;
        BufferedReader br= new BufferedReader(new InputStreamReader(System.in));
        System.out.println("Enter a no");
        n = Integer.parseInt(br.readLine());
        System.out.println("Enter your choice-1 for checking for palindrome choice-2 for checking for perfect number");
        p = Integer.parseInt(br.readLine());
        switch(p)
        {
            case 1: int num, digit, rev = 0;
            num = n;
            while(num != 0)
            {
                digit = num%10;
                rev = rev * 10 + digit;
                num = num/10;
            }
            if(n == rev)
                System.out.println(n + "is a palindrome");
            else
                System.out.println(n + "is not a palindrome");
            break;
            case 2 : int i, sum = 0;
            for(i = 1; i < n; i++)
            {
            if(n % i == 0)
            sum += i;
            }
            if(sum == n)
            System.out.println(n+"is a perfect no");
            else
            System.out.println(n+"is not a perfect no");
        }
    }
}
```

55. Write a program that encodes a word into Piglatin. To translate a word into a Piglatin word, convert the word into uppercase and then place the first vowel of the original word at the start of the new word along with the remaining alphabets. The alphabets present before the vowel being shifted towards the end followed by "AY".

Sample input (1) : London
Sample output (1) : ONDONLAY
Sample input (2) : Olympics
Sample output (2) : OLYMPICSAY

Ans.
```java
import java.io.*;
class Piglatin
{
    int l, i;
    String s, p;
    char ch;
    public Piglatin()
    {
        s = "RiteshSahu";
    }
    void display()
    {
        BufferedReader br = new BufferedReader(new InputStreamReader(System.in));
        System.out.println("Enter a string");
        s = br.readLine();
        s = s.toUpperCase();
        l = s.length();
        for(i = 0; i < l; i++)
        {
            ch = s.charAt(i);
            if(ch == 'A' || ch == 'E' || ch == 'I' || ch == 'O' || ch == 'U')
            {
            p = s.substring(i) + s.substring(0, i) + "AY";
            System.out.println(p);
            break;
            }
        }
    }
}
```

56. Write a program to calculate and print the sum of each of the following series :

(a) Sum (S) = 2 - 4 + 6 - 8 + ... - 20

(b) Sum (S) = x/2+x/5+x/7+.......+

(Value of x to be input by the user.)

Ans. (a)
```java
import java.io.*;
public class series
{
    public static void main(String args[])
    {
        int i, sum = 0, sign = -1;
        for(i = 2; i <= 20; i = i + 2)
        {
            sign = sign * - 1;
            sum = sum + i * sign;
        }
```

```java
        System.out.println("Sum of series" + sum);
    }
}
(b)  import java.io.*;
     public class sum
     {
         public static void series(int x)
         {
             double sum = 0;
             int i;
             for(i = 2; i <= 20; i = i + 3)
             {
                 sum = sum + (x / i);
             }
             System.out.println(sum);
         }
     }
```

57. Write a program to compute and display the sum of the following series :

$$\frac{1 + 2\ 1 + 2 + 3}{1 \times 2 + 1 \times 2 \times 3 + \ldots\ldots + 1 + 2 + 3 + 4 \ldots\ldots n}$$

$1 \times 2 \times 3 \times 4 \ldots\ldots n$

Ans.
```java
public class Test
{
    public static void series(int n)
    {
        double sum = 0;
        for(int k = 2; k <= n; k++)
        {
            int s = 0, m = 1;
            for(int x = 1; x <= k; x++)
            {
                s = s + x;
                m = m * x;
                sum = sum + (double) s/m;
            }
            System.out.println("Sum of series is" + sum);
        }
    }
}
```

58. An electronics shop has announced the following seasonal discounts on the purchase of certain items.

Purchase Amount in Rs	Discount on Laptop	Discount on Desktop PC
0-25000	0.0%	5.0%
25001-57000	5.0%	7.5%
57001-100000	7.5%	10.0%
More than 100000	10.0%	15.0%

Write a program based on the above criteria, to input name, address, amount of purchase and the type of purchase (L for Laptop and D for Desktop) by a customer. Compute and print the net amount to be paid by a customer along with his name and address.

(Hint : discount = (discount rate/100) * amount of purchase

Net amount = amount of purchase - discount)

Ans.
```java
import java.io.*;
public class EShop
{
    String name, add;
    double dis, amt, net;
    char type;
    void compute(String n, String a, double am, char t)
    {
    name = n;
    add = a;
    amt = am;
    type = t;
    if(type == 'l' || type == 'L')
    {
        if(amt > 0) && (amt <= 25000))
        {
            dis = 0;
        }
        else if(amt > 25000 && amt <= 57000)
        {
            dis = 5;
        }
        else if(amt > 57000 && amt <= 100000)
        {
            dis = 7.5;
        }
        else
        {
            dis = 10;
        }
    }
    else if(type == 'd' || type == 'D')
    {
        if(amt > 0 && amt <= 25000)
        {
            dis = 5;
        }
        else if(amt > 25000 && amt <= 57000)
        {
            dis = 7.5;
        }
        else if(amt > 57000 && amt <= 100000)
        {
            dis = 10;
```

```
        }
        else
        {
                dis = 15;
        }
    }
    else
    {
        System.out.println("Invalid Choice");
    }

        net = amt - dis/100 * amt;
        System.out.println("Customer Name : " + name);
        System.out.println("Customer Address :"+ add);
        System.out.println("Net Amount : " + net);

    }
}
```

59. Write a program to input a sentence and print the number of characters found in the longest word of the given sentence.

For example : if S = "India is my country" then the output should be 7

Ans.
```java
import java.io.*;
public class Longest
{
    String sen;
    int i, l, max = 0;
    void display(String s)
    {
        sen = s;
        sen = sen + " ";
        l = sen.length();
        for(i = 0; i < l; i++)
        {
            String w = "";
            while(sen.charAt(i) != ' ')
            {
                w = w + sen.charAt(i);
                i++;
            }
            if(w.length() > max)
            {
                max = w.length();
            }
        }
        System.out.println(max);
    }
}
```

60. Write a program to generate a triangle or an inverted triangle till n terms based upon the user's choice of triangle to be displayed.

Example 1.

Input : Type 1 for a triangle and type 2 for an inverted triangle

1

Enter the number of terms

5

Output :

1

2 2

3 3 3

4 4 4 4

5 5 5 5 5

Example 2.

Input : Type 1 for a triangle and type 2 for an inverted triangle

2

Enter the number of terms

6

Output :

6 6 6 6 6 6

5 5 5 5 5

4 4 4 4

3 3 3

2 2

1

Ans.
```java
import java.io.*;
public class Pattern
{
    int ch, n, i, j;
    void display()
    {
    BufferedReader br = new BufferedReader(new InputStreamReader(System.in));
    System.out.println("Type 1 for Triangle and \n Type 2 for Inverted Triangle");
    ch = Integer.parseInt(br.readLine());
    System.out.println("Enter no. of Terms");
    n = Integer.parseInt(br.readLine());
        if(ch == 1)
        {
            for(i = 1; i <= n; i ++)
            {
                for(j = 1; j <= i; j++)
                {
                System.out.print(i + " ");
                }
                System.out.println();
            }
        }
        else if(ch == 2)
        {
```

```java
        for(i = n; i >= 1; i--)
        {
            for(j = 1; j <= i; j++)
            {
            System.out.print(i + " ");
            }
        System.out.println();
        }
    }
    else
    {

        System.out.println("Invalid Choice");

    }

    }

}
```

61. Write a menu driven program to accept a number from the user and check whether it is a 'BUZZ' number or to accept any two numbers and print the 'GCD' of them.

   (i)   A BUZZ number is the number which either ends with 7 or is divisible by 7.

   (ii) GCD (Greatest Common Divisor) of two integers is calculated by continued division method. Divide the larger number by the smaller; the remainder then divides the previous divisor. The process is repeated till the remainder is zero. The divisor then results the GCD.

Ans.
```java
import java.io.*;
public class MenuDriven
{
    int n1, n2, ch;
    void display()
    {
        BufferedReader br = new Buffered Reader(new InputStreamReader(System.in));
        System.out.println("1. Buzz Number");
        System.out.println("2. GCD");
        System.out.println("Enter your choice");
        ch = Integer.parseInt(br.readLine());
        if(ch == 1)
        {
            System.out.println("Enter a number");
            n1 = Integer.parseInt(br.readLine());
            if(n1 % 7 == 0 || n1% 10 == 7)
            {
                System.out.println("Its a BUZZ number");
            }
            else
            {
                System.out.println ("Not a BUZZ number");
            }
        }
        else if(ch == 2)
        {
            System.out.println("Enter 2 numbers");
```

```
                n1 = Integer.parseInt(br.readLine());
                n2 = Integer.parseInt(br.readLine());
                if(n2 > n1)
                {
                    int x = n1;
                    n1 = n2;
                    n2 = x;
                }
                int t;
                while(n1 % n2 != 0)
                {
                    t = n1;
                    n1 = n2;
                    n2 = t % n2;
                }
                System.out.println("GCD is" + n2);
            }
            else
            {
            System.out.println("Invalid Choice");
            }
        }
    }
```

62. Convert the following segment into equivalent for loop.

```
int i;
i = 1;
while(i <= 20)
{
    System.out.println(i + " ");
    i++;
}
```

Ans.
```
int i;
for(i = 1; i <= 20; i++)
{
    System.out.println(i+" ");
}
```

63. Write a program using a method Palindrome( ), to check whether a string is a Palindrome or not by scanning characters of a string using for loop.

A Palindrome is a string that reads the same from left to right and vice versa.

E.g., MADAM, ARORA, ABBA, etc.

Ans.
```
import java.io.*;
public class Test
{
    public static void palindrome(String s)
    {
        String k = "";
        char e;
        for(int i = s.length() - 1; i >= 0; i--)
```

```
        {
            c = s.charAt(i);
            k = k + c;
        }
        if(s == k)
        System.out.println("String is palindrome")
        else
        System.out.println("String is not palindrome");
    }
}
```

64. Write a program to input any given string to calculate the total number of characters and vowels present in the string and also reverse the string :

Example :

INPUT :

Enter string : SNOWY

OUTPUT :

Total number of characters : 05

Name of vowels : 01

Reserve string : YWONS

Ans.
```
import java.io.*;
public class test
{
    public static void main(String args[]) throws IOException
    {
        String s, rev = "";
        char ch;
        int vowel = 0;
        BufferedReader br = new BufferedReader(new InputStreamReader(System.in));
        System.out.println("Enter a String ");
        s = br.readLine();
        int l = s.length();
    for(int i = 0; i < l; i++)
    {
        ch = s.charAt(i);
        if(ch == 'a' || ch == 'e' || ch == 'i' || ch == 'o' || ch == 'u')
        {
            vowel++;
        }
    }
    for(int i = l - 1; i >= 0; i--)
    {
        ch = s.charAt(i);
        rev = rev + ch;
    }
        System.out.println("Total number of characters " + l);
        System.out.println("Total number of vowels " + vowel);
        System.out.println("Reverse string is " + rev);
    }
}
```

Programming Based Questions

65. Write a program to print the sum of negative numbers, sum of positive even numbers and sum of positive odd numbers from a list of numbers (N) entered by the user. The list terminates when the user enters zero.

Ans.
```java
import java.io.*;
public class test
{
    public static void main(String args[]) throws IOException
    {
        String s;
        int num, sum1, sum2, sum3;
        sum1 = sum2 = sum3 = 0;
        BufferedReader br = new BufferedReader(new InputStreamReader(System.in));
        num = - 1;
        while(num != 0)
    {
        System.out.println("Enter a Number");
        s = br.readLine();
        num = Integer.parseInt(s);
        if(num < 0)
        sum1 = sum1 + num;
        else
        {
            if(num % 2 == 0)
            sum2 = sum2 + num;
            else
            sum3 = sum3 + num;
        }
    }
        System.out.println("Sum of negative numbers " + sum1);
        System.out.println("Sum of positive even numbers " + sum2);
        System.out.println("Sum of positive odd " + sum3);
    }
}
```

66. An employee is entitled to pay an income tax based on his gross annual income as follows :

Annual gross income Annual Tax deduction %

Less than or equal to ₹ 100000 0%

₹ 100001 to ₹ 500000 ₹ 1000 + 10% of income exceeding ₹ 100000

₹ 500001 to ₹ 800000 ₹ 5000 + 20% of income exceeding ₹ 500000

> 800000 ₹ 10000 + 30% of income exceeding ₹ 80000

Write a program to compute and print the tax payable by a salaried person.

Ans.
```java
import java.io.*;
public class IncomeTax
{
    public static void main(String args[]) throws IOException
    {
        BufferedReader A = new BufferedReader(new InputStreamReader(System.in));
        System.out.println("Enter the gross income");
        String x = A.readLine();
        int i = Integer.parseInt(x);
```

```java
        double t;
        if(i <= 100000)
        {
            t = (0.0/100) * i;
            System.out.println("TAX=" +t);
        }
        else if(i >= 100001 && i <= 5000000)
        {
            t = 1000 + (10.0/100) * (i - 100000);
            System.out.println("TAX = " + t);
        }
        else if(i >= 500001 && i <= 800000)
        {

            t = 5000 + (20.0 / 100) * (i - 500000);
            System.out.println("TAX = "+t);
        }
        else if(i > 800000)
        {
            t = 10000 + (30.0/100) * (i - 800000);
            System.out.println("TAX = " +t);
        }
    }
}
```

67. Write a menu driven program, defining methods to perform the following operations on strings :

   (i) Concatenate Strings.

   (ii) Check if a string terminates with a '.' (full stop).

Ans.
```java
import java.io.*;
public class test53
{
    static String concatenation(String s1, String s2)
    {
        String x = s1.concat(s2);
        return x;
    }
    static void check(String c)
    {
        int len = c.length();
        char e = c.charAt(len - 1);
        if(e == '.')
        System.out.print("The string terminates with a full stop");
        else
        System.out.print("The string doesn't terminate with a full stop");
    }
    public static void main(String args[]) throws IOException
    {
        BufferedReader buf = new BufferedReader(new InputStreamReader(System.in));
        System.out.println("****MENU*****");
        System.out.println("1. Concatenating strings");
```

```java
System.out.println("2. Check the terminating character as :");
System.out.println("Enter the choice :");
String ch1 = buf.readLine();
int ch = Integer.parseInt(ch1);
switch(ch)
{
    case 1 : System.out.println("Please enter the two strings");
    String b1 = buf.readLine();
    String b2 = buf.readLine();
    String d = concatenation(b1, b2);
    System.out.print("The concatenated string is"+d);
    break;
    case 2 : System.out.print("Enter the string to be checked :");
    String z = buf.readLine();
    check(z);
    break;
    default : System.out.print("Invalid choice");
}
}
}
```

68. Accept the length of three sides of a triangle and print appropriate message for the type it belongs to *e.g.,* Scalene, Equilateral or Isosceles.

Ans.
```java
import java.io.*;
public class Triangle
{
    public static void main(String args[]) throws IOException
    {
        BufferedReader A = new BufferedReader(new InputStreamReader(System.in));
        System.out.println("Enter the length of first side :");
        String x = A.readLine();
        double a = Double.parseDouble(x);
        System.out.println("Enter the length of second side :");
        String y = A.readLine();
        double b = Double.parseDouble(y);
        System.out.println("Enter the length of third side :");
        String z = A.readLine();
        double c = Double.parseDouble(z);
        if(a == b && a == c && b == c)
        System.out.println("It is an equilateral triangle");
        else if(a == b || a == c || b == c)
        System.out.println("It is an isosceles triangle");
        else
        System.out.println("It is a scalene triangle");
    }
}
```

69. (a) Define a method isVowel for a java class that accepts a character and checks whether it is a vowel or a consonant. It returns 1 if character is a vowel else it returns 0.

(b) Define main method to call isVowel.

Ans. import java.io.*;

```
public class Vowel
{
    public static int isVowel(char x)
    {
        if (x == 'A' || x == 'a' || x == 'E' || x == 'e' || x == 'I' || x == 'i' || x == 'O' || x == 'o' || x == 'U' ||
        x == 'u')
        return 1;
        else
        return 0;
    }
    public static void main(String args[]) throws IOException
    {
        BufferedReader buf = new BufferedReader(new InputStreamReader(System.in));
        System.out.println("Please enter a character :");
        char m = (char) buf.read();
        int a = isVowel(m);
        if(a == 1)
        System.out.print("The entered character is a vowel");
        else
        System.out.print("The entered character is not a vowel");
    }
}
```

70. Design a class Library, define a method for the class that accepts the data members : memberName, bookName. Define another method that computes the fine for a member. The fine is calculated depending on the number of days a book is returned late :

Days Fine per day in Rupees

First ten days ₹ 1

Next Ten days ₹ 5

Later than 20 days ₹ 8

Ans. import java.io.*;

```
public class Library
{
    static long mid;
    static String mname, bname;
    static double fine;
    static void acceptValues(long id, String n, String bn)
    {
        mid = id;
        mname = n;
        bname = bn;
    }
    static void calculate(int days)
    {
        if(days < 10)
        fine = days * 1;
        else if(days <= 20)
        fine = 10 + 5 * (days - 10);
```

```java
        else
        fine = 10 + 5 * 10 + 8 * (days - 20);
        System.out.print("The fine = " + fine);
    }
    public staitc void main(String args[]) throws IOException
    {
        BufferedReader buf = new BufferedReader(new InputStreamReader(System.in));
        System.out.println("Please enter the member id, name and the book name issued by him :");
        String i = buf.readLine();
        int x = Integer.parseInt(i);
        String n = buf.readLine();
        String b = buf.readLine();
        acceptValues(x, n, b);
        System.out.println("Please enter the number of days the books is returned late :");
        String b1 = buf.readLine();
        int d = Integer.parseInt(b1);
        calculate(d);
    }
}
```

71. Write a program in java to compute the railway fare depending on the criteria as given below :

Age (in years) Distance (in km)	Fare (in ₹)
Below 10	5
Between 10 and 50	20
Above 50	50
Between 10 and 60 below	10
Between 10 and 50	40
Above 50	80
Above 60 Below 10	4
Between 10 and 50	15
Above 50	35

Ans.
```java
import java.io.*;
public class Railway
{
    public static void main(String args[]) throws IOException
    {
        BufferedReader buf = new BufferedReader(new InputStreamReader(System.in));
        System.out.println("Please enter your age in years :");
        String a = buf.readLine();
        int age = Integer.parseInt(a);
        System.out.println("Please enter the distance to be travelled :");
        String d = buf.readLine();
        int dis = Integer.parseInt(d);
        if(age <= 10)
        {
            if(dis <= 10)
            System.out.print("Fair = ₹ 5.00");
            else if(dis <= 50)
```

```
            System.out.print("Fair = ₹ 20.00");
            else if(dis > 50)
            System.out.print("Fair = ₹ 50.00");
        }
        else if(age > 10 && age <= 60)
        {
            if(dis <= 10)
            System.out.print("Fair = ₹ 10.00");
            else if(dis <= 50)
            System.out.print("Fair = ₹ 40.00");
            else if(dis > 50)
            System.out.print("Fair = ₹ 80.000");
        }
        else
        {
            if(dis <= 10)
            System.out.print("Fair = ₹ 4.00");
            else if(dis <= 50)
            System.out.print ("Fair = ₹ 15.00");
            else if(dis > 50)
            System.out.print("Fair = ₹ 35.00");
        }
    }
}
```

72. Design a java class convert that is described as follows :

Private data member : centigrade

Default constructor : To initialise centigrade to its default value.

Parameterised constructor : To assign the temperature in centigrade scale to the data member.

CentiToFah()method : To compute the fahrenheit equivalent of the centigrade temperature and return the result.

main() method : To compute fahrenheit equivalents of centigrade temperatures from 10°C to 100°C in steps of 50°C.

Ans.
```
import java.io.*;
public class convert
{
        private double centigrade;
        convert()
        {
            centigrade = 0.0;
        }
        convert(double c)
        {
            centigrade = c;
        }
        double CentiToFah()
            {
            double f = 9.0/5 * centigrade + 32;
            return f;
```

```java
        }
        public static void main(String args[])
        {
            int i;
            for(i = 10; i<= 100; i = i + 5)
            {
            convert obj = new convert(i);
            double f = obj.CentiToFah();
            System.out.println("The temperature in C is "+i+" and Fahrenheit = "+f);
            }
        }
}
```

73. An electricity board charges the bill depending on the number of units consumed as follows :

Units Consumed   Rate per unit
first 100 units   40 P. per unit
next 200 units   60 P. per unit
above 300 units   ₹ 1 per unit

Write a program in java to print the bill for n customers of a town. Assume that a meter rent of ₹ 500 is paid by every customer.

Ans.

```java
import java.io.*;
public class bill
{
    public static void main(String args[]) throws IOException
    {
        int c, n;
        double b = 0, a = 0;
        BufferedReader buf = new BufferedReader(new InputStreamReader(System.in));
        System.out.println("Enter the number of customers");
        String x = buf.readLine();
        n = Integer.parseInt(x);
        for(int i =1; i <= n; i++)
        {
            System.out.println("Enter your number of units please :");
            String y = buf.readLine();
            c = Integer.parseInt(y);
            if(c <= 100)
            {
                b = c * 0.40;
            }
            else if(c > 100 && c <= 300)
            {
                b = 100 * 0.40 + (c - 100) * 0.60;
            }
            else if(c > 300)
            {
                b = 100 * 0.40 + 200 * 0.60 + (c - 300) * 1;
            }
            else
```

```
            {
                System.out.println("wrong choice");
            }
            a = 500 + b;
            System.out.println("The bill = "+a);
        }
    }
}
```

74. Write a program to print the following :
I, II, III, IIII, ... 10 terms.

Ans.
```
import java.io.*;
public class ABC
{
    public static void main(String args[])
    {
        String p = "", x;
        for(int i = 0; i < 10; i++)
        {
            x = "I";
            for(int j = 1; j <= i; j++)
            p = p + x;
            System.out.print(p + ", ");
        }
    }
}
```

75. Write program to print the following pattern :
```
*
* *
* * *
* * * *
* * * * *
```

Ans.
```
import java.io.*;
public class star
{
    public static void main(String args[])
    {
        int i, j;
        for(i = 1; i <= 5; i++)
        {
            for(j = 1; j <= i; j++)
            {
            System.out.print("*");
            }
        System.out.println();
        }
    }
}
```

76. Using switch statement, write a menu driven program for the following :

(i) To find and display the sum of the series given below :

S = x1 - x2 + x3 - x4 + x5 .... - x20

(where x = 2)

(ii) To display the following series :

1 11 111 1111 11111

For an incorrect option, an appropriate error message should be displayed.

Ans.
```java
import java.util.*; // importing package
class Menu
{
    int ch, x, i, sign = 1;
    double s = 0;
    void display()
    {
        Scanner sc = new Scanner(System.in);
        System.out.println("1. Sum of series");
        System.out.println("2. Display the series");
        System.out.println("Enter your choice");
        ch = sc.nextInt();
        switch(ch)
        {
            case 1 : x = 2;
            for(i = 1; i <= 20; i++)
            {
                s = s + Math.pow(x, i) * sign;
                sign = sign * -1;
            }
            System.out.println(s);
            break;
            case 2 : x = 0;
            for(i = 1; i <= 5; i++)
            {
                x = x * 10 + 1;
                System.out.print(x + " ");
            }
            break;
            default : System.out.println("Invalid Input");
        } // switch case ending
    }
}
```

Name Type Description

ch int To enter choice.

x int Variable of the given expression.

i int For loop.

sign int To store sign of the expression.

s double To store the sum.

77. Write a program to print the following :

```
1
1 1
1 2 1
1 3 3 1
1 4 6 4 1
```

Ans.
```java
import java.io.*;
public class ABC
{
    public static void main(String args[])
    {
        int h;
        for(int i = 0; i <= 4; i++)
        {
            h = 1;
            for(int j = 1; j <= i; j++)
            {
                h * = 11;
            }
            System.out.println(h);
        }
    }
}
```

78. Write a program to print the following pattern :

```
1
1 2
1 2 3
1 2 3 4
1 2 3 4 5
```

Ans.
```java
import java.io.*;
public class ABC
{
    public static void main(String args[])
    {
        for(int i = 1; i <= 5; i++)
        {
            for(int j = 1; j <= i; j++)
            {
            System.out.print(j+ " ");
            }
            System..our.println();
        }
    }
}
```

79. Consider a string "MEDIA REVOLUTION". Write a program that displays the number of times a letter 'O' exists in it.

Ans.
```java
import java.io.*;
public class Count
```

```java
{
    public static void main(String args[])
    {
        String a = "MEDIA REVOLUTION";
        int len = a.length();
        int c = 0;
        for(int i = 0; i < len; i++)
        {
            char x = a.charAt(i);
            if(x == 'O')
            c++;
        }
        System.out.print("The number of O's in the string are : "+c);
    }
}
```

80. What is nested if ?

Ans. Nested if is a multiple if statement within an if statement. The program can check as many number of conditions in an if statement.

Syntax :

```java
if(condition 1)
{
    if(condition 2)
    Statement 1;
    else
    Statement 2;
}
else
{
    if(condition 3)
    Statement 3;
    else
    Statement 4;
}
```

81. Using the switch-case statement, write a menu driven program to do the following :*

(a) To generate and print Letters from A to Z and their Unicode.

Letters	Unicode
A	65
B	66
.	.
.	.
.	.
Z	90

(b) Display the following pattern using iteration (looping) statement :

```
1
1  2
1  2  3
1  2  3  4
1  2  3  4  5
```

Ans.
```java
import java.util.*;
class Menu
{
int ch, i, j;
void display()
{
Scanner sc = new Scanner(System.in);
System.out.println("1. Letters");
System.out.println("2. Pattern");
    System.out.println("Enter Your Choice");
    ch = sc.nextInt();
switch(ch)
{
    case 1 : System.out.println
    ("Letters \t Unicode");
            for(i = 65; i <= 90; i++)
            {
            System.out.println
    ( (char)i + "\t" + i );
            }
            break;
            case 2 : for(i = 1; i <= 5; i++)
              {
                for(j = 1; j <= i; j++)
                {
                        System.out.print (j + " ");
                }
                System.out.println();
              }
            break;
        default: System.out.println
    ("Wrong Choice");
            }
        }
}
```

Name	Type	Description
Ch	int	To store the choice.
i, j	int	for loop variables.

82. A tech number has even number of digits. If the number is split in two equal halves, then the square of sum of these halves is equal to the number itself. Write a program to generate and print all four digit tech numbers.*

Example :

Consider the number 3025

Square of sum of the halves of 3025

$= (30 + 25)2$

$= (55)2$

$= 3025$ is a tech number.

Ans. class Tech
```
{
int i, a, b, s;
void display()
{
for(i = 1000; i <= 9999; i++)
{
    a = i % 100;
    b = i/100;
    s = a + b;
    if(s * s == i)
    {
    System.out.println(i);
    }
}
}
}
```

Name	Type	Description
a	int	To store the last two digits.
b	int	To store the first two digits.
s	int	To store the sum.
i	int	for loop variable.

Chapter 2. Class as the Basis of all Computation

1. Define a class called mobike with the following description : Instance variables/data members :

   int bno – to store the bike's number.

   int phno – to store the phone number of the customer. String name – to store the name of the customer.

   int days – to store the number of days the bike is taken on rent.

   int charge – to calculate and store the rental charge.

   Member methods :

   void input() – to input and store the detail of the customer.

   void compute() – to compute the rental charge.

   The rent for a mobike is charged on the following basis :

   First five days ₹ 500 per day.

   Next five days ₹ 400 per day.

   Rest of the days ₹ 200 per day.

   void display() – to display the details in the following format :

Bike No.	Phone No.	Name	No.of days	Charge
…………	…………......	…………......	…………..…	……………..…

Ans. import java.io.*;
```
class MoBike
{
    String name;
    int bno, phno, days, charge;
    void input() throws IOException
```

```java
    {
        BufferedReader br = new BufferedReader(new InputStreamReader(System.in));
        System.out.println("Enter name");
        name = br.readLine();
        System.out.println("Enter Bike number");
        bno = Integer.parseInt(br.readLine());
        System.out.println("Enter Phone number");
        phno = Integer.parseInt(br.readLine());
        System.out.println("Enter days");
        days = Integer.parseInt(br.readLine());
    }
    void compute()
    {
        if(days >= 1 && days <= 5)
        {
        charge = days * 500;
        }
        else if(days > 5 && days <= 10)
        {
            charge = 5 * 500 + (days - 5) * 400;
        }
        else
        {
            charge = 5 * 500 + 5 * 400 + (days - 10) * 200;
        }
    }
    void display()
    {
        System.out.println("Bike No. \t Phone No. \t Name \t No. of days \t Charge");
        System.out.println(bno + "\t" + phno + "\t" + name + "\t" + days +"\t" + charge);
    }
}
```

2. Define a class ElectricBill with the following specifications :

Class : ElectricBill

Instance variables/data members :

String n – to store the name of the customer

int units – to store the number of units consumed double bill – to store the amount to be paid Member methods :

void accept() – to accept the name of the customer and number of units consumed void calculate() – to calculate the bill as per the following tariff :

Number of units	Rate per unit
First 100 units	2.00
Next 200 units	3.00
Above 300 units	5.00

A surcharge of 2.5% charged if the number of units consumed is above 300 units.

Void print( ) – To print the details as follows :

Name of the customer : ....

Number of units consumed : ....

Bill amount : ....

Write a main method to create an object of the class and call the above member methods.

Ans.
```java
import java.util.*;// importing package
class ElectricBill
{
    String n;
    int units;
    double bill;
    void accept()
    {
        Scanner sc = new Scanner(System.in);
        System.out.println("Enter Name and units");
        n = sc.nextLine();
        units = sc.nextInt();
    }
    void calculate()
    {
        if(units <= 100)
        {
        bill = units * 2;
        }
        else if(units > 100 && units <= 300)
        {
            bill = 100 * 2 + (units – 100) * 3;
        }
        else
        {
            bill = 100 * 2 + 200 * 3 + (units – 300) * 5;
            if (units > 300)
            bill = bill + 2.5/100 * bill;
        }
    }
    void print()
    {
        System.out.println("Name of the customer : " + n);
        System.out.println("Number of units consumed : " + units);
        System.out.println("Bill amount :"+ bill);
    }
    public static void main(String args[])
    {
        ElectricityBill ob = new ElectricBill();
        ob.accept();// funcion calling
        ob.calculate();
        ob.print();
    }
}
```

Name	Type	Description
n	String	To store the name of the customer.
i	int	To store number of units consumed.
p	double	To store the amount to be paid.

3. Design a class to overload a function num_calc() as follows :

1. void num_calc(int num, char ch) — with one integer argument and one character argument, computes the square of integer argument if choice ch is 's' otherwise finds its cube.

2. void num_calc(int a, int b, char ch) — with two integer arguments and one character argument. It computes the product of integer arguments if ch is 'p' else adds the integers.

3. void num_calc(String s1, String s2) — with two string arguments, which prints whether the strings are equal or not.

Ans.
```
public class Overload
{
        void num_calc(int num, char ch)
        {
        int r;
                if(ch == 's')
                {
                 r = num * num;
                }
                else
                {
                r = num * num * num;
                }
        System.out.println(r);
        }
        void num_calc(int a, int b, char ch)
        {
        int r;
                if(ch == 'p')
                {
                r = a * b;
                }
                else
                {
                 r = a + b;
                }
        System.out.println(r);
        }
        void num_calc(String s1, String s2)
        {
            if(s1.equals(s2))
            {
            System.out.println("Equal String");
            }
            else
            {
             System.out.println("Unequal String");
            }
        }
}
```

4. Write a class with the name volume using function overloading that computes the volume of a cube, a sphere and a cuboid.

Formula :

Volume of a cube (vc) = s * s * s

Volume of a sphere (vs) = 4/3 * π* r * r * r

(where π = 3·14 or 22/7)

Volume of a cuboid (vcd) = 1 * b * h

Ans.
```
class volume
{
    void cube(int s)
    {
        System.out.println("Volume of cube is" + (s * s * s));
    }
    void cube(int l, int b, int h)
    {
        System.out.println("Volume of cuboid is" + (l * b * h));
    }
    double cube(double  r)
    {
        double v;
        v = (4/3) * 22·7 * r * r * r;
        return v;
    }
    void test()
    {
        cube(10);
        cube(5, 7, 9);
        double A1 = cube(3.5);
        System.out.println("Volume of sphere is" +Al);
    }
}
```

5. Write a class to demonstrate public and private specifier.

Ans.
```
class student
{
    public int RNO;
    private String name;
    private int m1, m2; int Avg;
    public void setdata(int R, String n1, int m, int n)
    {
        RNO = R;
        name = n1;
        m1 = m;
        m2 = n;
    }
    public void showdata()
    {
        System.out.println("Roll no is" + RNO);
        System.out.println("Name is" + name);
```

```java
        calculateAvg();
        System.out.println("Average makes is" + Avg);
    }
    private void calculateAvg()    //can be acessed in this class only.
    {
        Avg = (m1 + m2)/2;
    }
}
public class test
{
    public static void main(String[] args)
    {
    student s = new student();
    s.setdata(101, "RAJIV", 20, 19);
    s.RNO = 102;
    s.showdata();
    }
}
```

6. Define class student with the following specifications :

Private members of class student :

admno : integer

sname : string type

Eng., Math, Science : float

Total : float

get total() — A function to calculate Eng. + Math + Science with float return type.

Public members of functions of class student.

takedata() — function to accept values of admno, sname, Eng., Math, Science; invoke total() to calculate total.

showdata() — to display all data members on the screen.

Ans.
```java
class student
{
    private int admno;
    private String sname;
    private float eng, math, science, total;
    private float gettotal()
    {
        float t = eng + math + science;
        return t;
    }
    public void showdata()
    {
        System.out.println(admno);
        System.out.println(sname);
        System.out.println(eng);
        System.out.println(math);
        System.out.println(science);
        System.out.println(total);
    }
```

```java
        public void takedata(int a, String n, int e, int m, int s)
        {
            admno = a;
            sname = n;
            eng = e;
            math = m;
            science = s;
            total = gettotal( );
        }
    }
    public class stud
    {
        public static void main(String [] args)
        {
            student std1 = new student();
            std1.takedata(101, "RAM", 30, 48, 40);
            std1.showdata();
        }
    }
```

7. Write a program to accept name and total marks of N number of students in two single subscript array name[ ] and totalmarks[ ].

Calculate and print :

(i) The average of the total marks obtained by N number of students. [average = (sum of total marks of all the students)/N]

(ii) Deviation of each student's total marks with the average. [deviation = total marks of a student – average]

Ans.
```java
import java.util.*;//importing package
class Student
{
    int n, i, s = 0;
    double avg, d;
    void display()
    {
        Scanner sc = new Scanner(System.in);
        System.out.println("Enter number of students");
        n = sc.nextInt();
        String name[] = new String[n];
        int totalmarks[] = new int[n];
        for(i = 0; i < n; i++)
        {
            System.out.println("Enter name and total marks");
            name[i] = sc.nextLine();
            totalmarks[i] = sc.nextInt();
            s = s + totalmarks[i];
        }
            avg = (double)s/n;
            System.out.println("Average = " + avg);
        for(i = 0; i < n; i++)
```

```
            {
                d = totalmarks[i] – avg;
                System.out.println(name[i] + " Deviation is " + d);
            }
        }
} // class end
```

Name	Type	Description
n	int	To store the number of students.
i	int	For loop variable.
s	int	To store sum.
avg	double	To store average.
d	double	To store deviation.

8. Write a program which shows defining and using static members ?

Ans.
```
class math
{
    static float mul(float a, float b)
    {
        return a * b;
    }
    static float div(float a, float b)
    {
        return a/b;
    }
}
public class method
{
    public  static void main(String args [])
    {
    float x = math.mul(6.0f, 7.0f);
    float y = math.div(x, 2.0f);
    System.out.println("y = " + y);
    }
}
```

9. Write methods to display twin prime numbers that lie between a given range.

[Note : twin primes are prime numbers whose difference is 2 e.g., (11, 13), (17, 19) etc.]

Ans.
```
class test
{
    public void twinprime(int l, int n)
    {
        for(int i = l; i <= n; i++)
        {
            if(isprime(i) && isprime(i + 2))
                System.out.println(i + ", " + i + 2);
        }
    }
    public boolean isprime(int n)
    {
```

```
        int R;
        boolean fl = true;
        for (int x = 2; x < n; x ++)
        {
            if(n % x == 0)
            {
                fl = false;
                break;
            }
        }
        return fl;
    }
  :
}
```

Chapter 3. User - Defined Methods

1. Design a class to overload a function area() as follows :

(i) double area(double a, double b, double c) with three double arguments, returns the area of a scalene triangle using the formula :

area = s (s − a) (s − b) (s − c) where s = (a +b+c)/2

(ii) double area (int a, int b, int height) with three integer arguments, returns the area of a trapezium using the formula.

area = 1/2 height (a + b)

(iii) double area (doule diagonal 1, double diagonal 2) with two double arguments, returns the area of a rhombus using the formula :

area =1/2 (diagonal 1 × diagonal 2)

Ans.

```
class Overload
{
    double ar;
    double area(double a, double b, double c)
    {
        double s = (a + b + c) / 2;
        ar = Math.sqrt(s * (s − a) * (s − b) * (s − c));
        return(ar);
    }
    double area(int a, int b, int height)
    {
        ar = 0.5 * height * (a + b);
        return(ar);
    }
    double area(double diagonal1, double diagonal2)
    {
    ar = 0.5 * diagonal1 * diagonal2; return(ar);
    }
}
```

2. Define a class named FruitJuice with the following description :

Instance variables/data members :

int product_code — stores the product code number.

String flavour — stores the flavour of the juice (E.g. orange, apple, etc.).

String pack_type — stores the type of packaging (E.g. tetra-pack, PET bottle, etc.).

int pack_size — stores package size (E.g. 200 ml, 400 ml, etc.).

int product_price — stores the price of the product.

Member methods :

(i)   FruitJuice()— Default constructor to initialize integer data members to 0 and String data members to "".

(ii) void input()—To input and store the product code, flavour, pack type, pack size and product price.

(iii) void discount()—To reduce the product price by 10.

(iv) void display()—To display the product code, flavour, pack type, pack size and product price.

Ans.
```java
import java.io.*;
class FruitJuice
{
    int product_code, pack_size, product_price;
    String flavour, pack_type;
    public FruitJuice()
    {
        product_code = 0;
        pack_size = 0;
        product_price = 0;
        flavour = "";
        pack_type = "";
    }
    void input() throws IOException
    {
        BufferedReader br = new BufferedReader(new InputStreamReader(System.in));
        System.out.println("Enter Product Details");
        product_code = Integer.parseInt(br.readLine());
        flavor = br.readLine();
        pack_type = br.readLine();
        pack_size = Integer.parseInt(br.readLine());
        product_price = Integer.parseInt(br.readLine());
    }
    void discount()
    {
        product_price = product_price – 10;
    }
    void display()
    {
        System.out.println(product_code + " " + flavour + " " + pack_type + " " + pack_size + " " + product_price);
    }
}
```

3. Design a class to overload a function series() as follows :

1.   double series(double n) — with one double argument and returns the sum of the series,

$$\text{sum} = \frac{1}{1} + \frac{1}{2} + \frac{1}{3} + \ldots + \frac{1}{n}$$

2. double series(double a, double n) — with two double arguments and returns the sum of the series,

$$\text{sum} = \frac{1}{a^2} + \frac{1}{a^5} + \frac{1}{a^8} + \frac{10}{a^{11}} + \dots \text{ to } n \text{ terms}$$

Ans.
```java
class Overload
{
    double s;
    double series(int  n)
    {
        s = 0;
        int i;
        for(i = 1; i <= n; i++)
        {
        s = s + 1.0/i;
        }
        return(s);
    }
    double series(int a, int n)
    {
        s = 0;
        int i, c = 1;
        for(i = 1; i <= n; i++)
        {
        s = s + c/Math.pow(a, c + 1); c = c + 3;
        }
        return(s);
    }
}
```

4. Define a class called Library with the following description : Instance variables/data members :
int accnum — stores the accession number of the book. String title — stores the title of the book.
String author — stores the name of the author.
Member methods :
(i)   void input()– To input and store the accession number, title and author.
(ii) void compute()– To accept the number of days late, calculate and display the fine.
charged at the rate of ₹ 2 per day.
(iii) void display()–To display the details in the following format :
Accession Number   Title   Author
Write a main method to create an object of the class and call the above member methods.

Ans.
```java
import java.io.*;
class library
{
    int accnum;
    String title;
    String author;
    void input()throws IOException
    {
        BufferedReader Br = new BufferedReader(new InputStreamReader(System.in));
        System.out.println("Enter accession no, title, author");
```

```java
        accnum = Integer.parseInt(Br.readLine());
        title = Br.readLine();
        author = Br.readLine();
    }
    void compute() throws IOException
    {
        BufferedReader Bs = new BufferedReader(new InputStreamReader(System.in));
        System.out.println("No of DaysLate");
        int d = Integer.parseInt(Bs.readLine());
        int fine = d * 2;
        System.out.println("fine charged :"+ fine);
    }
    void display()
    {
        System.out.println("Accession Num" + '\t'+ "Title" + '\t' + "Author");
        System.out.println(accnum + '\t' + title + '\t' + author);
    }
}
public class LibraryTest
{
    public static void main(String args[])
    {
        library obj = new library();
        try
        {
        obj.input();
        obj.compute();
        obj.display();
        }
        catch(Exception e){}
    }
}
```

5. Define a class student described as below :

   Data members/instance variables :

   name, age, m1, m2, m3(marks in 3 subjects), maximum, average.

   Member methods :

   (i)   A parameterized constructor to initialize the data members.

   (ii) To accept the details of a student.

   (iii) To compute the average and the maximum out of three marks.

   (iv) To display the name, age, marks in three subjects, maximum and average.

   Write a main method to create an object of a class and call the above member methods.

Ans.
```java
import java.io.*;
public class Student
{
    String name;
    int age, m1, m2, m3, max;
    double avg;
    Student(String n, int a, int x, int y, int z)
```

```java
        {
            name = n;
            age = a;
            m1 = x;
            m2 = y;
            m3 = z;
        }
        void accept() throws IOException
        {

            BufferedReader br = new BufferedReader(new InputStreamReader(System.in));
            System.out.println("Enter name, age and marks in 3 subjects");
            name = br.readLine();
            age = Integer.parseInt(br.readLine());
            m1 = Integer.parseInt(br.readLine());
            m2 = Integer.parseInt(br.readLine());
            m3 = Integer.parseInt(br.readLine());
        }
        void compute()
        {
            avg = (m1 + m2 + m3) / 3.0;
            if(m1 > m2 && m1 > m3)
            {
                max = m1;
            }
            else if(m2 > m1 && m2 > m3)
            {
                max = m2;
            }
            else
            {
                max = m3;
            }
        }
void display()
{
System.out.println("Name : " + name);
System.out.println("Age : " + age);
System.out.println("Marks 1 : " + m1);
System.out.println("Marks 2 :" + m2);
System.out.println("Marks 3 :" + m3);
System.out.println("Maximum :"+ max);
System.out.println("Average : " + avg);
}
public static void main(String args[])
{
Student ob = new Student("Ritesh Sahu", 27, 97, 93, 84);
try
{
```

```
        ob.accept();
        ob.compute();
        ob.display();
        }
        catch(Exception e)
        {
            System.out.println("Error " );
        }
    }
}
```

6. Define a class employee having the following description :

Data Members :

| int pan | : to store personal account number. |

Instance variables :

String name	: to store name.
double tax income	: to store annual taxable income.
double tax	: to store tax that is calculated.

Member functions :

input()	: Store the pan number, name, taxable income.
calc()	: Calculate tax for an employee.
display()	: Output details of an employee.

Write a program to compute the tax according to the given conditions and display the output as per given format.

Total Annual Taxable Income	Tax Rate upto ₹ 1,00,000	No Tax
From ₹ 1,00,001 to ₹ 1,50,000	10% of the income exceeding	₹ 1,00,000
From ₹ 1,50,001 to ₹ 2,50,000	₹ 5000 + 20% of the income exceeding	₹ 1,50,000
Above ₹ 2,50,000	₹ 25,000 + 30% of the income exceeding	₹ 2,50,000

Output :

Pan Number	Name	Tax-Income	Tax
—	—	—	—
—	—	—	—
—	—	—	—
—	—	—	—

Ans.
```java
import java.io.*;
public class employee
{
    int pan;
    String name;
    double tax;
    double taxincome;
    public void input()
    {
        DataInputStream in = new DataInputStream(System.in);
        System.out.println("Enter the name of the employee");
        name = in.readLine();
        System.out.println("Enter pan number");
        pan = Integer.parseInt(in.readLine());
```

```java
            System.out.println("Enter your taxable income");
            taxincome = Double.parseDouble(in.readLine());
        }
        public void calc()
        {
            if(taxincome <= 100000)
            tax = 0;
            else if(taxincome >= 100001 && taxincome <= 150000)
                tax = ((taxincome - 100000) * 10) / 100;
            else if(taxincome >= 150001 && taxincome <= 250000)
                tax = 5000 + (((taxincome – 150000) * 20) / 100);
            else if(taxincome > 250000)
                tax = 25000 + (((taxincome - 250000) * 30) / 100);
        }
        public void display()
        {
            System.out.println("Pan number" + " " + " Name" + " " + "Tax-Income" + " "+ "Tax");
            System.out.println(pan + " " + name + " " + taxincome + " " + tax);
        }
    }
```

7. Define a class salary described as below :

Data Members :

Name, Address, Phone, Subject Specialization, Monthly Salary, Income Tax.

Member methods :

(i) To accept the details of a teacher including the monthly salary.

(ii) To display the details of the teacher.

(iii) To compute the annual Income Tax as 5% of the annual salary above ₹ 1,75,000/-. Write a main method to create object of a class and call the above member method.

Ans.
```java
class salary
{
    String Name, Address, Phone, subspec;
    int msalary;
    double itax;
    public void accept(String n, String ad, String ph, String s, int ms)
    {
        Name = n;
        Address = ad;
        phone = ph;
        subspec = s;
        msalary = ms;
    }
    public void display()
    {
        System.out.println("Name" + Name + " \nAddress" + Address + "\n Phone No." + Phone + "\n
        Subject.Specification" + subspec + "\n monthly salary" + msalary + "\n Income Tax" + itax);
    }
    public void compute()
    {
```

```java
        long Asalary = msalary * 12;
        if(Asalary > 175000)
            itax = 5/100.00 * Asalary;
        else
            itax = 0;
    }
    public static void main(String args[])
    {
    salary s = new salary();
    s.accept("Rahul", "New Agra", "285956", "computer science", 12000); s.compute();
    s.display();
    }
}
```

8. Write a class with name employee and basic as its data member, to find the gross pay of an employee of the following allowances and deduction. Use meaningful variable.

Dearness Allowance = 25% of Basic pay House Rent Allowance = 15% of Basic pay Provident Fund = 8.33% of Basic Pay

Net Pay = Basic Pay + Dearness Allowance + House Rent Allowance

Gross Pay = Net Pay – Provident fund

Ans.
```java
class employee
{
    private int basic;
    public employee(int b)
    {
        basic = b;
        double da, hra, pf, net, gross;
        da = (25.0/100.0) * basic;
        hra = (15.0/100.0) * basic;
        pf = (8.33/100.0) * basic;
        net = basic + da + hra; gross = net – pf;
        System.out.println(" Dearness Allowance " + da);
        System.out.println(" House Rent Allowance "+ hra);
        System.out.println(" Provident Fund " + pf);
        System.out.println(" Net pay " + net);
        System.out.println(" Gross Pay " + gross);
    }
}
```

9. Design a class to overload a function polygon() as follows :

  (i)   void polygon(int n, char ch) — with one integer argument and one character type argument that draws a filled square of side n using the character stored in ch.

  (ii) void polygon(int x, int y) — with two integer arguments that draws a filled rectangle of length x and breadth y, using the symbol '@'.

  (iii) void polygon() — with no argument that draws a filled triangle shown below.

     Example :

  (i)   Input value of n = 2, ch = 'O'

     Output :

     OO

     OO

(ii) Input value of x = 2, y = 5

Output :

@@@@@

@@@@@

(iii) Output :

```
*
* *
* * *
```

Ans.
```java
class overload
{
    void polygon(int n, char ch)
    {
        int i, j;
        for(i = 1; i <= n; i++)
        {
            for(j = 1; j <= n; j++)
            System.out.print(ch);
            System.out.println();
        }
    }
    void polygon(int x, int y)
    {
        int i, j;
        for(i = 1; i <= x; i++)
        {
            for(j = 1; j <= y; j++)
            {
                System.out.print('@');
            }
            System.out.println();
        }
    }
    void polygon()
    {
        int i, j;
        for(i = 1; i <= 3; i++)
        {
            for(j = 1; j <= i; j++)
            {
                System.out.print('*');
            }
            System.out.println();
        }
    }
}
```

10. Write a program to accept a word and convert it into lowercase if it is in uppercase, and display the new word by replacing only the vowels with the character following it.

Example :

Sample Input : computer Sample Output : cpmpvtfr.

Ans.
```java
import java.io.*;
class Change
{
    String s, s1 = "";
    int i, l; char ch;
    void change()
    {
        BufferedReader br = new BufferedReader(new InputStreamReader(System.in));
        System.out.println("Enter a string");
        s = br.readLine();
        s = s.toLowerCase(); l = s.length();
        for(i = 0; i < l; i++)
        {
            ch = s.charAt(i);
            if(ch == 'a' || ch == 'e' || ch == 'i' || ch == 'o' || ch == 'u')
            {
                ch = (char)(ch + 1);
            }
            s1 = s1 + ch;
        }
        System.out.println(" New Word is " + s1);
    }
}
```

11. Design a class to overload a function volume() as follows :

(i) double volume(double R) – with radius (R) as an argument, returns the volume of sphere using the formula.

$$V = 4/3 \times 22/7 \times R^3$$

(ii) double volume(double H, double R) – with height (H) and radius (R) as the arguments, returns the volume of a cylinder using the formula.

$$V = 22/7 \times R^2 \times H$$

(iii) double volume(double L, double B, double H) – with length (L), breadth (B) and Height (H) as the arguments, returns the volume of a cuboid using the formula.

$$V = L \times B \times H$$

Ans.
```java
class Overload
{// class beginning
    double V;
    double volume(double R)
    {
        V = ((4.0/3) * (22/7) * R * R * R);
        return(V);
    }
    double volume(double H, double R)
    {
        V = (22/7) * (R * R) * H;
        return(V);
    }
```

```java
double volume(double L, double B, double H)
{
    V = L * B * H;
    return(V);//returning the value of V
}
}
```

Name	Type	Description
V	double	To store Volume.
R	double	To store Radius.
H	double	To store Height.
L	double	To store Length.
B	double	To store Breadth.

12. Design a class to overload a function compare() as follows :

(i) void compare(int, int) — to compare two integer values and print the greater of the two integers.

(ii) void compare(char, char) — to compare the numeric value of two characters and print the character with higher numeric value.

(iii) void compare(String, String) — to compare the length of the two strings and print the longer of the two.

Ans.
```java
class Overload
{
    void compare(int a, int b)
    {
        if(a > b)
        {
            System.out.println(a);
        }
        else
        {
            System.out.println(b);
        }
    }
    void compare(char a, char b)
    {
        if((int)a > (int)b)
        {
            System.out.println(a);
        }
        else
        {
            System.out.println(b);
        }
    }
    void compare(String a, String b)
    {
        if(a.compareTo(b) > 0)
        {
            System.out.println(a);
```

```
            }
            else
            {
                System.out.println(b);
            }
        }
    }
```

13. Define a method to return the factorial of a number which is passed as an argument.

Ans.
```
class test
{
    long factorial(int n)
    {
    long f = 1;
    for(int i = 1; i <= n; i++)
    {
        f = f * i;
    }
    return f;
    }
    :
    :
}
```

14. Write a program using a function called area() to compute the area of a :

(i)   Circle(π * r * r) where π = 3.14

(ii) Square(side * side)

(iii) Rectangle(length * breadth)

Display the menu to output the area as per user's choice.

Ans.
```
import java.io.*;
public class test
{
    public static void circleArea(double r)
    {
        double a = 3.14 * r * r;
        System.out.println("Area of circle is " + a);
    }
    public static void squareArea(double side)
    {
        double a = side * side;
        System.out.println("Area of square is " + a);
    }
    public static void rectArea(double length, double breadth)
    {
        double a = length * breadth;
        System.out.println("Area of rectangle is " + a);
    }
    public static void main(String args[]) throws IOException
    {
        String s; int ch;
```

```java
BufferedReader br = new BufferedReader(new InputStreamReader(System.in));
System.out.println("\t\tMenu");
System.out.println("1. Circle Area");
System.out.println("2. Square Area");
System.out.println("3. Rectangle Area");
System.out.println("Enter A Choice ");
s = br.readLine();
ch = Integer.parseInt(s);
    switch(ch)
    {
    case 1 :
    System.out.println("Enter radius ");
    double r = Double.parseDouble(br.readLine());
    circleArea(r);
    break;
    case 2 :
    System.out.println("Enter side ");
    double side = Double.parseDouble(br.readLine());
    squareArea(side);
    break;
    case 3 :
    System.out.println("Enter length ");
    double l = Double.parseDouble(br.readLine());
    System.out.println("Enter breadth ");
    double b = Double.parseDouble(br.readLine());
    rectArea(l, b);
    break;
    default :
    System.out.println("Invalid choice");
    }

    }
}
```

15. What do you mean by function overloading ? Explain it with example.

Ans. Function overloading is the process of using the same name for two or more methods. Each redefinition of a function must use different type of parameters or different number of parameters.

Advantages : When an overloaded method is called, java uses no. of arguments/type of arguments to determine which version of overloaded function should be executed :

(i) This is one of the methods in java which is used to implement polymorphism (one interface, multiple implementation).

(ii) This gives the advantage of giving the same name to related functions.

(iii) This feature can be used when the objects have to perform a similar task but using different parameter inputs.

Example :

```java
public class test
{
    int Add(int a, int b)
    {
```

```java
        int x;
        x = a + b;
        return x;
    }
    double Add(double a, double b)
    {
        double x;
        x = a + b;
        return x;
    }
    public static void main(String args[])
    {
        test t = new test();
        int x, y, z;
        double n1, n2, R;
        x = 10;
        y = 20;
        n1 = 2.8;
        n2 = 2.98;
        z = t.Add(x, y);
        R = t.Add(n1, n2);
        System.out.println(z);
        System.out.println(R);
    }
}
```

16. (a) Write the java statement to invoke the method "calculate" using actual parameters, a = 20, b = 45.52.

(b) Write the java prototype to overload the method calculate to return a double result and accept three double parameters.

(c) Read the following overloaded method prototypes and answer the questions that follow :

```java
static Number calcMaths(Number num)
{
num.a++;
num.b++;
return num;
}
static Applymaths calcMaths(ApplyMaths num)
{
ApplyMaths ob = new ApplyMaths();
ob.x = ++num.x;
return ob;
}
```

(i) What is the first method calMaths computing ?

(ii) What are the returning types of overloaded method calcMaths ?

(iii) Write the statement to call the second method defintion of calcMaths.

Ans. (a) Java statement to invoke the method "calculate" using actual parameters, a = 20, b = 45.52.
obj.calculate(20, 45.52); //where obj is an object of the class in which calculate methods are defined

(b) double calculate(double x, double y, double z);

(c) (i) CalcMaths method increments the values of data members a and b for the object num by 1.

(ii) CalCMaths increments the value of data member by 1 and returns object as its returning type is the class name of which it is an object.

(iii) ApplyMaths obj = new ApplyMaths(); ApplyMaths obj2 = new ApplyMaths();
obj2 = calcMaths(obj);/*static function calcMaths can be directly invoked in another static method*/

17. Write a complete java program with the following members of its class.

Members	Member Name	Description
private data members	ac_num	Stores account number
	ac_name	Stores account holders name
	bal	Store balance amount in the account
constructor		To initialise all private data members to 0 (zero)
public methos	getValues()	To store data
	display()	To display the data
	deposit()	To modify balance according to the amount deposited.
	withdrawl()	To modify balance according to withdrawn amount.

Assume that above jobs have to be performed for a single account holder presently. [For many holders, the looping will be studied in further chapters]

Ans.
```java
public class Account
{
    private long ac_num;
    private String ac_name;
    double bal;
    Account()
    {
        ac_num = 0;
        bal = 0.0;
    }
    public void getvalues(long acNumber, String acName)
    {
        ac_num = acNumber; ac_name = acName;
    }
    public void deposit(double amt)
    {
        bal += amt;
    }
    public void withdraw(double amt)
    {
        bal -= amt;
    }
    public void display()
    {
        System.out.println("Account Number :" + ac_num);
        System.out.println("Account holder's Name" + ac_name);
        System.out.println("Account holder's balance :" + bal);
    }
    public static void main(String args[])
    {
        Account customer = new Account();
```

```
        customer.getvalues(20041961, "ANMOL ARORA");
        customer.deposit(5000);
        System.out.println("****AFTER DEPOSITING MONEY*****");
        customer.display();
        System.out.println();
        System.out.println("****AFTER WITHDRAWING MONEY****");
        customer.withdraw(1000);
        customer.display();
    }
}
```

Output :

```
****AFTER DEPOSITING MONEY****
Account Number          :    20041961
Account holder's Name   :    ANMOL ARORA
Account holder's balance :   5000.00
****AFTER WITHDRAWING MONEY****
Account Number          :    20041961
Account holder's Name   :    ANMOL ARORA
Account holder's balance :   4000.0
```

18. Write a complete java program with the following members of its class StoreCustomer :

Members	Member Name	Description
private data members	Cust_id	Stores character type customer id.
	Cust_name	Stores customer name.
	Cust_Add	Stores customer address.
	Due_Amt	Stores the amount due to the customer.
public methos	getValues()	To store the data of a customer.
	calculate()	To compute the total amount to be paid by the customer.
	display()	To modify balance according to the amount deposited.
		To show the data and amount.

Ans.
```
import java.io.*;
import java.io.*;
class StoreCustomer
{
    private char cust_id;
    private String cust_name, cust_add;
    double due_amt, amount;
    public void getValues(char cid, String nam, String add, double due) throws IOException
    {
    cust_id = cid;
    cust_name = nam;
    cust_add = add;
    due_amt = due;
    }
    public void calculate(double present_amt)
    {
    amount = due_amt + present_amt;
    }
```

```java
public void display()
{
System.out.println("*****CUSTOMER DETAILS******");
System.out.println();
System.out.println("CUSTOMER'S NAME :" + cust_name);
System.out.println("ADDRESS :" + cust_add);
System.out.println("AMOUNT DUE :" + due_amt);
System.out.println("TOTAL AMOUNT :" + amount);
}
}
//Calling the methods defined in above class import java.io.*;
public class call
{
    public static void main(String args[])
    {
    StoreCustomer obj = new StoreCustomer();
    System.out.println("Please enter the customers id code, name and address.");
    BufferedReader buf = new BufferedReader(new  InputStreamReader(System.in));
    try
    {
    char id = (char) buf.read();
    String mn = buf.readLine();
    String n = buf.readLine();
    String p = buf.readLine();
    System.out.println("Please enter the amount due on the customer :");
    String m = buf.readLine();
    double m1 = Double.parseDouble(m);
    obj.getValues(id, n, p, m1);
    System.out.println("Please enter the amount in Rs to be paid for the current purchase");
    String m2 = buf.readLine();
    double m3 = Double.parseDouble(m2);
    obj.calculate(m3);
    obj.display();
    }
    catch(Exception e)
    {
        System.out.println("Error");
    }
    }
}
```

19. Define a method 'Displacement' that calculates the displacement covered by a moving body according to Newton's second law of motion.

$s = ut + \frac{1}{2}at^2$, where u = 20 m/s, t = 20 min, a = 10 m/s2.

Ans.
```java
public class motion
{
    static void displacement()
    {
        double u = 20, t = 2 * 60, a = 10;
```

```
        double s= u * t + 1 / 2.0 * a * t * t;
        System.out.print("The displacement is :" + s + " metres");
    }
    public static void main(String args[])
    {
        displacement();
    }
}
```

20. A private Cab service company provides service within the city at the following rates:*

	AC CAR	NON AC CAR
Up to 5 Km	₹150/-	₹120/-
Beyond 5 Km	₹ 10/- Per Km	₹ 08/- Per Km

Design a class CabService with the following description:

Member variables /data members:

String Car-type   :   To store the type of car (AC or NON AC)

double km   :   To store the kilometer travelled

double bill   :   To calculate and store the bill amount

Member methods :

    CabService()   – Default constructor to initialize data members.
                 String data members to " " and double data members to 0.0.

    void accept()   – To accept car_type and km (using Scanner class only).

    void calculate() – To calculate the bill as per the rules given above.

    void display()   – To display the bill as per the following format

CAR TYPE:

KILOMETER TRAVELLED: TOTAL BILL:

Create an object of the class in the main method and invoke the member methods.

Ans.
```java
import java.util.*;
class CabServices
{
    String car_type;
    double km,bill;
    public CabServices()
    {
    car_type="";
    km=bill=0.0;
    }
    void accept()
    {
    Scanner sc = new Scanner(System.in);
    System.out.println("Enter Car Type and no. of Km");
    car_type=sc.nextLine();
    km=sc.nextDouble();
    }
    void calculate()
    {
    if(car_type.equalsIgnoreCase("AC"))
```

```
            {
                if(km<=5)
            {
                bill=150;
            }
                else
            {
            bill=150 + (km – 5) * 10;
            }
            }
            else if(car_type.equalsIgnoreCase("NON AC"))
            {
                if(km<=5)
            {
                bill=120
            }
                else
            {
            bill=120 + (Km – 5) * 8;
            }
            }
        else
        {
            System.out.println("Wrong Type");
        }
    }
    void display()
    {
    System.out.println("CAR TYPE : " + car_type);
    System.out.println("KILOMETER TRAVELLED : " + km);
    System.out.println("TOTAL BILL : " + bill);
    }
}
```


21. Design a class to overload a method number( ) as follows :*

   (i) *void Number (int num, int d)*   — *To count and display the frequency of a digit in a number.*

     Example:
     num = 2565685
     d = 5
     Frequency of digit 5 = 3

   (ii) void Number (int n1)   — To find and display the sum of even digits of a number.

     Example:
     n1 = 29865
     Sum of even digits = 16

Write a main method to create an object and invoke the above methods.

Ans. (i)   class Overload

```
class Overload
{
void Number(int num,int d)
    {
    int c=0,d1;
    while(num>0)
    {
        d1=num%10;
            if(d1==d)
        {
            c++;
        }
        num=num/10;
    }
    System.out.println("Frequency of digit " + d + " = " + c);
    }
```

(ii) void Number(int n1)

```
void Number(int n1)
{
int d,s=0;
while(n1>0)
{
    d=n1%10;
    if(d%2==0)
    {
        s=s+d;
    }
    n1=n1/10;
}
System.out.println("Sum of Even Digits = " + s);
}
}
```

22. Design a class name ShowRoom with the following description :*

Instance variables/Data members :

String name   :   To store the name of the customer

long mobno   :   To store the mobile number of the customer

double cost: To store the cost of the items purchased.

double dis :   To store the discount amount

double amount: To store the amount to be paid after discount.

Member methods :

ShowRoom()   – default constructor to initialize data members

void input()   – To input customer name, mobile number, cost

void calculate() – To calculate discount on the cost of purchased items, based on the following criteria :

Cost	Discount (in percentage)
Less than or equal to ₹ 10,000	*5%*
More than ₹ 10,000 and less than or equal to ₹ 20,000	*10%*

More than ₹ 20,000 and less than or equal to ₹ 35,000	15%
More than ₹ 35,000	20%

void display()   – To display customer name, mobile number, amount to be paid after discount.

Write a main method to create an object of the class and call the above member methods.

Ans.
```java
import java.util.*;
class ShowRoom
{
String name;
long mobno;
double cost, dis, amount;
public ShowRoom()
{
name = "";
mobno = 0L;
cost = 0.0;
dis = 0.0;
amount = 0.0;
}
 void input()
{
Scanner sc = new Scanner(System.in);
System.out.println("Enter the details");
name = sc.nextLine();
mobno = sc.nextLong();
cost = sc.nextDouble();
}
void calculate()
{
if(cost <= 10000)
{
        dis = 0.05 * cost;
}
else if(cost > 10000 && cost <= 20000)
{
        dis = 0.10 * cost;
}
else if(cost > 20000 && cost <= 35000)
{
        dis = 0.15 * cost;
}
else
{
        dis = 0.20 * cost;
}
amount = cost – dis;
}
```

```java
void display()
{
System.out.println("Customer Name : "+ name);
System.out.println("Customer Mobile Number : " + mobno);
    System.out.println("Amount to be Paid : " + amount);
    }
public static void main(String args[])
{
ShowRoom ob = new ShowRoom();
    ob.input();
ob.calculate();
    ob.display();
}
}
```

Name	Type	Description
name	String	To store the name of the customer.
mobno	long	To store the mobile number of the customer.
cost	double	To store the cost of the item purchased.
dis	double	To store the discount on the item purchased.
amount	double	To store the final amount to be paid.

23. Design a class to overload a function series( ) as follows :*

(a) void series(int x, int n) – To display the sum of the series given below :

x1 + x2 + x3 + ... xn terms

(b) void series(int p) – To display the following series :

0, 7, 26, 63 .... p terms

(c) void series() – To display the sum of the series given below :

$$\frac{1}{2} + \frac{1}{3} + \frac{1}{4} \,............\, \frac{1}{10}$$

Ans.
```java
class Overload
{
double s = 0;
int i;
void series(int x, int n)
{
for(i = 1; i <= n; i++)
{
        s = s + Math.pow(x, i);
}
System.out.println("Sum of the
 series is" + s);
}
void series(int p)
{
for(i = 1; i <= p; i++)
{
        System.out.print((i * i * i) – 1+ ", ");
}
```

```
}
void series()
{
for(i = 2; i <= 10; i++)
{
        s = s + 1.0/i;
}
System.out.println("Sum of the
 series is" + s);
}
}
```

Name	Type	Description
i	int	for loop variable.
s	double	To store the sum of the series.
x, n, p	int	To store the terms of the series.

Chapter 4. Constructors

1. Define a class, which accepts roll number and marks of a student. Write a constructor for the class, which accepts parameters to initialize the data members. Also take care of the case, where the student has not appeared for the test and just the roll number may be passed as the argument.

Ans.
```
class student
{
    private int roll no;
    private float marks;
    public student(int r, float m) // constructor with two arguments
    {
    rollno = r;
    marks = m;
    }
    public student(int r) // constructor with one argument
    {
    rollno = r;
    marks = 0;
    }
    student() // default constructor
    {
    rollno = 0;
    marks = 0;
    }
// methods omitted
}
```

2. (a) Write a class Number, define a constructor for the class to initialize a variable count as 0.

(b) Write the method main() for the above class to create its object.

Ans. (a)
```
class Number
    {
        private int count;
        public Number()/*Defining constructor*/
```

```
        {
            count = 0 /*Initialise count as 0*/
        }
    }
(b)  public static void main(String args[])
     { /*Creating object of class Number*/
     Number num = new Number();
     }
```

3. Write a Java class MyClass. The description of the class is as follows :

Members	Member Name	Description
Instance variable	age	To store age of a student
Constructor		Initialises age to 14.
Main method		Increment the age by 1.
		Display result.

Ans.
```
class MyClass
{
    int age; /*declaring instance variable age*/
    MyClass()
    {
        age = 14;    /* Initialises 14 to age*/
    }
    public static void main(String args[])
    {
        MyClass obj = new MyClass(); /*Creates object*/
        obj.age++;  /*Increments age by 1 */
        System.out.print("The changed age = "obj.age);  /*Displaying result*/
    }
}
```

4. Define a java class Employee with the following members :

Data members : code, name, basic, hra, da, PF.

Default constructor : Initialises, basic, hra, da and PF to zero.

Parameterised constructor : Initializes basic, computes hra, da and PF as per the following criteria :

hra = 10% of basic, da = 55% of basic, PF = ₹ 1000.

Main method : Computes and displays the net salary. Net Salary = basic + da + hra − PF

Ans.
```
public class Employee
{
    int code;/* Declaring Instance Variables*/ String name;
    public double basic, da, hra, PF;
    Employee()/* Default Constructor*/
    {
    /* Initialising instance variables to their default values*/
        code  = 0;
        name ="";
        basic = 0;
        da = 0;
        hra = 0;
        PF = 0;
    }
```

```java
/* Defining parameterised constructor*/
Employee(int c, String nam, double basSalary)
{
code = c;
name = nam;
basic = basSalary;
da = 55.0/100.00 * basic;
hra = 10.0/100.0 * basic;
    PF = 1000;

}
public static void main(String args[])
{
    int cd = 1;   /* Assigning initial values for an employee*/
        String n = "RADHESHYAM";
    double salary = 25000.85;
    /* Creating object and passing values of an employee*/
    Employee emp1 = new Employee(cd, n, salary); /*Computing net Salary*/
    double netSalary;
    netSalary = emp1.basic + emp1.da + emp1.hra - emp1.PF;
    System.out.println("EMPLOYEES PAYSLIP :");
    System.out.println();
    System.out.println("CODE :" + cd);
    System.out.println("NAME :" + n);
    System.out.println();
    System.out.print("NET SALARY : ₹" + netSalary);
}   /*End of main ()*/
}    /*End of class Employee*/
```

5. Define a class Colour as described below :

Members	Member Name	Description
Instance variable	coltop, colBottom	
Default Constructor		Initialise colTop as Pink and colBottom as Black
Parameterised		Initialise colTop and colBottom by accepted values.
Main method	main	Display the default colours as well as assigned ones through objects.

Ans.
```java
public class Color
{
    String colTop, colBottom; /*Declaring instance variables*/
    Color() /*Defining default Constructor*/
    {
        colTop = "Pink";   /*Initialising instance variables*/
        colBottom = "Black";
    }
    Color(String t, String B)    /*Defining parameterised constructor*/
    {
        colTop = t;
        colBottom = B;
    }
```

```
public static void main(String args[])
{
        Color Dress1 = new Color(); /*Creating object with default colours*/
        System.out.println("The colours for Dress are" + Dress1.colTop + " "+ Dress1.colBottom);
        String s1 = "WHITE", s2 = "BLACK";
        /* Creating object with default colours*/
        Color Dress2 = new Color(s1, s2);
        System.out.println("The colour of second Dress is " + Dress2.colTop + " and " +Dress2.colBottom);
}
}
```

Variables used :

colTop, colBottom	: Instance variables to store colours of top and bottom of an object.
t, B	: Formal parameteres of parameterised constructor to store passed values of colours of an object.
Dressl	: Dress object with default

colours Pink and Black. Dress2 : Dress object with colours White and Black.

s1, s2	: Store the new colours of Dress 2.

6. Consider a right angled triangle whose longest side is given as 6 cm and the base as 4 cm. Write a program that initialises the given sides of the triangle in a constructor and computes and displays the third side.

Ans.
```
public class TrianglesSide
{
        double longestSide, base; /* Defining paramterised constructor*/
        TrianglesSide(double L, double b)
        {
            longestSide = L;
            base = b;
        }
        public static void main(String args[])
        {
            double s1 = 6, s2 = 4;
            TrianglesSide triangle = new TrianglesSide(s1, s2);
            double s3, t1, t2;
            t1 = triangle.longestSide * triangle.longestSide;
            t2 = triangle.base * triangle.base;
            s3 = Math.sqrt(t1 - t2);
            System.out.print("The third side = " + s3);
        }
}
```

Variables used :

longestSide, base	: Members variables
L, b	: formal parameters to store the passed values of sides of triangle.
s1, s2	: actual parameters that store length of longest side & the base of triangle.
t1, t2	: store intermediate results of calculating third side.
s3	: stores the computed third side by applying the formula.
(hypotenuse)2	: (base)2 + (thirdSide)2
(thirdSide)2	: (hypotenuse)2 – (base)2

where hypotenuse is the longest side of a right angled triangle.

7. Write a class BankAccount that is described below :

Members	Member Names	Description
Instance variables	AcNumb, AcName	Store account number, holder's name and balance.
Default Constructor		Initialise AcNum, AcName and AcBalance.
Parameterised Constructor		Initialise AcNu7m, AcName and AcBalance with values accepted from object.

Ans. class BankAccount

```
{

    long AcNum;   /*Declaring Member variables*/ String AcName;
    double AcBalance;
    BankAccount()/*Defining constructor*/
    {
        AcNum = 0; /*Initialising member variables to default values*/
        AcName = "";
        AcBalance = 0.0;
    }
    /* Defining parameterised constructor*/
    BankAccount(in n, double bal, String nam)
    {
        Acnum = nam;
        AcName = nam;
        AcBalance = bal;
    }
}    /*End of class*/
```

Variables used :

AcNum	:	Member variables to store the account number.
AcName	:	Member variables to store the name of account holder.
AcBalance	:	Member variable to store the balance amount in the account.
n, bal, nam	:	Formal parameters to store the passed values of account number, balance amount and account holder's name respectively.

8. Create a class with one integer instance variable.

Initialize the variable using :

(i)   default constructor.

(ii) parameterized constructor.

Ans. class example

```
{

    int x;
    example() / default constructor
    {
        x = 2;
    }
    example(int x1) / parameterized constructor
    {
        x = x1;
    }
}
```

9. Define a class named movie Magic with the following description : Instance variables/data members :

int year	:	to store the year of release of a movie.
String title	:	to store the title of the movie.
float rating	:	to store the popularity rating of the movie. (minimum rating = 0.0 and maximum rating = 5.0)

Member methods :

(i)   movieMagic() :   Default constructor to initialize numeric data members to 0 and String data members to "".

(ii)   void accept()   :   To input and store year, title and rating.

(iii) void display() :   To display the title of a movie and a message based on the rating as per the table below :

Rating	Message to be displayed
0.0 to 2.0	Flop
2.1 to 3.4	Semi-hit
3.5 to 4.5	Hit
4.6 to 5.0	Super Hit

Write a main method to create an object of the class and call the above member methods.

Ans.
```java
import java.io.*;
public class movieMagic
{
        int year; String title; float rating;
        public movieMagic()
        {
            year = 0;
            title = "";
            rating = 0.0f;
        }
        void accept()throws IOException
        {
            BufferedReader br = new BufferedReader(new InputStreamReader(System.in));
            System.out.println("Enter year, title and rating");
            year = Integer.parseInt(br.readLine());
            title = br.readLine();
            rating = Float.parseFloat(br.readLine());
        }
        void display()
        {
            if(rating >= 0.0 && rating <= 2.0)
            {
            System.out.println("Flop");
            }
            else if(rating >= 2.1 && rating <= 3.4)
            {
                System.out.println("Semi Hit");
            }
            else if(rating >= 3.5 && rating <= 4.5)
            {
                System.out.println("Hit");
```

```
            }
            else
            {
                System.out.println("Super Hit");
            }
        }
    public static void main(String args[])
    {
            movieMagic ob = new movieMagic();
            try
            {
            ob.accept();
            ob.display();
            }
            catch(Exception e)
            {
                System.out.println("Error");
            }
        }
    }
```

10. Define a class Units that contains :

Private variables	:	kg, g, km, m, l
Parameterized Constructor	:	to initialise private variables kg, g, m, km and l with the values that are passed to the constructor.
Method "Convert"	:	to convert kg to g, km to m and l to m, where kg stands for kilograms, km for kilometres, l for litres and m for metres.

Ans.
```
public class Units
    {
        private double kg, g, m, km, l;
        Units(double kilogram, double gram, double met, double kilomet, double litre)
        {
            kg = kilogram;
            g = gram;
            m = met;
            km = kilomet;
            l = litre;
        }
        void convert()
        {
            double cong = kg * 1000;
            double conmet = km * 1000;
            double conmc = l / 1000;
            System.out.println(km + " kilometers = " +conmet + " metres");
            System.out.println(kg + "kilogram = " + cong + " grams");
            System.out.println(l + "litres = " +conmc + " metre cube");
        }
        public static void main(String args[])
        {
```

```
            Units obj = new Units(5,2500,500,5,21);
            obj.convert();
        }
    }
```

11. Define a java class 'Time' that has the following members described as below :

Private data members	: hr, min, sec.
Parameterized method "ACCEPT"	: To accept values for hr, min and sec.
method 'Convert'	: To convert the time entered in hr, min and sec to seconds.
method 'showResult'	: To display the result.

Ans.
```java
public class Time
{
    private long hr, min, sec, seconds;
    void accept(long hour, long minute, long second)
    {
        hr = hour;
        min = minute;
        seconds = second;
    }
    void convert()
    {
        seconds = hr * 3600 + min * 60 + seconds;
    }
    void showResult()
    {
        System.out.print("The total seconds :" + seconds);
    }
}
```

12. Define a class ConvertCurrency that contains the following member methods :

DollorToRupee()	: Accepts dollors as parameter and returns the amount in rupees.
Euro ToRupee()	: Accepts euro currency as parameter and returns the amount in rupees.
main()	: Calls the above methods and displays the result.

Ans.
```java
import java.io.*;
public class ConvertCurrency
{
    static double DollorToRupee(double doll)
    {
        return doll * 69;
    }
    static double EuroToRupee(double euro)
    {
        return euro * 72;
    }
    public static void main(String args[])
    {
        System.out.println("Rupees :" + DollorToRupee(55));
        System.out.print("Rupees converted from 20 euro : " + EuroToRupee(20));
    }
}
```

13. Write a class TriangleArea that contains the overloaded methods area, one that accepts the length of the base of triangle and the height of triangle as parameter.

The other area method accepts the length of three sides of a triangle.

The two formulas for computing the area are :

Area 1 =1/2 *base *height

Area 2 = s (s – a) (s – b) (s – c)

Ans.
```java
import java.io.*;
public class TriangleArea
{
    static double area(int len, int h)
    {
        return(1/2.0 * len * h);
    }
    static double area(int s1, int s2, int s3)
    {
        double s = (s1 + s2 + s3)/2.0;
        return(Math.sqrt(s * (s - s1) * (s - s2) * (s - s3)));
    }
    public static void main(String args[]) throws IOException
    {
        System.out.println("Enter the sides of a triangle :");
        BufferedReader inp = new BufferedReader(new  InputStreamReader(System.in));
        String side1 = inp.readLine();
        String side2 = inp.readLine();
        String side3 = inp.readLine();
        int ss1 = Integer.parseInt(side1);
        int ss2 = Integer.parseInt(side2);
        int  ss3 = Integer.parseInt(side3);
        System.out.println("The area computed by hero's formula =" + area(ss1, ss2,ss3));
        System.out.print("Enter the base length and height of triangle :");
        String l = inp.readLine();
        String he = inp.readLine();
        int b = Integer.parseInt(l);
        int height = Integer.parseInt(he);
        System.out.print("The area computed ="+area(b, height));
    }
}
```

14. Write a complete java program that defines the following methods :

assign()	:	that assigns value to a number.
doublenumber()	:	that doubles the number assigned above.
display()	:	that displays the result.
main()	:	that calls the above methods.

Ans.
```java
import java.io.*;
public class P1
{
private static double num, d;
static void assign(double n)
{
```

```java
        num = n;
}
static void doublenumber()
{
    d = 2 * num;
}
static void display()
{
    System.out.println("The double of " + num + "="+d);
    }
public static void main(String args[]) throws IOException
    {
        BufferedReader buf = new BufferedReader(new  InputStreamReader(System.in));
        System.out.println("Please enter a number :");
        String x = buf.readLine();
        int n = Integer.parseInt(x);
        assign(n);
        doublenumber();
        display();
    }
}
```

15. Write a complete java program that contains the following methods :

assign()   : that accepts values of the digit at unit's place, the digit at ten's place and the digit at hundred's place.

findNumber()   : that finds the number corresponding to the accepted digits.

main()   : that calls the above methods and displays the computed number.

Ans.
```java
import java.io.*;
public class ABC
{
        private static int unit, tens, hundreds;
        static void assign(int u, int t, int h)
        {
        unit = u; tens = t;
        hundreds = h;
        }
        static long findnumber()
        {
        return hundreds * 100 + tens * 10 + unit;
        }
        public static void main(String args[]) throws IOException
        {
        BufferedReader buf = new BufferedReader(new  InputStreamReader(System.in));
        System.out.println("Please enter a units place digit, the tens place digit and hundred place digit :");
        String x = buf.readLine();
        int n = Integer.parseInt(x);
        String x2 = buf.readLine();
        int n2 = Integer.parseInt(x2);
        String x3 = buf.readLine();
```

```
        int n3 = Integer.parseInt(x3);
        assign(n, n2, n3);
        System.out.print("The number is :" + findnumber());
    }
}
```

Chapter 5. Library Classes

1. Write a program that outputs the results of the following evaluations based on the number entered by the user.

(i)   Natural logarithms of the number.

(ii) Absolute value of the number.

(iii) Square root of the number.

(iv) Random numbers between 0 and 1.

Ans.
```
import java.io.*;
public class test
{
    public static void main(String args[]) throws IOException
    {
        int n;
        BufferedReader b = new BufferedReader(new InputStreamReader(System.in));
        System.out.println("Enter A Number ");
        n = Integer.parseInt(b.readLine());
        System.out.println("Log of number is " + Math.log(n));
        System.out.println("Absolute value of number is " + Math.abs(n));
        System.out.println("Square root is " + Math.sqrt(n));
        System.out.println("Random Numbers are : ");
        System.out.println(Math.random());
    }
}
```

2. Write a program to input 10 numbers and find their sum and average.

Ans.
```
import java.io.*;
public class Peo
{
    public static void main(String args[]) throws IOException
    {
        DataInputStream br = new DataInputStream(System.in);
        int c = 1, sum = 0, num;
        double av;
        System.out.println("Enter 10 numbers ");
        while(c <= 10)
        {
            String S = br.readLine();
            num = Integer.parseInt(S);
            sum = sum + num;
            c++;
        }
        av = (double) sum/10;
        System.out.println("Sum is" + sum);
```

```
            System.out.println("Average is" + av);
        }
    }
```

3. Write a program to input 10 real numbers and find the greatest and the smallest numbers.

Ans.
```
import java.io.*;
public class Peo
{
    public static void main(String args[]) throws IOException
    {
    DataInputStream br = new DataInputStream(System.in);
    int c = 1;
    double num, gr = 0, sm;
    String S;
    S = br.readLine();
    num = Double.parseDouble(S);
    gr = num;
    sm = num;
    System.out.println("Enter 9 numbers ");
    while(c <= 9)
    {
        S = br.readLine();
        num = Double.parseDouble(S);
        if(num > gr)
        gr = num;
        if(num < sm)
        sm = num;
        c++;
    }
    System.out.println("greatest number is" + gr);
    System.out.println("smallest number is" + sm);
    }
}
```

4. Define a method areaTriangle() that computes the area of a triangle using the hero's formula; $s(s-a)(s-b)(s-c)$ where $s = (a + b + c)/2$

Ans.
```
import java.io.*;
public class test
{
    static void areaTriangle(double a, double b, double c)
    {
        double s = (a + b + c)/2;
        double ar = Math.sqrt(s * (s - a) * (s - b) * (s - c));
        System.out.print("The area of the triangle is :"+ar);
    }
    public static void main(String args[]) throws IOException
    {
        BufferedReader buf = new BufferedReader(new  InputStreamReader(System.in));
        System.out.print("Please enter three sides of the triangle :");
```

```
        String sd1 = buf.readLine();
        double s1 = Double.parseDouble(sd1);
        String ad2 = buf.readLine();
        double s2 = Double.parseDouble(sd1);
        String sd3 = buf.readLine();
        double s3 = Double.parseDouble(sd1);
        areaTriangle(s1, s2, s3);
    }
}
```

5. (a) Create a package myPackage that contains the following classes. The description of each class is given along with it.

Class : Square

method :

(i) compute() — to calculate area of square accepting the required values from the calling module.

(ii) perimeter()— tocalculateperimeterofthesquare, acceptingrequiredvaluesfromcalling module.

Class Circle :

Methods — (i) circumference() (ii) area()

Class Rectangle :

Methods — (i) Area() (ii) Perimeter()

(b) Define another java class myClass that can access the methods of myPackage and prints the area of square, area of circle and the area of rectangle taking the side of square = 4.5 cm, length of rectangle = 5 cm, breadth = 3 cm and the radius of circle as 7 cm.

Ans. (a)

```
package myPackage;
import java.lang.Math.*;
public class Square
{
        public static void compute(double side)
        {
                double ar = side * side;
                System.out.print("The area of square ="+ar);
        }
        public static void parameter(double side)
        {
                double p = 4 * side;
                System.out.print("The perimeter of square =" + p);
        }
}
    public class Circle
    {
        public static void circumference(int r)
        {
        double c = 2 * Math.PI * r;
        System.out.print("Circumference is :" + c);
        }
        public static void area(double r)
        {
            double a = Math.PI * r * r;
            System.out.print("Area is :" +a);
```

```
                }
            }
        public class Rectangle
        {
            public static void perimeter(int s1, int s2)
            {
                double c = 2 * (s1 + s2);
                System.out.print("perimeter is :" + c);
            }
            public static void area(int s1, int s2)
            {
                double a = s1 * s2;
                System.out.print("Area is :" +a);
            }
        }
```

(b) import myPackage;
```
    public class myClass
    {
        public static void main(String [] args)
        {
        double s = 4.5;
        Square ob = new Square();
        ob.compute(s);
        Circle obj = new Circle();
        double r = 6;
        obj.area(r);
        Rectangle objt = new Rectangle();
        objt.area(5, 3);
        }
    }
```

6. Write a program to assign a full path and file name as given below. Using library functions, extract and output the file path, file name and file extension separately as shown.Input C :\Users\admin\Pictures\flower.jpg

Output path   :   C :\users\admin\Pictures\
File name   :   flower
Extension   :   jpg

Ans.
```
class Path
{
        String s, pth, fname, file, ext;
        int i, j;
        void display()
        {
            s = "C :\\ Users\\ admin\\ Pictures\\ flower.jpg";
            i = s.lastIndexOf('\\ ');
            pth = s.substring(0, i + 1);
            fname = s.substring(i + 1);
            j = fname.indexOf('.');
            file = fname.substring(0, j);
```

```
            ext = fname.substring(j + 1);
            System.out.println("Path : " + pth);
            System.out.println("File name : " + file);
            System.out.println("Extension : " + ext);
        }
    }
```

Chapter 6. Encapsulation

1. In the program given below, state the name and the value of the:

(i)   method argument or argument variable.

(ii) class variable.

(iii) local variable.

(iv) instance variable

```
class myClass.
{
        static int x = 7;
        int y = 2;
        public static void main(String args[])
        {
            myClass obj = new myClass();
            System.out.println(x);
            obj.sampleMethod(5);
            int a = 6;
            System.out.println(a);
        }
        void sampleMethod(int n)
        {
            System.out.println(n);
            System.out.println(y);
        }
}
```

Ans. (i)   int n; (argument variable)

(ii) x = 7; (class variable)

(iii) a = 6; (local variable)

(iv) y = 2; (instance variable)

2. Consider the following code and answer the questions that follow :

```
class academic
{
        int x, y;
        void access()
        {
            int a, b;
            academic student = new academic();
            System.out.println("Object created");
        }
}
```

(i)   What is the object name of class academic ?

(ii) Name the class variables used in the program.

(iii) Write the local variables used in the program.

(iv) Give the type of function used and its name.

Ans. (i)   The class academic has the object name student.

(ii)   There is no Class Variable.

(iii) Local variables : a, b;

(iv) Function name is access() and its return type is void. It is a member function of the class.

Chapter 7. Arrays

1. Write a program to accept the year of graduation from school as an integer value from the user. Using the Binary Search technique on the sorted array of integers given below :

Output the message "Record exists". If the value input is located in the array. If not, output the message "Record does not exist".

{1982, 1987, 1993, 1996, 1999, 2003, 2006, 2007, 2009, 2010}

Ans.
```java
import java.io.*;
class Search
{
        int A[] = {1982, 1987, 1993, 1996, 1999, 2003, 2006, 2007, 2009, 2010};
        int n, l, h, mid, flag = 0;
        void display()throws IOException
        {
            BufferedReader br = new BufferedReader(new InputStreamReader(System.in));
            System.out.println("Enter year");
            n = Integer.parseInt(br.readLine());
            l = 0;
            h = A.length - 1;
            while(l <= h)
            {
                    mid = (l + h)/2;
                    if(n > A[mid])
                {
                    l = mid + 1;
                }
                else if(n < A[mid])
                {
                    h = mid - 1;
                }
                else
                {
                    flag = 1;
                    break;
                }
            }
            if(flag == 1)
            {
                    System.out.println("Record exists");
            }
            else
```

Programming Based Questions

```java
                {
                        System.out.println("Record does not exists");
                }
        }
}
```

2. Write a program to input 10 integer elements in an array and sort them in descending order using the bubble sort technique.

Ans.
```java
import java.io.*;
class Arrange
{
        int A[] = new int[10];
        int i, j, t;
        void display()throws IOException
        {
            BufferedReader br = new BufferedReader(new InputStreamReader(System.in));
            for(i = 0; i < 10; i++)
            {
                System.out.println("Enter a number");
                A[i] = Integer.parseInt(br.readLine());
            }
            for(i = 0; i < 10; i++)
            {
                for(j = 0; j < 9 - i; j++)
                {
                    if(A[j] < A[j + 1])
                    {
                        t = A[j];
                        A[j] = A[j + 1];
                        A[j + 1] = t;
                    }
                }
            }
            for(i = 0; i < 10; i++)
            {
                System.out.println(A[i]);
            }
        }
}
```

3. Write a program to accept the names of 10 cities in a single dimension string array and their STD (Subscribers Trunk Dialing) codes in another single dimension integer array. Search for a name of a city input by the user in the list. if found, display "Search Successful" and print the name of the city along with its STD code, or else display the message "Search Unsuccessful, No such city in the list".

Ans.
```java
import java.io.*;
public class STD
{
        public static void main(String args[]) throws IOException
        {
        int S[] = new int [10];
```

```java
String n[] = new String [10];
String sn;
BufferedReader br = new BufferedReader(new InputStreamReader(System.in));
int pos = -1, i;
for(i = 0; i < 10; i++)
{
        System.out.println("Enter City Name and STD");
        n[i] = br.readLine();
        S[i] = Integer.parseInt(br.readLine());
}
System.out.println("Enter city name to search");
sn = br.readLine();
for(i = 0; i <= 9; i++)
{
        if(n[i].equalsIgnoreCase(sn))
        {
        pos = i;
        break;
        }
}
if(pos != - 1)
        System.out.println("STD of the entered city = "+S[pos]);
else
        System.out.println("Search Unsuccessful, No such city in the list");
}
}
```

4. Write a program to input and store the weight of ten people. Sort and display them in descending order using the bubble sort technique.

Ans.
```java
import java.io.*;
class Sort
{
        int A[] = new int[10];
        int i, j, t;
        void display()throws IOException
        {
            BufferedReader br = new BufferedReader(new InputStreamReader(System.in));
            for(i = 0; i < 10; i++)
        {
            System.out.println("Enter Weight");
            A[i] = Integer.parseInt(br.readLine());
        }
        for(i = 0; i < 10; i++)
        {
            for(j = i + 1; j < 10; j++)
            {
                if(A[i] < A[j])
                {
                t = A[i];
```

```
                A[i] = A[j];
                A[j] = t;
                }
            }
        }
        for(i = 0; i < 10; i++)
        {
        System.out.println(A[i]);
        }
    }
}
```

5. Write a program to perform binary search on a list of integers given below, to search for an element input by the user, if it is found display the element along with its position, otherwise display the message "Search element not found".

5, 7, 9, 11, 15, 20, 30, 45, 89, 97

Ans.
```
.import java.io.*;
public class BSearch
{
        int A[] = {5, 7, 9, 11, 15, 20, 30, 45, 89, 97};
        int low, high, mid, flag = 0;
        void display(int n)
        {
            low = 0;
            high = A.length - 1;
            while(low <= high)
            {
                mid = (low + high)/2;
                if(n > A[mid])
            {
                low = mid + 1;
            }
            else if(n < A[mid])
            {
                high = mid - 1;
            }
            else
            {
            flag = 1;
            break;
            }
        }
        if(flag == 1)
        {
        System.out.println(n + " Found at position " + (mid + 1));
        }
        else
        {
        System.out.println("Search element not found");
```

```
      }
    }
  }
```

6. Write a program to store 6 elements in an array P, and 4 elements in an array Q and produce a third array R, containing all the elements of array P and Display the resultant array.

EXAMPLE :	INPUT	OUTPUT
P[]	Q[]	R[]
4	19	4
6	23	6
1	7	1
2	8	2
3		3
10		10
		19
		23
		7
		8

Ans.
```java
import java.io.*;
class Merge
{
        int P[] = new int[6];
        int Q[] = new int[4];
        int R[] = new int[10];
        int i, j;
        void display()throws IOException
        {
            BufferedReader br = new BufferedReader(new InputStreamReader(System.in));
            for(i = 0; i < 6; i++)
            {
                System.out.println("Enter a number");
                P[i] = Integer.parseInt(br.readLine());
            }
            for(i = 0; i < 4; i++)
            {
                System.out.println("Enter a number");
                Q[i] = Integer.parseInt(br.readLine());
            }
            for(i = 0; i < 6; i++)
            {
                R[i] = P[i];
            }
            for(i = 6, j = 0; j < 4; j++, i++)
            {
                R[i] = Q[j];
            }
            for(i = 0; i < 10; i++)
            {
```

```
                System.out.println(R[i]);
            }
        }
    }
```

7. Write a program that creates an integer array of 10 elements, puts some values in it, and displays the values.

Ans.
```
public class ArrayDemo
{
        int[] anArray = new int[10]; // create an array of integers;
        //d eclare an array of integers
        public void demo()
        {
            for(int i = 0; i < anArray.length; i++)
            {
                anArray[i] = i;
                System.out.print(anArray[i] + " ");
            }
        System.out.println();
        }
}
```

8. The annual examination results of 50 students in a class is tabulated as follows :

Roll no.	Subject ₹ A	Subject ₹ B	Subject ₹ C
……………	……………	……………	……………

Write a program to read the data, calculate and display the following :

(i)   Average mark obtained by each student.

(ii) Print the roll number and average marks of the students whose average mark is above 80.

(iii) Print the roll number and average marks of the students whose average mark is below 40.

Ans.
```
import java.io.*;
public class AnExam
{
        int rno[] = new int[50];
        double a[] = new double[50];
        double b[] = new double[50];
        double c[] = new double[50];
        double avg[] = new double[50];
        int i;
        void readData()throws IOException
        {
            BufferedReader br = new BufferedReader(new InputStreamReader(System.in));
            for(i = 0; i =< 50; i++)
            {
                System.out.println("Roll no and marks in 3 subjects of a student");
                rno[i] = Integer.parseInt(br.readLine());
                a[i] = Double.parseDouble(br.readLine());
                b[i] = Double.parseDouble(br.readLine());
                c[i] = Double.parseDouble(br.readLine());
                avg[i] = (a[i] + b[i] + c[i])/3;
            }
```

```java
        }
        void display()
        {
            System.out.println("Roll No.\t Subject A\tSubject B\t Subject C\t Average");
            for(i = 0; i < 50; i++)
            {
            System.out.println(rno[i] + "\t" + a[i] + "\t" + b[i] + "\t" + c[i] + "\t" + avg[i]);
            }
        System.out.println("Students whose average is above 80");
        for(i = 0; i < 50; i++)
        {
            if(avg[i] > 80)
            {
                System.out.println(rno[i] + "\t" + a[i] + "\t" + b[i] + "\t" + c[i] + "\t"+ avg[i]);
            }
        }
        System.out.println("Students whose average is below 40");
        for(i = 0; i < 50; i++)
        {
            if(avg[i] < 40)
            {
                System.out.println(rno[i] + "\t" + a[i] + "\t" + b[i] + "\t" + c[i] + "\t" + avg [i];
            }
        }
    }
}
```

9. Define a class and store the given city names in a single dimensional array. Sort these names in alphabetical order using the Bubble Sort technique only.

INPUT   :   Delhi, Bengaluru, Agra, Mumbai, Kolkata

OUTPUT   :   Agra, Bengaluru, Kolkata, Delhi, Mumbai

Ans.
```java
import java.io.*;
public class city
{
        public static void main(String args[])
        {
        int i, j;
        String t;
        String m[] = {"Delhi", "Bengaluru", "Agra", "Mumbai", "Kolkata"};
        for(i = 0; i < 4; i++)
        {
            for(j = 0; j <= 3 - i; j++)
            {
                if(m[j].compareTo(m[j + 1]) > 0)
                {
                    t = m[j];
                    m[j] = m[j + 1];
                    m[j + 1] = t;
                }
```

```
            }
        }
        System.out.println("The names in alphabetical order are");
        for(i = 0; i < 5; i++)
        System.out.println(m[i]);
        }
    }
```

10. Write a program to initialize the given data in an array and find the minimum and maximum values along with the sum of the given elements.

    Numbers : 2 5 4 1 3

    Output : Minimum value : 1

    Maximum value : 5

    Sum of the elements : 15

Ans.
```
.import java.io.*;
public class Test
{
        public static void main(String args[])
        {
            int x[] = {2, 5, 4, 1, 3};
            int min, max, sum;
            sum = min = max = x[0];
            for(int i = 1; i <= 4; i++)
            {
                sum = sum + x [i];
                if(x [i] > max)
                    max = x [i];
                if(x [i] < min)
                    min = x [i];
            }
            System.out.println("Maximum No." + max + " \n Minimum No." + min + "sum of All Nos."
            + sum);
        }
    }
```

11. Write a program that creates an integer array of 10 elements, accepts values for array elements from the user and displays the values.

Ans.
```
import java.io.*;
public class ArrayDemo
{
        int[] anArray = new int[10];
        public void accept()throws IOException
        {
            int num;
            String str;
            BufferedReader bReader = new BufferedReader(new InputStreamReader(System.in));
            System.out.println("Enter a number and press return");
            for(int i = 0; i < anArray.length; i++)
            {
                str = bReader.readLine();
```

```
                num = Integer.parseInt(str);
                anArray[i] = num;
            }
            for(i = 0; i < anArray.length; i++)
            {
                System.out.println("Element" + (i + 1) "is :" + anArray[i]);
            }
        }
    }
}
```

12. Write a program that finds the average marks of students stored in stu Array.

Ans.
```
import java.io.*;
public class ArrayDemo
{
        int[] anArray = new int[10];
        public void accept()throwsIOException
        {
            int sum;
            int avg = 0;
            int num;
            String str;
            BufferedReader bReader = new BufferedReader(new InputStreamReader(System.in));
            System.out.print("Enter marks of students");
            for(int i = 0; i < anArray.length; i++)
            {
                str = bReader.readLine();
                num = Integer.parseInt(str);
                anArray[i] = num;
                sum += anArray[i];
            }
            avg = sum/10;
            System.out.println("Average marks is :" +avg);
        }
}
```

13. The marks obtained by 50 students in a subject are tabulated as follows :

```
Name        Marks
.........    .........
.........    .........
.........    .........
```

Write a program to input the names and marks of the students in three subjects.
Calculate and display :

(i) The subject average marks (subject average marks = subject total/50)

(ii) The highest marks in the subject and the name of the student.

(The maximum marks in a subject are 100)

Ans.
```
import java.io.*;
public class Exam
{
        string name[] = new string[50];
        double a[] = new double[50];
```

```java
double b[] = new double[50];
double c[] = new double[50];
double avg1 = 0;
double avg2 = 0;
double avg3 = 0;
double hm[] = new double[3];
string namehm[] = new string[3];
int i;
void readData()throws IOException
{
    BufferedReader br = new BufferedReader(new InputStreamReader(System.in));
    for(i = 0; i =< 50; i++)
    {
        System.out.println("Name and marks in 3 subjects of a student");
        name [i] = br.readLine();
        a[i] = Double.parseDouble(br.readLine());
        b[i] = Double.parseDouble(br.readLine());
        c[i] = Double.parseDouble(br.readLine());
        avg1 = avg1 + a[i];
        avg2 = avg2 + b[i];
        avg3 = avg3 + b[i];
    }
    avg1 = avg1/50;
    avg2 = avg2/50;
    avg3 = avg3/50;
}
void display()
{
    System.out.println("Name \t Subject 1\t Subject 2\t Subject 3");
    for(i = 0; i < 50; i++)
    {
    System.out.println(name[i] + "\t" + a[i] + "\t" + b[i] + "\t" + c[i]);
    }
    System.out.println("Average in 1st subject : "+avg1);
    System.out.println("Average in 2nd subject : "+avg2);
    System.out.println("Average in 3rd subject : "+avg3);
    System.out.println("Students having highest marks in subject");
    for(i = 0; i < 50; i++)
    {
        hm[0] = 0;
        hm[1] = 0;
        hm[2] = 0;
        if(a[i] > hm[0])
        {
            hm[0] = a[i];
            namehm[0] = name[i];
        }
        if(b[i] > hm[1])
```

```
        {
            hm[1] = b[i];
            namehm[1] = name[i];
        }
        if(c[i] > hm[2])
        {
            hm[2] = c[i];
            namehm[2] = name[i];
        }
    }
    System.out.println("Student Name and Highest marks in 1st subject :" + namehm[0]+"\t"+hm[0]);
    System.out.println("Student Name and Highest marks in 2nd subject :" + namehm[1]+"\t"+hm[1]);
    System.out.println("Student Name and Highest marks in 3rd subject :" + namhm[2]+"\t"+hm[2]);
    }
}
```

14. Write a program to accept 15 integers from the keyboard, assuming that no integer entered isa zero. Perform bubble sort on the integers and then print them in ascending order.

Ans.
```
import java.io.*;
public class test
{
    public static void main(String args[]) throws IOException
    {
        int n[ ] = new int[15];
        int I, t;
        BufferedReader b = new BufferedReader(new InputStreamReader(System.in));
        for(I = 0; I <= 14; I++)
        {
            System.out.println("Enter a Number ");
            n[I] = Integer.parseInt(b.readLine());
        }
        for(I = 0; I < 14; I++)
        {
            for(int j = I + 1; j <= 14; j++)
            {
                if(n[I] > n[j])
                {
                t = n[I];
                n[I] = n[j];
                n[j] = t;
                }
            }
        }
        for(I = 0; I <= 14; I++)
        {
        System.out.println(n[I]);
        }
    }
}
```

15. Write a program to initialize an array of 5 names and initialize another array with their respective telephone numbers. Search for a name input by the users, in the list. If found display "Search successful" and print the name along with the telephone number, otherwise display "Search unsuccessful. Name not enlisted".

Ans.
```java
import java.io.*;
public class test
{
    public static void main(String args[]) throws IOException
    {
        BufferedReader br = new BufferedReader(new InputStreamReader(System.in));
        String nm[] = {"Harish", "Dev", "Rakesh", "Sudheer", "Nishant"};
        String telno[] = {"9897605811","9412163232","9891102002", "9837000144", "9893299877"};
        String s;
        boolean found = false;
        System.out.println("Enter Name to search");
        s = br.readLine();
        for(int i = 0; i <= 4; i++)
        {
            if(s.equals(nm[i]))
            {
            found = true;
            System.out.println("Search Successful ! The telephone number of " + s + " Is " + telno[i]);
            break;
            }
        }
        if(found == false)
        System.out.println("Search Unsuccessful. Name not enlisted");
    }
}
```

16. Assume that marks have already been entered in array stuArray. Write a method to find the maximum and minimum marks.

Ans.
```java
public void check()
{
    int min = max = 0;
    min = stuArray[0];
    for(int i = 0; i < stuArray.length; i++)
    {
        if(max < stuArray[i])
        max = stuArray[i];
        if(min > stuArray[i])
        min = stuArray[i];
    }
    System.out.println("The maximum is :" + max);
    System.out.println("The minimum is :" + min);
}
```

17. Write a method that reverses the characters in a character array.

Ans.
```java
public void string()
{
```

```java
char[] array = {'a', 'b', 'c', 'd', 'e', 'f', 'g', 'h', 'i', 'j'};
for(int last = array.length; last > 0; last--)
{
    System.out.print(array[last]);
}
}
```

18. Write a method that reads a character array and stores the reverse of the array in another array.

Ans.
```java
public void stringrev()
{
        char[] array = {'a', 'b', 'c', 'd', 'e', 'f', 'g', 'h', 'i', 'j'};
        int len = array.length;
        char[] reverse = new char[len];
        for(int last = len, ctr = 0; last > 0; last - -, ctr++)
        {
        reverse [ctr] = array[last];
        }
}
```

19. Write a program that reads a character array and checks if it is a **palindrome**.

Ans.
```java
.import java.io.*;
public class Palindrome
{
        char[] array = {'a', 'b', 'c', 'd', 'e', 'f', 'g', 'h', 'i', 'j'};
        int flag = 0;
        public void demo()
        {
            int len = array.length;
            int ctr = 0;
            for(int last = len; last > 0 && ctr < len; last - -, ctr++)
            {
                if(array[ctr] == array[last])
                {
                    continue;
                }
                else
                {
                    flag = 1;
                    break;
                }
            }
            if(flag == 1)
                    System.out.println("It is not a palindrome");
            else
                    System.out.println("It is a palindrome");
        }
}
```

20. Write a program which accepts an integer array as parameter and doubles all the elements of the array. Also, write another method to pass an array to the method and display the original array.

Ans.
```
public class Arrdemo
{
        public void Array(int[] arr)
        {
            for(int ctr = 0; ctr < arr.length; ctr++)
            arr[ctr] = arr[ctr] + arr[ctr];
        }
        public void display(int[] arr1)
        {
            for(int ctr = 0; ctr < arr1.lenth; ctr++)
            System.out.print(arr1[ctr] +" ");
        }
}
```

21. Write a program which accepts an integer array as parameter and copies it to another array.

Ans.
```
public class Arrdemo
{
        public void display(int[] arr)
        {
                int[] arrcopy = new int[arr.length];
                for(int ctr = 0; ctr < arr.length; ctr++)
                arrcopy[ctr] = arr[ctr];
        }
}
```

22. Write a program which accepts 10 names and displays them in uppercase.

Ans.
```
import java.io.*;
public class Arrdemo
{
        String[] Name = new String[10];
        String str;
        public void accept()
        {
            BufferedReader bReader = new BufferedReader(new InputStreamReader(System in));
            for(int i = 0; i < anArray.length; i++)
            {
                    System.out.print("Enter a number and press return");
                    Str = bReader.readLine();
                    anArray[i] = str;
            }
            for(int j = 0; j < anArray.length; j++)
            {
                    if(anArray[i] != null)
                    System.out.println("Name" + j + ";"+anArray[j].toUpperCase());
                    else
                    System.out.println("Name" + j +"empty");
            }
        }
}
```

23. Suppose a 10-element array A contains the values a1, a2……a10. Find the values in A after each loop.

    (i)   for(i = 0; i < 9; i++)

         A [i + 1] = A[i];

    (ii) for(i = 8; i >= 0; i - -)

         A[i + 1] = A[i];

Ans. (i) In the first loop, the A[0] elemtnt is assigned to the A[1] , A[1] to A[2] and so on.

    (ii) In the 2nd Loop A[8] element is assigned to A[9], A[7] to A[8] and so on.

24. Write a Java program to find the largest and smallest elements in a vector.

Ans.

```java
import java.io.DataInputStream;
public class Array1
{
        public static void main(String args[]) throws IOException
        {
            DataInputStream in = new DataInputStream(System.in);
            final int size = 25;
            int i, n = 0, large, small;
            int v[] = new int[size];
            System.out.println("Enter how many elements(max 25) :");
            n = Integer.parseInt(in.readLine());
            System.out.println("Enter elements of a vector - - >");
            for(i = 0; i < n; i++)
            {
                v[i] = Integer.parseInt(in.readLine());
            }
            large = v[0];
            small = v[0];
            for(i = 0; i < n; i++)
            {
                if(v[i] > large)
                large = v[i];
                if(v[i] < small)
                small = v[i];
            }
            System.out.println("Largest element :" + large);
            System.out.println("Smallest element : "+ small);
        }
}
```

25. Define a class with a method to sort an array by bubble sort method.

Ans.

```java
import java.io.*;
public class test
{
    public void sort(int A[])
    {
        int a, b, c;
        for(a = 0; a < A.length - 1; a++)
        {
            for(b = a + 1; b < A - length; b + +)
            {
```

```java
            if(A[a] > A[b])
            {
            c = A[a];
            A[a] = A[b];
            A[b] = C;
            }
        }
    }
}
```

26. Write a program to store weight of 10 students into an array and display those ages which are greater than average age.

Ans.
```java
import java.io.*;
public class Test
{
    public static void main(String args[])
    {
        double weight[] = {40.8, 44.9, 50.5, 70.00, 80.5, 38.5, 50.00, 55.00, 30.5, 34.0};
        double sum = 0, Avg = 0;
        for(int i = 0; i < weight.length; i++)
        {
            sum = sum + weight[i];
        }
        Avg = sum/10.0;
        for(i = 0; i < weight - length; i++)
        {
            if(weight[i] > Avg)
            System.out.println(weight [i]);
        }
    }
}
```

27. Define a method to search a value into an array using binary search method.

Ans.
```java
import java.io.*;
public class test
{
    public void search(int A [], int n) // n is the value to be search in an Array A.
    {
        int low = 0, high = A.length - 1;
        int f = 0;
        while(low <= high && f == 0)
        {
            mid = (low + high)/2;
            if(A[mid] == n)
            {
                f = 1;
                System.out.println(n+ "found at" + mid + "th position");
                break;
            }
        }
```

```java
            else if(A[mid] > n)
            high = mid - 1;
            else
            low = mid + 1;
        }
        if(f == 0)
        System.out.print(n + "is not found in array");
    }
}
```

28. Define a method to sort an array using bubble sort method.

Ans.
```java
import java.io.*;
public class test
{
        public void sort(int A[])
        {
            int a, b, c;
                int l = A.length - 1;
                for(a = 0; a <= l; a++)
                {
                        for(b = 0; a <= l - 1 - a; b++)
                        {
                                if(A[b] > A[b + 1])
                                {
                                c = A[b];
                                A[b] = A[b + 1];
                                A[b + 1] = c;
                                }
                        }
                }
        }
}
```

29. Define a method to search a value into an array using linear search techniques.

Ans.
```java
import java.io.*;
public class test
{
        public void search(int A[], int n) // n is the value to be search and || A[] is the Array.
        {
        int f = 0;
        int l = A.length;
            for(int i = 0; i <= l - 1 && f == 0; i++)
            {
                if (A[i] == n)
                {
                    System.out.print(n + "is found at" + i + "positon");
                    f = 1;
                }
            }
```

```
        if(f == 0)
        System.out.print(n+ "not found in list");
        }
    }
```

30. Give an array of 6 elements, the difference of successive elements may be difference of previous numbers as follows :

e.g.; [2, 6, 12, 20, 30, 42]

```
    2  6  12  20  30  42
    4  6  8  10  12
    2  2  2  2
    0  0  0
    0  0
```

Ans.

```java
import java.io.*;
public class Previous
{
    public static void main(String args[]) throws IOException
    {
        int [] a = new int [6];
        int k = 4, n = 6;
        BufferedReader input = new BufferedReader(new InputStreamReader(System. in));
        System.out.println("Enter Six values");
        for(int i = 0; i < n; i++)
        {
            String x = input.readLine();
            a[i] = Integer.parseInt(x);
        }
        for(i = 0; i < 6; i++)
        {
            for(int j = 0; j < n - i; j++)
            {
                if(i == 0)
                    System.out.print(a[j]+" ");
                else
                {
                    a[j] = a[j + 1] - a[j];
                    System.out.print(a[j]+" ");
                }
            }
        }
    }
}
```

31. Write a Java program to create a single dimensional array for N numbers and transfer the smallest element to the left side and the second smallest element to the right side and as so on up to n numbers.

Ans.

```java
import java. io.*;
public class transfer
{
    public static void main(String args[]) throws IOException
    {
```

```java
        int a[] = new int[50];
        BufferedReader input = new BufferedReader(new InputStreamReader(System.in));
        int n;
        System.out.print("Enter Number of Elements You Want To Input");
        String d = input.readLine();
        n = Integer.parseInt(d);
        String numb;
        for(int i = 0; i < n; i++)
{

    System.out.print("Enter any number");
    numb = input.readLine();
    a[i] = Integer.parseInt(numb);
}
int s, e, m, p, min = 0, t, j, i;
s = 0;
e = n - 1;
for(i = 1; i <= n; i++)
{
        min = a[s];
        p = s;
        for(j = s; j <= e; j++)
        {
            if(a[j] < min)
        {
        min = a[j];
        p = j;
        }
        }
    if(i % 2 == 1)
    {
            t = a[s];
            a[s] = a[p];
            a[p] = t;
            s++;
    }
    else
    {
            t = a[e];
            a[e] = a[p];
            a[p] = t;
            e--;
        }
    }
    System.out.println("Now Output is");
    for(m = 0; m < n; m++)
    {
        System.out.print(a[m] + " ");
    }
```

```
            }
    }
Output :
Enter Number of Elements You Want To Input - - > 5
Enter Any Number - - > 25
Enter Any Number - - > 36
Enter Any Number - - > 15
Enter Any Number - - > 2
Enter Any Number - - > 26
Now Output Is :
2 25 36 26 15
```

32. Write a Java program which searches an element from an array and locates the position of the searched element.

Ans.
```java
// Program for searching an element in an Array.
import java.io.*;
public class search
{
        public static void main(String args[]) throws IOException
        {
                int i;
                int[] array = new int[50];
                int look = 0;
                int location = 0;
                BufferedReader input = new BufferedReader(new InputStreamReader(System.in));
                System.out.print("Enter Numbers in Array = ");
                String x = input.readLine();
                String numb;
                int n = Integer.parseInt(x);
                for(i = 0; i < n; i++)
                {
                    System.out.print("Enter Number =" + (i + 1) + " : : ");
                    numb = input.readLine();
                    array[i] = Integer.parseInt(numb);
                }
                System.out.print("Enter Number to be searched = ");
                String a = input.readLine();
                look = Integer.parseInt(a);
                for(i = 0; i < n; i++)
                {
                    if(array[i] == look)
                    location = i + 1;
                }
                if(location > 0)
                        System.out.println("The Required Number " + look + " Found at = " + location);
                else
                        System.out.println("The Required Number" + look + "Not Found !!");
        }
}
```

Output :

Enter Number in Array = 6

Enter Number = 1 : : 7

Enter Number = 2 : : 9

Enter Number = 3 : : 10

Enter Number = 4 : : 5

Enter Number = 5 : : 77

Enter Number = 6 : : 22

Enter Number to be Searched = 77

The Required Number 77 Found at = 5

33. The marks obtained by 50 students in a subject are tabulated as follows :

Name   Marks

....

....

....

Write a program to input the names and marks of the students in the subject. Calculate and display :

(i)   The subject **average marks** (subject average marks = subject total/50)

(ii) The highest marks in the subject and the name of the student.

(The maximum marks in the subject are 100)

Ans.

```java
import java.io.*;
public class test
{
        public static void main(String [] args)throws IOException
        {
                String n, m, nm = "";
                int mk, g = 0, sm = 0;
                BufferedReader b = new BufferedReader(new InputStreamReader(System.in));
                for(int I = 0; I <= 50; I++)
                {
                        System.out.println("Enter Name");
                        n = b.readLine();
                        System.out.println("Enter marks");
                        mk = Integer.parseInt(b.readLine());
                        sm = sm + mk;
                        if(mk > g)
                        {
                                g = mk;
                                nm = n;
                        }
                }
                av = sm/50;
                System.out.println("Average marks " + av);
                System.out.println("Highest marks are " + g + " Student Name " + nm);
        }
}
```

34. Write a program to accept 15 integers from the keyboard, assuming that no integer entered is a zero. Perform bubble sort on the integers and then print them in ascending order.

Ans.
```java
import java.io.*;
public class test
{
        public static void main(String args[]) throws IOException
        {
                int n[] = new int[15], l, I, t;
                BufferedReader b = new BufferedReader(new InputStreamReader(System.in));
                for(I = 0; I <= 14; I++)
                {
                        System.out.println("Enter a Number ");
                        n[I] = Integer.parseInt(b.readLine());
                }
                for(I = 0; I < 14; I++)
                {
                        for(int j = I + 1; j <= 14; j++)
                        {
                            if(n[I] > n[j])
                            {
                            t = n[I];
                            n[I] = n[j];
                            n[j] = t;
                            }
                        }
                }
                for(I = 0; I <= 14; I++)
                {
                System.out.println(n[I]);
                }
        }
}
```

35. Write a program to input forty words in an array. Arrange these words in descending order of alphabets, using selection sort technique. Print the sorted array.

Ans.
```java
import java.util.*;// importing package
class selectSort
{
        String A[] = new String[40];
        int i, j, min;
        String t;
        void display()
        {
                Scanner sc = new Scanner(System.in);
                for(i = 0; i < 40; i++)
                {
                        System.out.println("Enter a name");
                        A[i] = sc.next();
                }
                  for(i = 0; i < 40; i++)
                  {
```

```
                    min = i;
                    for(j = i +1; j < 40; j++)
                    {
                            if(A[i].compareTo(A[j]) < 0)
                            {
                                    min = j;
                            }
                    }
                    t = A[i];
                    A[i] = A[min];
                    A[min] = t;
            }
            for(i = 0; i < 40; i++)
            {
                    System.out.println(A[i]);
            }
        }
} // class ending
```

Name	Type	Description
A[]	String	To store forty words
i, j	int	Loop variable
t	String	Temporary variable to store a string
min	int	To store index value of smaller string of the array

36. WAP to accept 15 integers from the console. Sort the list in ascending order using :

(i)   Selection Sort Method.

(ii) Bubble Sorting Method.

Ans. (i)
```
import java.io.*;
public class SelectionSorting
{
        public static void main(String args[]) throws IOException
        {
        int arr[] = new int[20];
        BufferedReader buf = new BufferedReader(new InputStreamReader(System.in));
        System.out.println("Enter 15 numbers :");
        for(int i = 0; i < 15; i++)
        {
                String h = buf.readLine();
                arr[i] = Integer.parseInt(h);
        }
        int n = 15;
        int min, minPosition = 0;
        for(int i = 0; i < n - 1; i++)
        {
                min = arr[i];
                for(int j = i + 1; j < n; j++)
                {
                        if(min > arr[j])
```

```java
                                {
                                    min = arr[j];
                                    minPosition = j;
                                }
                        }
                        int t = arr[i];
                        arr[i] = min;
                        arr[minPosition] = t;
                }
                System.out.println("The sorted values in ascending order are : ");
                for(int k = 0; k < n; k++)
                {
                        System.out.println(arr[k]);
                }
            }
        }
```

(ii) ```java
     import java.io.*;
     public class BubbleSorting
     {
             public static void main(String args[]) throws IOException
             {
                     int arr[] = new int[20];
                     BufferedReader buf = new BufferedReader(new InputStreamReader(System.in));
                     System.out.println("Enter 15 numbers :");
                     for(int i = 0; i < 15; i++)
                     {
                             String h = buf.readLine();
                             arr[i] = Integer.parseInt(h);
                     }
                     int n = 15;
                     for(int i = 0; i < n - 1; i++)
                     {
                             for(int j = 0; j < n - 1; j++)
                             {
                                     if(arr[j] > arr[j + 1]
                                     {
                                             int t = arr[j];
                                         arr[j] = arr[j + 1];
                                         arr[j + 1] = t;
                                     }
                             }
                     }
                     System.out.println("The numbers in ascending order are :");
                     for(int k = 0; k < n; k++)
                     System.out.println(arr[k]);
             }
     }
```
```

37. A company keeps a linear array year (k) that contains the number of employees born in the year k. WAP to perform the following tasks :
    (i)   To print each year in which no employee is born.
    (ii) To find and print the number of years in which no employee is born.
    (iii) To find the number of employees who will be atleast 60 years old at the end of the year 2004.

Ans.
```java
import java.io.*;
public class test2
{
        public static main(String args[]) throws IOException
        {
            int year[] = new int[1000];
            System.out.println("Please enter the minimum year in which an employee can be born of :");
            BufferedReader buf = new BufferedReader(new InputStreamReader(System.in));
            String n = buf.readLine();
            int num = Integer.parseInt(n);
            System.out.println("Please enter the maximum year in which an employee can be born of :");
            String n1 = buf.readLine();
            int num 1 = Integer.parseInt(n1);
            String n2;
                for(int k = num; k <= num1; k++)
                {
                System.out.println("Please enter the number of employees born in the year" + k);
                n2 = buf.readLine();
                year[k] = Integer.parseInt(n2);
                }
            int c = 0, d = 0;
            int yr = 2004 - 60;
            int S = 0;
            System.out.println("The years in which no employee was born are :");
            for(int k = num; k <= num1; k++)
            {
                    if(year[k] == 0)
                    {
                            c ++;
                            System.out.println(year[k]);
                    }
                    if(k <= yr)
                S = S + year[k];
            }
            System.out.println("The number of years in which no employee was born :"+c);
            System.out.println("The number of employees who will be at least 60 yrs old in year 2004 are : " + S);
        }
}
```

38. WAP in Java that accepts the name of a student and his marks in three subjects. Compute his total marks and percentage. Assume that there are 40 students in a class.
    The final output should be the Report of all the students printed as follows :
    ****STUDENT REPORT****

Name	Eng. Marks	Math Marks	Comp. Marks	Total Percent
....	....	....	....	....
....	....	....	....	....
....	....	....	....	....
....	....	....	....	....

Ans.

```java
import java.io*;
public class test3
{
        public static void main(String args[]) throws IOException
        {
                BufferedReader buf = new BufferedReader(new InputStreamReader(System.in));
                String n[] = new String[40];
                int m1[] = new int[40];
                int m2[] = new int[40];
                int m3[] = new int[40];
                int t[] = new int[40];
                double p[] = new double [4];
                for(int i = 0; i < 1; i++)
                {
                        System.out.println("Enter the name of a student");
                        n[i] = obj.readLine();
                        System.out.println("Enter the English marks of a student");
                        String y = obj.readLine();
                        m1[i] = Integer.parseInt(y);
                        System.out.println("Enter the maths marks of a student");
                        String z = obj.readLine();
                        m2[i] = Integer.parseInt(z);
                        System.out.println("Enter the computer marks of a student");
                        String a = obj.readLine();
                        m3[i] = Integer.parseInt(a);
                        t[i] = m1[i] + m2[i] + m3[i];
                        p[i] = t[i]/300 * 100.0;
                }
                System.out.println("****STUDENT REPORT*****");
                System.out.println("Name EngMarks MathMarks CompMarks Total Percent");
                for(int i = 0; i < 1; i++)
                System.out.println(n[i] + " "+m1[i] + " "+m2[i] + ""+m3[i]+ "=" +t[i] + " "+p[i]);
        }
}
```

39. WAP in Java that reads the following list of countries and their respective cities into arrays. The program should accept the name of a country in the list as input and print the corresponding city name as output. The program should give an error message when a city or a country is not in the list.

Ans.

```java
import java.io*;
public class test4
{
        public static void main(String args[]) throws IOException
        {
                String count[] = {"India", "China", "Japan", "Russia", "Sri Lanka"};
```

```
String city[] = "Delhi", "Beijing", "Tokyo", "Moscow", "Columbo"};
boolean v = false;
System.out.println("Enter the country whose city you want to know");
BufferedReader obj = new BufferedReader(new InputStreamReader(System.in));
String x = obj.readLine();
for(int i = 0; i < 5; i++)
{
if(x.compareTo(count[i]) == 0)
{
        v = true;
        System.out.println("City is" + city[i]);
}
}
if(v == false)
{
        System.out.println("Country not found");
}
    }
}
```

40. A dealer sells (1) Badminton rackets (2) Shuttlecocks in boxes containing 10 each (3) Nets.
WAP to create a bill using the information given below :
Input : Date of purchase, name of buyer, price of each item, quantity of each item.
Output : BILLING DETAILS

S.No.	Item	Price	Quantity	Amount
....	....	....	....	....
....	....	....	....	....

Add 8% sales tax and print the net amount to be paid.

Ans.
```
import java.io.*;
public class test5
{
        public static void main(String args[]) throws IOException
        {
                BufferedReader obj = new BufferedReader(new InputStreamReader(System.in));
                String item[] = new String[3];
                double price[] = new double[3];
                String date;
                int qty[] = new int[3];
                double amt[] = new double[3];
                System.out.println("Enter date of purchase");
                date = obj.readLine();
                System.out.println("Enter name");
                String nam = obj.readLine();
                double s = 0.0, sum = 0.0;
                for(int i = 0; i < 3; i++)
                {
                        System.out.println("Enter the article");
                        item[i] = obj.readLine();
                        System.out.println("price of item");
```

```
                String p = obj.readLine();
                price[i] = Double.parseDouble(p);
                System.out.println("Quantity of item");
                String q = obj.readLine();
                qty[i] = Integer.parseInt(q);
                amt[i] = qty[i] * price[i];
                s = s + amt[i];
            }
            sum = s * (8.0/1000) + s;
            System.out.println("BILLING DETAILS");
            System.out.println("S.No., Item Price, Quantity, Amount");
            for(int k = 0; k <= 2; k++)
            {
                int p = k + 1;
                System.out.println(p+ " "+item[k]+ " " +price[k]+ " "+qty[k]+ " "+amt[k]);
                System.out.println("net amount after adding 8% sales tax = Rs "+sum);
            }
        }
    }
```

41. Write a program to assign 5 names in an array and display it on the screen.

Ans.
```
public class Name5
{
    public static void main(String args[])
    {
        String name[] = {"John", "Mary", "Jake", "Pete", "Amanda"};
        int j;
        for(j = 0; j < 5; j++)
        {
            System.out.println(name[j]);
        }
    }
}
```

42. Create a matrix of dimension 3 × 4 and display the elements in the form of rows and columns.

Ans.
```
public class matrix1
{
    public static void main(String args[])
    {
        int a[][] = {{1, 3, 4, 9}, {2, 4, 6, 7}, {3, 6, 8, 1}};
        int i, j;
        for(i = 0; i < 3; i++)
        {
            for(j = 0; j < 4; j++)
            {
                System.out.print(a[i][j] +" ");
            }
            System.out.println();
        }
    }
}
```

43. Accept a matrix of dimension 3 × 3 and print the sum of each row of the matrix.

Ans.
```java
public class matrix2
{
        public static void main(String args[])
        {
        int a[][] = {{3, 4, 9}, {4, 6, 7}, {6, 8, 1}};
        int i, j;
        int sum;
                for(i = 0; i < 3; i++)
                {
                        sum = 0;
                        for(j = 0; j < 3; j++)
                        {
                        System.out.print(a[i][j]+" ");
                        sum += a[i][j];
                        }
                        System.out.print("=" +sum);
                        System.out.println();
                }
        }
}
```

44. Accept a matrix of dimension 4 × 3 and print the sum of each column of the matrix.

Ans.
```java
public class matrix3
{
        public static void main(String args[])
        {
                int a[][] = {{3, 4, 9}, {4, 6, 7}, {6, 8, 1}, {1, 2, 3}};
                int i, j;
                int sum = 0;
                for(i = 0; i < 4; i++)
                {
                        for(j = 0; j < 3; j++)
                        {
                                System.out.print.(a[i][j]+" ");
                        }
                        System.out.println();
                }
                for(i = 0; i < 3; i++)
                {
                        sum = 0
                        for(j = 0; j < 4; j++)
                        {
                                sum += a[j][i];
                        }
                        System.out.print(sum + "");
                }
        }
}
```

45. Create a matrix of dimension 4 × 4 and print the diagonal elements of the matrix.

Ans.
```
public class matrix4
{
        public static void main(String args[])
        {
                int a[][] = {{3, 4, 9, 6}, {4, 6, 7, 2}, {6, 8, 1, 2}, {1, 2, 3, 5}};
                int i, j;
                int sum = 0;
                for(i = 0; i < 4; i++)
                {
                        for(j = 0; j < 4; j++)
                        {
                                if(i == j || i + j == 3)
                                System.out.print(a[i][j]+ "");
                                else
                                System.out.print(" ")
                        }
                        System.out.println();
                }
        }
}
```

46. Create a matrix of dimension 3 × 3 and print the upper elements of the main diagonal.

Ans.
```
public class matrix5
{
        public static void main(String args[])
        {
                int a[][] = {{4, 9, 6}, {6, 7, 2}, {8, 1, 2}};
                int i, j;
                for(i = 0; i < 3; i++)
                {
                        for(j = 0; j < 3; j++)
                        {
                                if(i < j)
                                System.out.print(a[i][j] +" ");
                        }
                }
        }
}
```

47. Create a java program to create an array of size 3 × 3 and display the sum of its diagonal elements.

Ans.
```
public class matrix6
{
        public static void main(String args[])
        {
        int a[][] = {{4, 9, 6}, {6, 7, 2}, {8, 1, 2}};
        int i, j;
        int s1 = 0, s2 = 0;
        for(i = 0; i < 3; i++)
        {
```

```java
                for(j = 0; j < 3; j++)
                {
                        if(i == j)
                        s1 += a[i][j];
                        if(i + j == 2)
                        s2 += a[i][j];
                }
        }
        System.out.println("sum of 1st diagonal = "+s1);
        System.out.println("sum of 2nd diagonal = "+s2);
        }
}
```

48. Write a java program to print the transpose of a matrix of dimension 3 × 2.

Ans.
```java
public class matrix7
{
        public static void man(String args[])
        {
                int a[][] = {{9, 6}, {7, 2}, {1, 3}};
                int i, j;
                for(i = 0; i < 2; i++)
                {
                        for(j = 0; j < 3; j++)
                        {
                                System.out.print(a[j][i]+" ");
                        }
                        System.out.println();
                }
        }
}
```

49. Write a program to search for an integer value input by the user in the sorted list given below using binary search technique. If found display "Search Successful" and print the element, otherwise display "Search Unsuccessful"*

$$\{31, 36, 45, 50, 60, 75, 86, 90\}$$

Ans.
```java
import java.util.*;
class Search
{
int A[]={31,36,45,50,60,75,86,90};
int n,low,high,mid,flag=0;
void display()
{
low=0;
        high=A.length-1;
        Scanner sc=new Scanner(System.in);
System.out.println("Enter a no.");
n=sc.nextInt();
        while(low<=high)
{
```

```java
        mid=(low+high)/2;
            if(n>A[mid])
        {
            low=mid+1;
        }
        else if(n<A[mid])
        {
            high=mid-1;
        }
        else
        {
            flag=1;
            break;
        }
    }
    if(flag==1)
    {
        System.out.println("Search Successful"+n+"Found");
    }
    else
    {
        System.out.println("Search Unsuccessful ");
    }
    }
}
```

50. Write a menu driven program to perform the following operations as per user's choice:*

  (i) To print the value of c = a2 + 2ab, where a varies from 1.0 to 20.0 with increment of 2.0 and b = 3.0 is a constant.

  (ii) To display the following pattern using for loop:

```
A
AB
ABC
ABCD
ABCDE
```

     Display proper message for an invalid choice.

Ans.
```java
import java.util.*;
class Menu
{
int ch;
double a,b=3.0,c;
char :i,j;
void display()
{
Scanner sc=new Scanner(System.in);
System.out.println("1. Value of c");
System.out.println("2. Pattern");
System.out.println("Enter Your Choice");
```

```
ch=sc.nextInt();
    if(ch==1)
    {
                for(a=1.0;a<=20.0;a=a+2)
                {
                c=a*a + 2*a*b;
                System.out.println(c);
                }
    }
    else if(ch==2)
        {
            for(i='A';i<='E';i++)
            {
                for(j='A';j<=i;j++)
                {
                    System.out.print(j);
                }
                System.out.println();
            }
        }
    else
    {
        System.out.println("Wrong Choice");
    }
    }
    }
```

51. Write a program to input and store integer elements in a double dimensional array of size 3 × 3 and find the sum of elements in the left diagonal.*

Example :

1	3	5
4	6	8
9	2	4

Output: Sum of the left diagonal elements = (1 + 6 + 4) = 11

Ans.
```
import java.util.*;
class Matrix
{
int A[][]=new int[3][3];
int i,j,s=0;
void display()
{
Scanner sc=new Scanner(System.in);
for(i=0;i<3;i++)
{
                for(j=0;j<3;j++)
                {
                System.out.println("Enter a no.");
                A[i][j]=sc.nextInt();
```

```
                }
        }
        for(i=0;i<3;i++)
        {
                for(j=0;j<3;j++)
                {
                        if(i == j)
                        {
                        s=s + A[i][j];
                        }
                }
        }
        System.out.println("Sum of the left diagonal
        elements = " + s);
    }
}
```

52. Write a program to input 15 integer elements in an array and sort them in ascending order using the bubble sort technique.*

Ans.
```
import java.util.*;
class Bsort
{
int A[] = new int[15];
int i, j, t;
void display()
{
Scanner sc = new Scanner(System.in);
for(i = 0; i < 15; i++)
{
        System.out.println("Enter a number");
        A[i] = sc.nextInt();
}
for(i = 0; i < 15; i++)
{
        for(j = 0; j < 14 – i; j++)
        {
        if(A[j] > A[j + 1])
        {
                t = A[j];
                A[j] = A[j + 1];
                A[j + 1] = t;
        }
        }
}
for(i = 0; i < 15; i++)
    {
        System.out.println(A[i]);
    }
```

}
}

Name	Type	Description
A[]	int	Array to store 15 numbers.
i, j	int	for loop variables.
t	int	Temporary variable to store value to swap.

Chapter 8. String Handling

1. Write a program to input a string and print out the text with the uppercase and lowercase letters reversed, but all other characters should remain the same as before.

Example :

INPUT :　　　　　　WelComE TO School OUTPUT　　　　　: wELcOMe to sCHOOL

Ans.
```java
import java.io.*;
public class demo
{
        public static void main(String [] args)throws IOException
        {
                String S; int i, len; char ch;
                BufferedReader br = new BufferedReader(new InputStreamReader(System.in));
                System.out.println("Enter a string");
                S = br.readLine();
                len = S.length();
                for(i = 0; i <= len - 1; i++)
                {
                        ch = S.charAt(i);
                        if(Character.isUpperCase(ch))
                        ch = Character.toLowerCase(ch);
                        else if(Character.isLowerCase(ch))
                        ch = Character.toUpperCase(ch);
                        System.out.print(ch);
                }
        }
}
```

2. What do the following function return for :

String x = "Hello"; String y = "World";

(i)　System.out.println(x + y);

(ii) System.out.println(x.length());

(iii) System.out.println(x.charAt(3));

(iv) System.out.println(x.equals(y));

Ans. (i)　HelloWorld　　　　(ii)　5　　　　(iii) l　　　　(iv) false

3. Design a class to overload a function check( ) as follows :

(i)　void check(String str, char ch) – to find and print the frequency of a character in a string. Example :

Input	Output
str = "success"	number of s present is = 3
ch = 's'	

(ii) void check(String s1) – to display only vowels from string s1, after converting it to lower case. Example:

Input :

sl = "computer"　　Output : o u e

Ans. class Overload

```
class Overload
{ // class beginning int i;
        void check(String str, char ch)
        {
                int c = 0;
                str = str.toLowerCase();
                for(i = 0; i < str.length(); i++)
                {
                        if(ch == str.charAt(i))
                        {
                        c++;
                        }
                }
                System.out.println("number of" + ch + " present is " +c);
        }
        void check(String s1)
        {
                char ch;
                s1 = s1.toLowerCase();
                for(i = 0; i < s1.length(); i++)
                {
                        ch = s1.charAt(i);
                        if(ch == 'a' || ch == 'e' || ch == 'i' || ch == 'o' || ch == 'u')
                        {
                                System.out.print(ch + " ");
                        }
                }
        }
} // class ending
```

Name	Type	Description
str	String	To store the given string.
c	int	To store the count value.
ch	char	To store the given character.
i	int	For loop variable.
sI	string	To store a string.

4. Write a statement each to perform the following task on a string :

(i) Extract the second last character of a word stored in the variable wd.

(ii) Check if the second character of a string str is in uppercase.

Ans. (i) int len = wd.length();

      char ch = wd.charAt(len – 2)

(ii) char ch = str.charAt(1);

     if(ch >= 65 && ch <= 90)

     {

     System.out.println("Upper Case");

     }

     else

     {

```
                System.out.println("Not an Upper Case");
    }
```

5. Write a program to display a given string into reverse.

Ans.
```
class test
    {
                public static void reverse(String s)
                {
                        int l = s.length() – 1;
                        for(int i = l; i > 0; i--)
                        {
                                System.out.print(s.charAt(i));
                        }
                }
    :
    :
    }
```

6. Define a method to count the number of vowels in a string.

Ans.
```
class test
    {
                public int count vowels(String s)
                {
                        int l = s.length();
                        int v = 0;
                for(int i = 0; i < l; i ++)
                {
                        e = s.charAt(i);
                        if(e == 'a' | e == 'e' || e == 'i' | c == 'o' | c == 'u')
                        v++;
                }
                return v;
                }
    }
```

7. Write a program to display :

   (i)   length.

   (ii) String in uppercase.

   (iii) String in lowercase.

Ans.
```
public class test
    {
                public static void main(String args[])
                {
                        String s = "Hello";
                        System out println("String length is" + s.length());
                        System out println("String in uppercase" + s.toUpperCase());
                        System out println("String in Lower Case" + s.toLowerCase());
                }
    }
```

8. Input a sentence and display the longest word.

Ans.
```java
import java.io.*;
public class Peo
{
        public static void main(String args[]) throws IOException
        {
                DataInputStream Br = new DataInputStream(System.in);
                String S = Br.readLine();
                S = S + " ";
                String w, wL="";
                int i1;
                i1 = 0; w = "";
                int len = S.length();
                char c;
                for(int i = 0; i < len; i++)
                {
                        c = S.charAt(i);
                        if(c != ' ')
                        w = w + c;
                        else
                        {
                                if(w.length() > i1)
                                {
                                        wL = w;
                                        i1 = w.length();
                                }
                                w = "";
                        }
                }
                System.out.println("Longest word is " + wL + "length is" + i1);
        }
}
```

9. Write a program to enter a sentence from the keyboard and count the number of times a particular word occurs in it. Display the frequency of the search word.

Example :

INPUT :

Enter a sentence : the quick brown fox jumps over the lazy dog.

Enter a word to be searched : the

OUTPUT :

Searched word occurs : 2 times.

Ans.
```java
import java.io.*;
public class test
{
        public static void main(String args[]) throws IOException
        {
                char c;
                int ent = 0;
                BufferedReader br = new BufferedReader(new InputStreamReader(System.in));
                System.out.println("Enter a sentence");
```

```
                String s = br.readLine();
                System.out.println("Enter a word to be searched");
                String w = br.readLine();
                String n = "";
                for(int i = 0; i < s.length(); i++)
                {
                        c = s.charAt(i);
                        if(c == ' ' || c == '.')
                        {
                                if(n.equals(w))
                                ent = ent + 1;
                                n = "";
                        }
                        else
                        {
                                n = n + c;
                        }
                }
                System.out.println("frequency of word is "+ ent);
        }
}
```

10. Consider the following statement—"January 26 is celebrated as the Republic Day of India".

    Write a program to change 26 to 15, January to August, Republic to Independence and finally print" August 15 is celebrated as the Independence Day of India".

Ans.
```
public class test
{
        public static void main(String [] args)
        {
                String N;
                String s ="January 26 is celebrated as the Republic Day of India";
                int I = s.indexOf("26");
                N = "August 15" + s.substring(I + 2);
                I = N.indexOf("Republic");
                N = N.substring(0, I) + "Independence" + N.substring(I + 8);
                System.out.println("new string \n" + N);
        }
}
```

11. Define a class Student that has the following member methods and data members :

    Data members :   roll_num,   name,   marksEng,   marksMaths.

    Member methods :

    1. ComputeGrade() — to assign grade of a student to variable grade.
    2. replaceName() — to replace a word in the name of a student by the desired word as entered by the user.

Ans.
```
import java.io.*;
public class Student
{
        static int roll_num, marksEng, marksMaths, marksComp;
        static double total, percent;
```

```java
        static char grade;
        static String name;
        static void computeGrade(char g) /*Method to assign grade*/
        {
                grade = g;
        }
        static void replaceName(String nam) throws IOException /*Method to replace the name*/
        {
                BufferedReader buf = new BufferedReader(new  InputStreamReader(System.in));
                System.out.print("Please enter the word to replace");
                String n = buf.readLine();
                System.out.println("Please enter the new word");
                int len = n.length();
                String n1 = buf.readLine();
                int x = nam.indexOf(n);
                if(x >= 0)
                {
                        x = x - 1;
                        String str1 = nam.substring(0, x+1);
                        String str2 = nam.substring(x + len );
                        String str3 = str1.concat(n1);
                        str3 = str3.concat(str2);
                        System.out.print("The resulting string is :"+str3);
                }
                else
                System.out.print("name not found to be replaced");
        }
        public static void main(String args[]) throws IOException
        {
                computeGrade('A');
                replaceName("Shiva Kumar Sardesai");
        }
}
```

12. (a) Write a java method Palindrome to check whether a string str is a palindrome or not. A palindrome is a string that reads the same from left to right and right to left. e.g., MADAM, ARORA, MALAYALAM, NITIN, etc., are plaindromes.

    (b) Write main() to call the plaindrome().

Ans. (a)
```java
import java.io.*;
public class test2
{
        static void Palindrome()
        {
                BufferedReader buf = new BufferedReader(new InputStreamReader(System.in));
                System.out.print("Please enter a string :");
                String stt = buf.readLine();
                StringBuffer t = new StringBuffer(stt);
                StringBuffer strr = t.reverse();
                String h = new String(strr);
```

```
                if(stt.equalsIgnoreCase(h))
                System.out.print("The string is a palindrome");
                else
                System.out.print("The string is not a palindrome");
            }
        }
```

(b)
```
    public class test
    {
            public static void main(String args[])
            {
            test2 obj = new test2();
            obj.Palindrome();
            }
    }
```

13. Write a program in Java to accept a string in lower case and change the first letter of every word to upper case.

Display the new string.

Sample input : we are in cyber world.

Sample output : We Are In Cyber World.

Ans.
```
import java.util.*;//importing package
public class Demo
{
        public static void main( String [] args)
        {
        String s,w;
        char ch;
        int i, l;
                Scanner sc = new Scanner(System.in);
                System.out.println("Enter a Sentence");
                s = sc.nextLine();
                s = s + " ";
                l = s.length();
                for(i = 0; i < l; i++)
                {
                        w = "";
                        while(s.charAt(i) != ' ')
                        {
                                w = w + s.charAt(i);
                                i++;
                        }//while loop ending
                        ch = w.charAt(0);
                        ch -= 32;
                        w = ch + w.substring(1);
                        System.out.print(w + " ");
                }
        }
}
```

Name	Type	Description
s	String	To store a string.
w	String	To store a word.
ch	char	To store a character.
i	int	For loop variable.
l	int	To store length of string.

14. Write a java method that accepts two strings as parameters, compares them exactly and returns true if they match and false if they don't match.

Ans.
```
import java.io.*;
public class test
{
        static boolean comparison(String str1, String str2)
        {
                if(str1.equals(str2))
                return true;
                else
                return false;
        }
        public static void main(String args[]) throws IOException
        {
                BufferedReader buf = new BufferedReader(new  InputStreamReader(System.in));
                System.out.print("Enter two strings please.");
                String s1 = buf.readLine();
                String s2 = buf.readLine();
                boolean v = comparison(s1, s2) ;
                    if(v == true)
                    System.out.print("The strings are same");
                    else
                    System.out.print("The strings are not same ");
        }
}
```

15. Write a java method that extracts first five characters of a string and middle characters of another string. Compares them and Prints 'EQUAL' if they match else it prints 'NOT EQUAL'.

Ans.
```
import java.io.*;
public class test
{
        static void extract(String str1, String str2)
        {
                int l = str2.length();
                int m = l/2 - 1;
                int st = (0 + m) / 2 + 1;
                int end = st + 5;
                String s1 = str1.substring(0, 5);
                String s2 = str2.substring(st, end);
                System.out.println("First five characters of "+str1+" are "+ s1);
                System.out.println("Mid five characters of "+str2 + " are " + s2);
                if(s1.equals(s2))
```

```
                System.out.print("They are equal");
                else
                System.out.print("They are not equal");
        }
        public static void main(String args[]) throws IOException
        {
                BufferedReader inp = new BufferedReader (new InputStreamReader(System.in));
                System.out.println("Please enter two strings :");
                String a = inp.readLine();
                String a2 = inp.readLine();
                extract(a, a2);
        }
}
```

16. Write a program to accept a string. Convert the string to uppercase. Count and output the number of double letter sequences that exist in the string.

    Sample input : "SHE WAS FEEDING THE LITTLE RABBIT WITH AN APPLE"

Ans.
```
import java.io.*;
public class str
{
        void main(String S)
        {
        S = S.toUpperCase();
        int i, l, c = 0;
        char ch, ch1;
        l = s.length();
        for(i = 0; i < l; i++)
        {
        ch = s.charAt(i);
        ch1 = s.charAt(i + 1);
        if(ch == ch1)
        c++;
        }
        System.out.println(c);
        }
}
```

17. Write a program to input a sentence and convert it into uppercase and display each word in a separate line.*

    Example: Input : India is my country

    Output : INDIA
            IS
            MY
            COUNTRY

Ans.
```
import java.util.*;
class Sentence
{
    String s,w;
    int i,l;
```

```java
public Sentence()
{
s="Destination Point Computers";
}
    void display()
{
Scanner sc=new Scanner(System.in);
System.out.println("Enter a Sentence");
    s=sc.nextLine();
    s=s.toUpperCase();
    s=s+" ";
    l=s.length();
    for(i=0;i<l;i++)
{
    w="";
        while(s.charAt(i)!=' ')
    {
        w=w+s.charAt(i);
        i++;
    }
        System.out.println(w);
}
}
}
```

18. Write a program to input a sentence and convert it into uppercase and count and display the total number of words starting with a letter 'A'.*

    Example :

    Sample Input : ADVANCEMENT AND APPLICATION OF INFORMATION TECHNOLOGY ARE EVER CHANGING.

    Sample Output : Total number of words starting with letter 'A' = 4.

Ans.
```java
import java.util.*;
class Count
{
    String s;
    int l, i, c = 0;
    void display()
    {
        Scanner sc = new Scanner(System.in);
        System.out.println("Enter a sentence");
        s = sc.nextLine();
        s = s.toUpperCase();
        s = " " + s;
        l = s.length();
        for(i = 0; i < l; i++)
        {
            if(s.charAt(i) == ' ' && s.charAt(i + 1) == 'A')
```

```
            {
                c++;
            }
        }
        System.out.println("Total number of words starting with letter A = " + c);
    }
}
```

Name	Type	Description
s	String	To store a sentence.
l	int	To store the length.
i	int	for loop variable.
c	int	Counter variable.

Output Based Questions | Set **5** |

1. System.out.print("BEST");

System.out.println("OF LUCK");

Choose the correct option for the output of the above statements :

(i) BEST OF LUCK

(ii) BEST OF LUCK

Ans. (i) BEST OF LUCK is the correct option.

2. What are the final values stored in variable x and y below ?

double a = - 6.35;

double b = 14.74;

double x = Math.abs(Math.ceil(a));

double y = Math.rint(Math.max(a, b));

Ans. x = 6.0

y = 15.00

3. Give the output of the following program segment :

double x = 2.9, y = 2.5;

System.out.println(Math.min(Math.floor(x), y));

System.out.println(Math.max(Math.ceil(x), y));

Ans. 2.0

3.0

4. Write a Java statement to input/read the following from the user using the keyboard.

(i) Character.   (ii) String.

Ans.

(i) char ch;	(ii) String S;
BufferedReader br = new BufferedReader(new InputStreamReader(System.in));	BufferedReader br = new BufferedReader(new InputStreamReader(System.in));
ch = (char)br.read();	S = br.readLine();

5. What is the output of the following :

(i) System.out.println("four :" + 4 + 2);

System.out.println("four :" + (2 + 2));

(ii) String S1 = "Hi";

String S2 = "Hi";

String S3 = "there";

String S4 = "HI";

System.out.println(S1 + "equals" + S2 + "" + S1.equals(S2));

System.out.println(S1 + "equals" + S3 + "" + S1.equals(S3));

System.out.println(S1 + "equals" + S4 + "" + S1.equals(S4));

System.out.println(S1 + "equalsIgnoreCase" +S4 + "" + S1.equalsIgnoreCase(S4));

Ans. (i) four : 42

four : 4

(ii) Hi equals Hi true
      Hi equals there false
      Hi equals HI false
      Hi equalsIgnoreCase HI true.

6. Find the output of the following program segment, when :

(i) val = 200

```
System.out.println(val);
```

(ii) val = 1600

```
int val, sum, n = 550;
sum = (n + val) > 1750 ? 400 : 200;
System.out.println(sum);
```

Ans. (i) 200

(ii) 400

7. Declare a class that has the following members :

(i) Roll number of student, which is in the range 1-50.

(ii) Name

(iii) Division which is in the range 1-10.

(vi) Section, which can be A or B.

(v) Average marks, with decimal precision.

     Member function declarations :

(vi) Function to return average marks of a student.

Ans.

```
Public class student
{
        private int rollno;
        private String name;
        private int div;
        private char section;
        private float avgmarks;
        public float calavg()
        {
                return avgmarks;
        }
}
```

8. Give the output of the following java statements :

(a) `System.out.printIn(Math.cbrt(125));`

(b) `System.out.printIn(Math.cbrt(0.027));`

(c) `double n = 3.56;`
    `System.out.printIn(Math.ceil(n));`

(d) `double n = 7.86;`
    `System.out.printIn(Math.floor(n));`

(e) `double n = 9.4;`
    `System.out.printIn(Math.round(n));`

(f) `double m = 9.99;`
    `System.out.printIn(Math.floor(m));`

(g) `double n = 5.01;`
    `System.out.printIn(Math.ceil(n));`

(h) `double j = 8.5;`
    `System.out.printIn(Math.round(j));`

(i) System.out.println(Math.ceil(7.9));

Ans. (a) 5   (c) 4.0   (e) 9.0   (g) 6.0   (i) 8.0

(b) 0.3   (d) 7.0   (f) 9.0   (h) 9.0

9. Write the output for the following :

System.out.println("Incredible"+ "\n"+"world");

Ans. Incredible world

10. State the data type and values of a and b after the following segment is executed.

String s1 = "Computer", s2 = "Applications";

a = (s1.compareTo(s2));

b = (s1.equals(s2));

Ans. int type, a = 2

boolean type, b = false

11. Write an equivalent Java syntax for the following expression :

$$a = \frac{0.05 - 2y^3}{x - y}$$

Ans. double a = (0.05 - 2 * math.pow(y, 3))/(x - y);

12. Give the output of the following method :

```
public static void main(String [] args)
{
    int a = 5;
    a++;
    System.out.println(a);
    A - = (a--) - (--a);
    System.out.println(a);
}
```

Ans. 6

4

13. What is meant by precedence of operators ?

Ans. The order in which operators of an expression are going to be evaluated and resolved in a predetermined order is called operator precedence.

14. Write a Java statement to create an object mp4 of class digital.

Ans. digital mp4 = new digital();

15. What will be the output of the following code ?

```
(i)  int k = 5, j = 9;
     k += k++ - ++j + k;
     System.out.println(" k = "+k);
     System.out.println(" j = "+j);
(ii) double b = - 15.6;
     double a = Math.rint(Math.abs(b));
     System.out.println("a ="+a);
```

Ans. (i) k = 6

j = 10

(ii) 16.0

16. What will be the output for the following program segment ?

```
int a = 0, b = 30, c = 40;
a = b + c++ + b;
System.out.println("a = "+a);
```

Ans. a = 100.

17. What will be the output for the following program segment ?

```
int a = 0, b = 30, c = 40;
a = --b + c++ + b;
System.out.println("a = "+a);
```

Ans. a = 98.

18. Find the output of the following program segment, when :

```
val = 500
val = 1600
int val, sum, n = 550;
sum = n + val > 1750 ? 400 : 200;
System.out.println(sum);
```

Ans. (i) 750 (ii) 950.

19. What will be the output of the following, if x=5 initially ?

```
(i)  5 * ++x;          (ii)  5 * x++;
```

Ans. (i) 30

(ii) 25

20. What is the output of the following ?

```
char c = 'A';
short m = 26;
int n = c + m;
System.out.println(n);
```

Ans. 91

21. int res = 'A';

What is the value of res ?

Ans. res = 65

22. Write the output :

```
char ch = 'F';
int m = ch;
m = m + 5;
System.out.println(m+ " " + ch);
```

Ans. 75 F

23. Give the output of the following code :

```
String A ="26", B = "100";
String D = A + B + "200";
int x = Integer.parseInt(A);
int y = Integer.parseInt(B);
int d = x + y;
System.out.println("Result 1 = " + D);
System.out.println("Result 2 = " + d);
```

Ans. Result 1 = 26100200

Result 2 = 126

24. Give output of the following :

```
class test
{
        public void check()
        {
                int fine = 0;
```

```
              boolean paid = false;
              fine = paid ? 0 : 200;
              System.out.println(fine)
         }
      }
```

Ans. 200

25. What will be the answer of the following statements when int a = 10, b = 15, c = 20 ?

  (i) System.out.println("Result" + (a >= 10));

  (ii) System.out.println("Result"+ !(a >= 10);

  (iii) System.out.print ln("Result" + (a + 5 > c);

  (vi) System.out.println("Result"+ ((a + c) == (b + 15)));

Ans. (i) Result true   (ii) Result false   (iii) Result false   (iv) Result true.

26. What will be the output of the following program segment ?

```
{
int a = 10, b = 20, c = 9;
a = --c + b++ + a;
System.out.println(a);
}
```

Ans. Output will be 38

27. In m = 5 and n = 2 output the values of m and n after execution in (i) and (ii) :

  (i) m -= n;

  (ii) n = m + m/n;

Ans. (i) 3

  (ii) 7.5 if m or n are of double type, 7 if m and n are integer.

28. Give the output of the following program segment and also mention how many times the loop is executed:

```
int i;
    for (i = 5; i > 10; i ++)
    System.out.println(i);
    System.out.println(i * 4);
```

Ans. Loop will be executed 0 times since the test condition is initially false.

  Output will be : 20.

29. What are the values of x and y when the following statements are executed ?

```
int a = 63, b = 36
boolean x = (a > b) ? true : false;
int y = (a < b) ? a : b;
```

Ans. x = true.

  y = 36

30. Rewrite the following using ternary operator :

```
if(bill > 1000)
discount = bill * 10.0/100;
else
discount = bill * 5.0/100;
```

Ans. discount = bill > 10000 ? (bill * 10.0 / 100) : (bill * 5.0 / 100);

31. Give the output of the following program segment and also mention the number of times the loop is executed :

```
int a, b;
for(a = 6, b = 4; a <= 24; a = a + 6)
{
        if(a % b == 0)
        break;
}
System.out.println(m + " " + ch);
```

Ans. 12

The loop will be executed 2 times.

32. What will be the output of the following code ?

```
(i)   int m = 2; int
      n = 15;
      for(int i = 1; i < 5; i++);
      m++;
      --n;
      System.out.println("m ="+m);
      System.out.println("n ="+n);
```

```
(ii) char x = 'A';
     int m;
     m = (x == 'a') ? 'A' : 'a';
     System.out.println(m =+ m);
```

Ans. (i)   m = 3

n = 14

(ii) 65

33. Give the output of the following code fragment :

When :

(i)   opn = 'b'

(ii) opn = 'x'

(iii) opn = 'a'

```
switch(opn)
{
case 'a':
System.out.println("Platform Independent");
break;
case 'b':
System.out.println("Object Oriented");
case 'c':
System.out.println("Robust and Secure");
break;
default:
System.out.println("Wrong Input");
}
```

Ans. (i)   Object Oriented

Robust and Secure

(ii) Wrong Input

(iii) Platform Independent

34. Convert the following if else if construct into switch case:

```
if(var == 1)
System.out.println("good");
else if(var == 2)
System.out.println("better");
elseif(var == 3)
System.out.println("best");
else
System.out.println("invalid");
```

Ans. switch(var)

{

case 1 : System.out.println("good");

break;

case 2 : System.out.println("better");

break;

case 3 : System.out.println("best");

break;

default : System.out.println("invalid");

}

35. The following is a segment of a program :

int x = 1, y = 1;

if(n > 0)

{

x = x + 1;

y = y - 1;

}

What will be the value of x and y, if n assumes a value :

(i) 1   (ii) 0

Ans. (i) x = 2, y = 0   (ii) x = 1, y = 1

36. Analyze the following program segment and determine how many times the body of the loop will be executed (show the working) :

x = 5; y = 50;

while(x <= y)

{

y = y/x;

System.out.println(y);

}

Ans. Working :

x y condition output

5 50 5 <= 50 (true) 10

5 10 5 <= 10 (true) 2

5 2 5 <= 2 (false)

Output :

10

2

37. Analyze the given program segment and answer the following questions :

for(int i = 3; i <= 4; i++)

{

      for(int j = 2; j < i; j++)

      {

      System.out.print(" ");

      }

System.out.println("WIN");

}

(i) How many times does the inner loop execute ?

(ii) Write the output of the program segment.

Ans. (i)   Inner loop will be executed 3 times.

(ii)   WIN

WIN

38. Give the output of the following expressions :

(i)   If x == - 999, calculate Math.abs(x);

(ii)   If x= = 9.0, calculate Math.sqrt(x);

Ans. (i)   999   (ii) 3.0

39. Display the output of the following program :

(i)   class test

```
class test
{
        public static void main(String[] args)
        {
                int x, y;
                x = y = 1;
            if (x == y)
            System.out.print("1");
            else
            System.out.print("0");
        }
}
```

(ii) int x = 1;

```
int x = 1;
    while(x <= 10)
    {
        if(x == 3)
        break;
        System.out.print(x);
        x++;
    }
```

(iii) int k = 2, x = 1;

```
int k = 2, x = 1;
    while(k <= 10)
    {
            x = x + k;
            System.out.print(x);
            k += 2;
    }
```

(iv) for(int k = 1; k <= 5; k++)

```
for(int k = 1; k <= 5; k++)
    {
            if(k == 5)
            System.out.print(k);
            else
            System.out.print(k * k);
    }
```

(v) char ch='a';

```
char ch='a';
    while(ch <= 'z')
    {
        System.out.print(ch);
        ch += 1;
    }
```

Ans. (i) Output : 1

(ii) Output :

1

2

(iii) Output : 3

7

13

21

31

(iv) Output : 1

4

9

16

5

(v) Output : a

b

c

d

:

:

z

40. Analyze the following program segment and determine how many times the loop will be executed and what will be the output of the program segment ?

```java
int p = 200;
while(true)
{
        if(p < 100)
        break;
        p = p - 20;
}
System.out.println(p);
```

Ans. Loop will execute 7 times and the output will be 80.

41. Give the output of the following program segments :

(i)
```java
for(int i = 11; i <= 20; ++i)
{
        if(i > 13 && i < 19)
        {
                continue;
        }
        System.out.println(i);
}
```

(ii)
```java
int a = 1;
while(a <= 6)
{
        if(a > 3)
        {
        break;
        }
```

```
        System.out.println(a);
        a++;
        }
```

(iii) public class output1
```
{
        public static void main(String args[])
        {
        int a = 0;
        int sum = 0;
        while(a <= 7)
        {
                sum + = a;
                if(a > 4)
                {
                        break;
                }
                a++;
        }
        System.out.println(sum);
        }
}
```

(iv) public class output2
```
{
        public static void main(String args[])
        {
        int p[] = {7, 3, 6, 10, 4, 6, 9};
        int sum = 0, a = -1;
        while(a < 6)
        {
                a++;
                if(a == 3 || a == 6)
                {
                        continue;
                }
                sum += p[a];
        }
        System.out.println(sum);
        }
}
```

(v) int a = 7;
```
    int sum = 0;
    do
    {
            sum = sum + a;
            a++;
    }while(a < 6);
    System.out.println(sum);
```

(vi)   int i = 3;
       int sum = 0;
       do
       {
               sum = sum + i;
               i++;
       }while(i < 7);
       System.out.println(sum);

(vii) int i;
       for(i = 1; i < 10; i++);
       System.out.print(i);

(viii) int i;
       for(i = 1; ; i++);
       System.out.print(i);

(ix)   int i = 5;
       while(i > 1)
       {
               System.out.println(i);
               i--;
       }

(x)   char a[] = {'A', 'I', 'D', 'N', 'I'};
       int i, l;
       l = a.length;
       i = l - 1;
       while(i >= 0)
       {
               System.out.print(a[i]);
               i--;
       }

Ans. (i)   11
              12
              13
              19
              20

(ii)   1
       2
       3

(iii) 15

(iv)   26

(v)   7

(vi)   18

(vii) 10

(viii) (no output, loop is infinite)

(ix)   5
       4
       3
       2

(x)   INDIA

42. Give the output of the following code :*

```
String P = "20", Q = "19";
int a  = Integer.parseInt(P);
int b = Integer.valueOf(Q);
System.out.println(a+""+ b);
```

Ans. 2019

43. If the value of basic = 1500, what will be the value of tax after the following statement is executed ?*

```
tax = basic > 1200 ? 200 : 100;
```

Ans. 200

44. Give the output of the following code and mention how many times the loop will execute ?*

```
int i;
for(i = 5; i >= 1; i-- )
{
        if(i%2 == 1)
            continue;
        System.out.print(i+"");
}
```

Ans. 4 2

The loop will get executed 5 times.

45. Give the output of the following :*

```
Math.sqrt(Math.max(9, 16))
```

Ans. 4.0

Chapter 2. Class as the Basis of all Computation

1. What will be the output of the following code program ?

```
class Test
{
        public static int varone = 10;
        public static void method1()
        {
                int varone = 25;
            System.out.println(varone);
        }
        public static void method2()
        {
            System.out.println(varone);
        }
        public static void main(String args[])
        {
        method1();
        method2();
        }
}
```

Ans. 25

10

---

2. What is the final value of ctr when the iteration process given below; executes ?

```
int ctr = 0;
for(int i = 1; i <= 5; i++)
for(int j = 1; j <= 5; j += 2)
++ctr;
```

Ans. ctr = 15

Chapter 3. User - Defined Methods

1. Display the output of the following program segments :

```
public boolean f(int a, int b)
{
        boolean e = false;
        while(a > 1 && b > 1)
        {
                if(a > b)
                a = a - b;
                else
                b = b - a;
        }
        if(a == 1 || b == 1)
        e = true;
        return e;
}
```

What will be the output when the above function will be called as ?

(i)   f(28, 39)   (ii) f(27, 39)

Ans. (i)   Result will be true   (ii) Result will be false.

2. Enter any two variables through constructor parameters and write a program to swap and print the values.

Ans.
```
public class test
{
        public test(int a, int b)
        {
                int t;
                t = a;
                a = b;
                b = t;
                System.out.print("Value of a is " + a);
                System.out.print("Value of b is " + b);
        }
}
```

Chapter 4. Constructors

1. What will be the output of the following ?

```
class Main
{
        Main()
```

```java
        {
                calculate()
                System.out.println("constructor");
        }
        void calculate()
        {
                show();
                System.out.println("calculating")
        }
        void show()
        {
                System.out.println("I am displaying");
        }
        public static void main()
        {
                Main obj = new Main();
        }
}
```

Ans. The output produced will be :

I am displaying calculating constructor.

Chapter 5. Library Classes

1. What is the data type returned by the library functions ?

(i)   compareTo()   (ii) equals()

Ans. (i)   int

e.g. : int result ="computer".compareTo("applications");

(ii) boolean

e.g. : boolean result = "computer"equals("science");

2. What will the following functions return when executed ?

(i)   Math.max(- 17, - 19)   (ii) Math.ceil(7.8)

Ans. (i)   - 17   (ii) 8

3. Give the output of the following :

(i)   Math.floor(-4.7)   (ii) Math.ceil(3.4) + Math.pow(2, 3)

Ans. (i)   - 5.0   (ii) 12.0

4. Study the method and answer the given questions :

```java
public void sampleMethod()
{
        for(int i = 0; i < 3; i++)
        {
                for(int j = 0; j < 2; j++)
                {
                        int number = (int)(Math.random() * 10);
                        System.out.println(number);
                }
        }
}
```

(i) How many times does the loop execute ?

(ii) What is the range of possible values stored in the variable number ?

Ans. (i) Outer loop will execute 3 times whereas inner loop will get executed 6 times.

(ii) 0 to 9

5. What will be the output when the following code segments are executed ?

(i) ```
String s = "1001";
int x = Integer.valueOf(s);
double y = Double.valueOf(s);
System.out.println("x = "+x);
System.out.println("y = "+y);
```

(ii) ```
System.out.println("The king said\"Begin at the beginning !\"to me.");
```

Ans. (i) x = 1001

y = 1001.0

(ii) The king said "Begin at the beginning!" to me.

6. If int n[]={1, 2, 3, 5, 7, 9, 13, 16}, what are the values of x and y ?

```
x = Math.pow(n[4], n[2]);
y = Math.sqrt(n[5] + n[7]);
```

Ans. x = 343.0 and y = 5.0

7. Name the methods of Scanner class that :

(i) is used to input an integer data from the standard input stream.

(ii) is used to input a String data from the standard input stream.

Ans. (i) nextInt()   (ii) next()

8. Complete the code below to create an object of Scanner class :

```
Scanner sc = Scanner()
```

Ans. Scanner sc = new Scanner(System.in);

9. State the data type and value of res after the following is executed :*

```
char ch = '9';
res = Character.isDigit(ch);
```

Ans. Data type of **res** is boolean and it's value is true.

Chapter 7. Arrays

1. Consider the following String array and give the output :

```
String arr[] = {"delhi", "chennai", "mumbai", "lucknow", "jaipur"};
System.out.println(arr[0].length() > arr[3].length());
System.out.print(arr[4].substring(0, 3));
```

Ans. false

JAI

2. ```
String x[] = {"SAMSUNG", "NOKIA", "SONY", "MICROMAX", "BLACKBERRY"};
```

Give the output of the following statements :

(i) System.out.println(x[1]);

(ii) System.out.println(x[3].length());

**Ans.** (i) NOKIA   (ii) 8

**3.** Write the output of the following program segments :

(i) ```
char a[][] = new char[5][5];
int i, j;
for(i = 0; i < 4; i++)
```

---

* Frequently asked previous years Board Exam Questions.

```java
        {
            for(j = 0; j < 4; j++)
            {
                    if(i == j || i + j == 3)
                    a[i][j] = 'A';
                    else
                    a[i][j] = ' ';
            }
            for(i = 0; i < 4; i++)
            {
                    for(j = 0; j < 4; j++)
                    System.out.print(a[i][j]);
                    System.out.println();
            }
        }
```

(ii)
```java
    int a[] = {10, 11, 12, 13, 14};
    a[4] = ++a[2];
    a[3] = a[2] - a[1];
    System.out.print(a[3]+ " " +a[4]);
```

(iii)
```java
    int i, j, a[][] = new int[3][2];
    for(i = 0; i < 3; i++)
    {
            for(j = 0; j < 2; j++)
            {
            a[i][j] = i * j + 2;
            }
    }
    System.out.println(a[1][1]+"\t" +a[0][1]+"\t" +a[2][0] + "\t" + a[2][1];
```

(iv)
```java
    int a[][] = {{1, 2}, {3, 4}};
    int i, j;
    for(i = 0; i < 2; i++)
    {
    for(j = 0; j < 2; j++)
    System.out.println(a[i][j]);
    }
```

Ans. (i)   A A
       AA
       AA
       A A

(ii) 2 13

(iii) 3 2 2 4

(iv) 1
     2
     3
     4

Chapter 8. String Handling

1. State the output of the following program segment :
```
String s = "Examination";
int n = s.length();
System.out.println(s.startsWith(s.substring(5, n)));
System.out.println(s.charAt(2) == s.charAt(6));
```
Ans. false

True

2. What will be the output of the following code :
```
String s = "malayalam";
System.out.println(s.substring(1).length - 8);
System.out.println(s.substring(1).length);
```
Ans. 0

8

3. Give the output of the following :
```
String n = "Computer Knowledge.";
String m = "";
System.out.println(n.substring(0, 8).concat(m.substring(9)));
System.out.println(n.endsWith("e"));
```
Ans. ComputerApplications

True

4. Write the output of the following :
   (i) System.out.println(Character.isUpperCase('R'));
   (ii) System.out.println(Character.toUpperCase('j'));

Ans. (i) True   (ii) J

5. What will be the output for the following program segment ?
```
String s = new String("abc");
System.out.println(s.toUpperCase());
```
Ans. ABC

6. Give the output of the following string functions :
   (i) "ACHIEVEMENT".replace('E', 'A')
   (ii) "dedicate".compareTo("devote")

Ans. (i) ACHIAVAMANT   (ii) – 18

7. State the value of characteristic and mantissa when the following code is executed :
```
String s = "4.3756";
int n = s.indexOf('.');
int characteristic = Integer.parseInt(s.substring(0, n));
int mantissa = Integer.valueOf(s.substring(n + 1));
```
Ans. characteristic = 4

mantissa = 3756

8. State the values stored in the variables str1 and str2 :
```
String s1 = "good";
String s2 = "world matters";
String str1 = s2.substring(5).replace('t', 'n');
String str2 = s1.concat(str1);
```
Ans. str1 = manners and str2 = good manners

9. If, String x = "Computer";

String y = "Applications";

What do the following functions return for :

(i) System.out.println(x.substring(1, 5));

(ii) System.out.println(x.indexOf(x.charAt(4)));

(iii) System.out.println(y + x.substring(5));

(iv) System.out.println(x.equals(y));

Ans. (i) ompu   (ii) 4   (iii) Applicationster   (vi) false

10. Write the output for the following :

String s = "Today is Test";

System.out.println(s.indexOf('T'));

System.out.println(s.substring(0, 7) +" " + "Holiday");

Ans. 0

Today is Holiday

11. State the output of the following program segment :

String str1 = "great", str2 = "minds";

System.out.println(str1.substring(0, 2).concat(str2.substring(1)));

System.out.println(("WH"+(str1.substring(2).toUpperCase())));

Ans. grinds

WHEAT

Chapter 1. Revision of Class IX Syllabus

1. Find out the errors (if any) :

```
class test
{
        public static main();
        {
                int a = 10;
                system.out.print line (" values a is" a);
        }
}
```

Ans.
```
public class test
{
        public static void main(String [] args)
        {
                int a = 10;
                System.out.println("value of a is" + a);
        }
}
```

2. Rewrite the following using Ternary operator if :

```
if (income <= 10000)
    tax = 0;
else
    tax = 12;
```

Ans. tax = income <= 10000 ? 0 : 12

3. Rewrite the following using Ternary operator :

```
if(var1 == 10)
    t = 50;
else
    t = 120;
```

Ans. t = var1 == 10 ? 50 : 120;

4. Rewrite the following program segment using if-else statements instead of the ternary operator.

```
String grade = (mark >= 90)? "A" : (mark >= 80) ? "B": "C";
```

Ans.
```
String grade;
if(mark >= 90)
    grade = "A";
else if(mark >= 80)
    grade = "B";
else
    grade = "C";
```

5. Rewrite the following program segment using while instead of for statement :

```
int f = 1, I;
for(I = 1; I < 5; I++)
{
        f * = I;
        System.out.println(f);
}
```

Ans.
```
int I = 1, f = 1;
while(I <= 5)
{
        f * = I;
        System.out.println(f);
        I++;
}
```

6. Rewrite the following program segment using the if...else statement:

```
comm = (sale > 15000) ? sale 5/100 : 0;
```

Ans.
```
if(sale > 15000)
{
        comm = sale * 5/100;
}
else
{
        comm = 0;
}
```

7. How many times will the following loop execute ? What value will be returned ?

```
int x = 2, y = 50;
do
{
        ++x;
        y − = x++;
}
while(x <= 10);
return y;
```

Ans. Loop will execute 4 times and y will be returned as 2.

8. Convert the following segment into an equivalent do loop.

```
int x, c;
for(x = 10, c = 20; c >= 10; c = c − 2)
x++;
```

Ans.
```
int x = 10, c = 20;
do
{
x++;
c = c − 2;
}
while(c >= 10);
```

9. Convert following do-while loop into for loop.

```
int i = 1;
int d = 5;
```

```
        do
        {
                d = d * 2;
                System.out.println(d);
                i++;
        } while(i <= 5);
```

Ans.
```
int i, d = 5;
    for(i = 1; i <= 5; i++)
    {
            d = d * 2;
            System.out.println(d);
    }
```

Chapter 6. Encapsulation

1. Point out the errors (if any) :

```
class sample
{
        private int, num;
        public void square(int n)
        {
                int var;
                var = n * n;
                result = var;
        }
        public void twice()
        {
                int twice = var * 2;
                if (twice > 100)
                {
                        int store;
                        store = twice;
                        twice = 100;
                }
                System.out.println("The value passed as parameter was : "+n);
                System.out.println("The original value of twice is :"+ store);
                System.out.println("The new value of twice is :"+ twice);
        }
}
```

Ans. The variable var is local variable and cannot be used in twice() method.

The variable store is local variable and can only be used inside the if block. The parameter n can only be used in the method to which it is passed.

Chapter 7. Arrays

1. Find the errors in the given program segment and re-write the statements correctly to assign values to an integer array.

```
int a = new int (5);
```

```
for(int i = 0; i <= 5; i++)
a[i] = i;
```

Ans. . (i) int a[] = new int[5]; (square brackets [] must be used)

(ii) for(int i = 0; i < 5; i++) a[i] = i; (i must be less than 5)

2. Find and correct the errors in the following program segment :

```
int n[] = (2, 4, 6, 8, 10)
for(int i = 0; i <= 5; i++)
System.out.println("n["+I+"] = " + n[I]);
```

Ans. (i)   In first line curly brackets ({}) should be used and the statement should end with semicolon(;).

int n[] = {2, 4, 6, 8, 10};

(ii) for(int i = 0; i < 5; i++) (i must be less than 5)

(iii) System.out.println("n["+i+"] = " + n[i]); (i is case sensitive)

3. Find and correct the errors in the following program segment :

```
int n[] = (1, 2, 3, 4, 5, 6, 7, 8)
for(int i = 0; i <= 8; i++)
System.out.println("n["+I+"] = " + n[I]);
```

Ans. (i)   In first line curly brackets ({ }) should be used and statement should end with a semicolon (;).

int n[] = {1, 2, 3, 4, 5, 6, 7, 8};

(ii) for condition is wrong, it should be

for(int I = 0; I <= 7; I++)

1. Evaluate the following expressions, if the values of the variables are a = 2, b = 3 and c = 9.

   (i)   a – (b++) * (– –c)   (ii) a * (++b) % c

Ans. (i) 2 – 3 * 8

          = 2 – 24

          = – 22

  (ii) 2 * 4 % 9

          = 8 % 9

          = 8

2. Write the corresponding expressions for the following mathematical expressions :

   (i) $a^2 + b^2$

   (ii) $z = x^3 + y^3 - xy/z$

Ans. (i) (a * a) + (b * b);

    (ii) z = (x * x * x) + (y * y *y) – (x * y / z);

3. Give value of x for the given expressions :

   (i)   int x = 50;

         x % = 4;

   (ii)   boolean x;

         x = 10 > 5;

   (iii)   int a = 10, B = 20;

         boolean x;

         x = a > 5 && b > 5;

   (iv)   int a = 5;

         boolean x;

         x = a >= 2 !! a == 10;

   (v)   int a = 5;

         boolean x;

         x = a > 10 !! a >= 7;

   (vi)   int a = 5, b = 10;

         boolean x;

         x = a > 10 !! (b + 5 >= 15 && b – 5 < 7);

   (vii) int a = 5, x;

         x = a++ + 10;

   (viii) int x, y, z;

         x = 0;

         y = 9;

         z = 10;

         x = z + ++y/z;

Ans. (i)   2

    (ii)   true

(iii) true

(iv) true

(v) false

(vi) true

(vii) 15

(viii)x = 10 + 10/10 = 10 + 1 = x = 11

4. What is the value of x1 if x = 5 ?

x1 = ++x − x++ + − − x

Ans. x1 = 6

5. Write the value of variable result after the execution of the following expressions :

(i)   result = 10 + 5 * 10 − 4

(ii) result = 10 + (3 * 8 / 2 * (7 + 1))

(iii) result = (n1< n2) && (n1== 5) (here n1= 15, n2= 20)

(iv) result = 6 + 4 / 3 * 2

Ans. (i)   = 10 + 50 − 4

            = 60 − 4

            = 56

(ii)   = 10 + (24/2 * (7 + 1))

            = 10 + (12 * 8)

            = 10 + 96

            = 106

(iii)   = true && false

            = false

(iv)   = 6 + 1 * 2

            = 6 + 2

            = 8

6. What will be the value of x after the execution of the following expression if ?

x = 10 and y = 20

x = x > y ? 10 : y + 2;

Ans. x will be 22.

7. What will be the result stored in x after evaluating the following expression ?

int x = 5;

x = x++ * + 2 + 3 * --x;

Ans. x will be 25.

8. What is the value of y after evaluating the expression given below ?

y += ++y + y−− + − −y; when int y = 8

Ans. 33

9. If a = 5, b = 9 calculate the value of a += a++ − ++b + a.

Ans. a += a ++ − ++b + a

        = 5 − 10 + 6 = 1

        Final value of a = 5 + 1 = 6

10. What will be the result of the following two expressions if I = 10 initially.

(i)   ++I <= 10   (ii) I++ <= 10

Ans. (i) false.   (ii) true.

11. Explain each given the following two expressions :

(i)   Val = 3   (ii) Val == 3

Ans. (i)   Val = 3

            In the above case variable val is assigned the value 3.

(ii) Val == 3

In the above case variable val is being compared, whether it is equal to 3.

Chapter 5. Library Classes

1. Write a Java expression for the following :

$$\frac{\sqrt{3x} + x^2}{a+b}$$

Ans. Math.sqrt((3 * x) + (x * x))/(a + b);

2. Write a Java expression for $ut + 1/2ft^2$

Ans. u * t + 1.0/2 * f * Math.pow(t, 2)

OR

u * t + 1.0/2 * f * t * t.

3. Write a Java expression for :

$$\frac{(a+b)^n}{\sqrt{3+b}}$$

Ans. double x = Math.pow($a + b$, n) / (Math.sqrt(3) + b);

4. Write a Java expression for the following :

$$ax^5 + bx^3 + c$$

Ans. a * Math.pow(x, 5) + b * Math.pow (x, 3) + c.

5. Write compounding or corresponding java statements for given expressions :

(a) $x = a^2 + b^2$ (b) $x = \dfrac{\sqrt{a+b}}{\sqrt{a^2 + b^2}}$

(c) $a = k^2 + \sqrt{a^2}$ (d) $x = a^3 + b^4 + \dfrac{\sqrt{a+b}}{\sqrt{a^2 + b^2}}$

Ans. (a) $x = a * a + b * b$;

OR

x = Math.pow(a, 2) + Math.pow(b, 2);

(b) x = Math.sqrt($a + b$)/Math.sqrt(Math.pow(a, 2) + Math.pow(b, 2));

OR

x = Math.sqrt($a + b$)/Math.sqrt($a * a + b * b$);

(c) a = ($k * k$) + Math.sqrt(Math.pow(a, 2));

(d) x = Math.pow(a, 3) + Math.pow(b, 4) + Math.sqrt($a + b$)/Math.sqrt(Math.pow(a, 2) + Math.pow(b, 2));

6. Write the corresponding expressions for the following mathematical expressions :

(i) $a^3 + b^2$

(ii) $z = x^3 + y^2 - xy/z$

Ans. (i) $x = (a * a * a) + (b * b)$;

OR

x = Math.pow(a, 3) + Math.pow(b, 2);

(ii) $z = (x * x * x) + (y * y) - (x * y)/z)$;

OR

z = Math.pow(x, 3) + Math.pow(y, 2)- (($x * y$) / z);

7. Write a Java expression for $2as + u^2$

Ans. Java expression : Math.sqrt(2 * a * s + Math.pow(u, 2));

8. Write an expression in Java for

$$z = \frac{5x^3 + 2y}{x + y}$$

Ans. $z = 5 * \text{Math.pow}(x, 3) + 2 * y)/(x + y);$

9. What are the values stored in variables r1 and r2;

   (i)   double r1 = Math.abs(Math.min(–2.83, –5.83));

   (ii) double r2 = Math.sqrt(Math.floor(16.3));

Ans. (i)   r1 = 5.83   (ii) r2 = 4.0

Chapter 7. Arrays

1. Given that :

   int A[] = {35, 26, 19, 76, 50};

   What will be value contained in A[3] ?

Ans. 76

2. If int $x[]$ = {4, 3, 7, 8, 9, 10}; what are the values of p and q if :

   (i) $p = x$.length

   (ii) q = $x[2] + x[5] * x[1]$

Ans. (i) $p = 6$

      (ii) $q = 37$

3. The following numbers (89, 20, 31, 56, 20, 64, 48) are required to be sorted using selection sort. Show how the list would appear at the end of each pass.

Ans. Step I. 20, 89, 31, 56, 20, 64, 48

     Step II. 20, 20, 31, 56, 89, 64, 48

     Step III. 20, 20, 31, 56, 89, 64, 48

     Step IV. 20, 20, 31, 48, 89, 64, 56

     Step V. 20, 20, 31, 48, 56, 64, 89

     Step VI. 20, 20, 31, 48, 56, 64, 89

     Step VII. 20, 20, 31, 48, 56, 64, 89

4. Given an array : 89, 20, 31, 56, 20.

   Sort this array in ascending order using Bubble Sort.

Ans. Given array is 89, 20, 31, 56, 20

     Bubble Sort.

     Step I 20, 89, 31, 56, 20

     Step II 20, 31, 89, 56, 20

     Step III 20, 31, 56, 89, 20

     Step IV 20, 31, 56, 20, 89

     Step V 20, 31, 56, 20, 89

     Step VI 20, 31, 56, 20, 89

     Step VII 20, 31, 20, 56, 89

     Step VIII 20, 31, 20, 56, 89

     Step IX 20, 31, 20, 56, 89

     Step X 20, 20, 31, 56, 89

Chapter 1. Revision of Class IX Syllabus

1. State the difference between token and identifier.

Ans. The smallest individual unit of a Java program is known as a token. Symbolic names given to variables, objects classes etc., are known as identifiers.

2. Differentiate between print() and println() method.

Ans. The system.out.println() method changes the line after displaying output on the console and the cursor moves to the beginning of the next line.

The system.out.print() method does not change line after giving output on the console, the cursor remains at the end of the text.

3. What is the difference between a source code and an object code ?

Ans.

Source Code	Object Code
(a) The code which is written in Java is source code.	(a) The intermediate code produced by the java compiler is called object code.
(b) Source code is un-compiled code.	(b) Object code is compiled code.
(c) Source codes are human readable codes.	(c) Object codes are used by JVM(Java Virtual Mechine) to produce machine executable code.

4. State the difference between a boolean literal and a character literal.

Ans. A Boolean literal can have any of these two values, true or false.

A Character literal is one character enclosed in single quotes, ex : 'a', 'T', '9'.

5. Differentiate between static and non-static data members.

Ans. Static data members are the members which maintain a single copy for the whole class and are shared by all the objects of that class. They are also known as class variables.

Non static data members are the members which maintain a separate copy for each and every individual object of that class. They are also known as instance variables.

6. Give one point of difference between unary and binary operators.

Ans. Operators that act on a single operand are called unary operators whereas operators that act on two operands are called binary operators.

7. What is the difference between / and % operator ?

Ans. /operator is used to find the quotient between two operands while % operator is used to find the remainder between two operands.

E.g. : 10/2 = 5 whereas 10 % 2 = 0

8. State the difference between = and ==.

Ans.

= operator	== operator
(i) This is called assignment operator.	(i) This is called equality operator.
(ii) Used to assign value to a variable.	(ii) Used to compare two values for equality.

9. Differentiate between an operator and an expression.

Ans.

Operator	Expression
(i) Action symbols like +, −, %, *, / are called operators.	(i) String with variable and operator is called an expression e.g., x + y * 10
(ii) (ii) Operators may be unary, binary or ternary.	(ii) The expression may be simple or composite.

10. What is the differnce between x = a++ and x = ++a; when a and x are int variables and variable a is 10 ?

Ans. (i)   x = a++;

In this expression postfix form of increment operator is used, so the value of a is assigned to x first, after assignment, value of a will be incremented. Therefore, the value of x will be 10 and a will be 11 after execution.

(ii)   x = ++a;

In this expression, prefix form of increment operator is used, so value of a is incremented first, after that assignment will be performed. The value of x will be 11 and the value of a will also be 11 after execution.

11. Give two differences between the switch statement and the if-else statement.

Ans.

switch	if-else
(i) It only tests for equality for selected values (integer or character).	(i) It can work with all relational operators.
(ii) It cannot handle floating points.	(ii) It can handle floating point constants.
(iii) Used to take two way decisions.	(iii) Used for multiple branching.

12. What is the difference between a break statement and a continue statement when they occur in a loop ?

OR

Differentiate between break and continue statements.

Ans.

Break	Continue

The break statement is used to quit from the loop without executing any of the remaining statements in the loop, exiting the loop entirely.
For example :
for(int i = 1; i <= 10; i++)
{
    if(i == 7)
        break;
    System.outpintln(i);
}
	The continue statement stops execution of the current iteration and goes back to the beginning of the loop to began the next iteration.
	For example :
	for(int i = 1; i <= 15; i++)
	{
	    if(i == 3)
	        continue;
	    System.out.println(i);
	}

13. State the difference between while and do-while loop.

Ans.

while	do-while loop
(i) The condition is tested before entering into the loop.	(i) Condition is tested after the first execution of the loop.
(ii) If the conditon evaluates to false the very first time, the loop Statements will not be executed.	(ii) The loop statements will be executed at least once even if the condition is false.

(iii) while (condition)
{
    statements
}
	(iii) do
	{
	    statements
	}
	while (condition);

14. State the difference between entry controlled loop and exit controlled loop.

Ans. The loops in which the condition is checked first and then the loop body gets executed are called entry controlled loops. They are also called pre-tested loop e.g. : for, while.

The loops in which the loop body gets executed first and then the condition is checked are called exit controlled loops. They are also called post-tested loops e.g. : do-while.

15. Differentiate between finite and infinite loop.

Ans.

Finite loop	Infinite loop

Finite loop exits after a definite iteration.
It has an exit condition.
For example :
int c;
for(int i = 0; i < 10; i++)
{
    c = 7 * i;
    System.out.println(c);
}
	It executes infinite number of times.
	It does not have an exit condition.
	For example :
	int c;
	for(int i = 0; ; i++)
	{
	    c = 7 * i;
	    System.out.println(c);
	}

Chapter 2. Class as the Basis of all Computation

1. What is the difference between an object and a class ?

Ans. Class is a set of objects that shares common characteristics and behaviour. It is also known as an object factory or producer of objects.

Object is an identifiable entity with some characteristics and behaviour. It is also known as an instance of a class.

2. What is the difference between Primitive and User-Defined Data Types ?

Ans.

Primitive data types	User-Defined data types
(i) These are built-in data types. Java provides these data types.	(i) These data types are created by the users.
(ii) The sizes of these data types are fixed.	(ii) The sizes of these data types are variable as their sizes depend upon their constituent members.
(iii) These data types are available in all parts of a Java program.	(iii) The availability of these data types depend upon their scope.

Chapter 3. User - Defined Methods

1. Differentiate between call by value or pass by value and call by reference or pass by reference.

Ans.

Call by Value	Call by Reference
(i) The actual parameter are copied to the formal parameter.	(i) The actual parameters are not copied to the formal parameters. They are just referred to another name.
(ii) Memory is allocated separately for actual and formal parameters.	(ii) The memory is not allocated separately for actual and formal parameters.

2. Differentiate between pure and impure functions.

Ans. Pure functions are the functions which do not alter the state of an object received as a parameter.

e.g. :
```
int f1(int a)
{
        int b = a + 5;
        return(b);
}
```

Impure functions are the functions which alter the state of an object received as a parameter.

e.g. :
```
int f1(int a)
{
        a = a + 5;
```

```
    return(a);
  }
```

3. Differentiate between actual parameter and formal parameter.

Ans. The parameters specified in the method call are known as actual parameters and the parameters specified in the header of a function/method are called formal parameters.

Chapter 4. Constructors

1. Give a difference between a constructor and a method.

OR

Differentiate between constructor and function.

Ans.

Constructor	Method or Function
(i) Constructors have the same name as that of the class.	(i) Functions have different name than that of the class.
(ii) Constructors do not have a return type, not even void.	(ii) Functions have to a return type.
(iii) Constructors are called automatically at the time of object creation.	(iii) Functions need to be called.

Chapter 5. Library Classes

1. What are library classes ? Give an example.

Ans. The classes which are already built in java are called library classes. These classes are grouped together and stored in packages. Eg: Math, String, StringBuffer, Scanner etc.

2. Write the difference between length and length().

Ans. length is an attribute used with arrays which returns the number of elements present in it. length() is a function used with string objects which returns the number of characters present in it.

3. Write a difference between the functions isUpperCase() and toUpperCase().

Ans.

isUpperCase()	toUpperCase()
(i) This function is used to check whether a character is in upper case.	(i) This function is used to convert a character to upper case.
(ii) Return type is boolean.	(ii) Return type is char.

4. Differentiate between toLowerCase() and toUpperCase() methods.

Ans. toLowerCase() is used to change uppercase letters or a string into lowercase whereas toUpperCase() is just reverse of it.

5. What is the difference between the Scanner class functions next( ) and nextLine( ) ?

Ans.

next()	nextLine()
It is used to accept a string input without any space.	It is used to accept a string input with spaces.

Chapter 6. Encapsulation

1. Explain the different types of access specifiers.

Ans. Access specifier can be of following types :

(i) **Public :** The class members declared as public can be accessed outside the class definition.

(ii) **Private :** The class members declared as private cannot be accessed from outside the class, it is only accessed by the methods in the same class.

(iii) **Protected :** It means that the class members declared as protected can be accessed in the current class and in the methods of any subclasses.

2. Differentiate class variables, instance variables and local variables.

Ans. **Class variables :** These variables belong to class and not to the object. These variables have one copy in the memory, this copy is shared by all the objects of that class.

Instance variables : These variables are also declared inside the class. Each object has a different copy of an instance variable. Instance variables belong to the object.

Local variables : The variables declared inside a method block are called local variables.

3. What is the difference between a static and a non-static class ?

Ans. A static class is one which has the static modifier applied. Because, it is static, it must access the members of its enclosing class through an object. An inner class is a non-static nested class.

It has access to all of the variables and methods of its outer class and may refer to them directly in the same way that other non-static members of the outer class do.

4. Differentiate between public and private modifiers for members of a class.

Ans. Private members of a class are accessible only within the class. Keyword private is used to declare a member as private.

Public members of a class are available to all the classes of all the packages.

5. Differentiate between private and protected visibility modifiers.

Ans. Private is the most restricted access specifier which is accessible only in its own class.

Protected members are accessible by the classes of the same package or by a child class in any other package.

Chapter 7. Arrays

1. Differentiate between Binary Search and Linear Search.

Ans.

	Linear Search		Binary Search
(i)	Can be used in an unsorted array.	(i)	This takes place only in a sorted array. It may be in ascending or descending order and should be known to the programmer.
(ii)	(ii) The value is looked for in a sequence starting form the Ist element until it is searched or till the end of the array if it is not found.	(ii)	The middle subscript of the array is calculated. The value to be searched is compared with the middle positioned element. If element is less than the middle array element (Assume array in ascending order). The upper bound changes to get the middle value, so that the search now takes place only in the upper half of the array, or in the lower half of the array. The process is repeated until the value is found at the middle.
(iii)	This process takes more time when size of the array is large.	(iii)	This process takes less time.

2. Differentiate between searching and sorting.

Ans.

	Searching		Sorting
(i)	It is the process of checking whether the element is present in the array or not.	(i)	It is the process of arranging the data in ascending or descending order in the array.
(ii)	Examples of searching techniques are linear and binary search.	(ii)	Examples of sorting techniques are Selection sort, bubble sort, etc.

3. What is bubble sort ?

Ans. In bubble sort, each pair of adjacent data elements of the array are compared and elements are swapped if they are not in correct order.

4. What is the difference between text files and binary files ?

Ans. In text files, data are stored as per a specific character encoding scheme e.g., ASCII text or unicode text is stored.

In binary files, data are stored in the form of bytes that are in machine readable form.

Chapter 8. String Handling

1. What is the difference between equals() and compareTo() methods.

Ans. equals() methods gives true if both the strings are exactly the same otherwise gives false.

e.g. : String S1 = "Hello", S2 = "Hi", S3 = "Hello";

boolean b;

b = S1.equals(S2);

// value of b will be false.

b = S1.equals(S3);

// value of b will be true.

compareTo() : This function also checks strings for similarity.

This will return :

Zero : when both strings are the same.

Negative value : when first string is less than the second string.

Positive value : when second string is greater than the first string.

Example : System.out.println("Hello" compare to ("Hello"))// 0.

System.out.println("ABC".compareTo("XYZ")); // negative value.

System.out.println("XYZ".compareTo("ABC")); // positive.

Explanatory Based Questions

Chapter 1. Revision of Class IX Syllabus

1. What do you mean by type casting ?

Ans. Coversion of one type of data into another type is called type casting or type conversion.

Type casting is of two types :

(i) Implicit or automatic type casting : This type of conversions are performed by java automatically when any expression contains operands of different data types. The lower type values are counted into higher type values automatically. This is also called type promotion. The following table suggests the conversion with no loss of data.

From	Convert to
byte	short, char, int, long, float, double
short	int, long, float, double
char	int, long, float, double
int	long, float, double
long	float, double
float	double

e.g. : int x = 9;

double y = 2.8;

double z = x + y;

In this example, (x) is int type, whereas (y) is double. So int will be automatically casted to double. The result will be of double type. The value z will be 11.8.

(ii) Explicit type casting : In this type of conversion the values as type casted according to the user requirement. This conversion can be done by the following syntax : (type) expession.

Note : When large values are converted into smaller type, the result will be loss of data.

e.g. : int x = 5, y = 2;

double z;

z = (double) x /(double) y;

if the value of z is 2.5, without type casting it will give only 2.

2. What are comments ? Explain their usage and types.

Ans. Comments are non-executable lines of programs. Comments play a vital role in a program, they are used for the documentation purpose and to explain the purpose of a program, purpose of statements and variables. In commercial applications comments are used to explain each part of a program, to make a program easily understandable and modifiable. There are two types of comments available in java :

// (single line comment) : This will comment the line from // to the end of line.

/*.........

......*/ (multiple line comment) : When we want to comment more than one continuous line,

we can use it.

e.g.:

/* This is a Bluej program to give a sum of two numbers by Preeti */

public class sample

{

```
public static void main(String[] args)
{
        int n1, n2; // to store numbers to be add.
        int R; // to store the sum.
        n1 = 10;
        n2 = 20;
        R = n1 + n2;
        System.out.println("sum is" + R);
}
}
```

3. Explain different types of numeric constants. Also give examples.

Ans. There are two types of numeric constants :

(i) Integer constants

(ii) Real constants

(i) Integer constants refer to a sequence of digits.

   e.g. : 121, – 246, etc.

(ii) Real constants are inadequate to represent quantities that vary continuously, such as distance, heights, temp. and so on.

   e.g. : 0.47, 0.0064 etc.

4. Explain types of character constants with example.

Ans. There are two types of character constants :

(i) Single character constants   (ii) String constants

   Single character constants contain single characters within a pair of single quote marks.

   e.g. : '5', 'X' etc.

(ii) String constants are a sequence of characters enclosed between double quotes. The characters may be alphabets, numbers, special characters or blank spaces.

   e.g. : "Hello world", "1456", "?#$–+", etc.

5. Explain logical OR and logical AND operator.

Ans. Logical OR (||) : When two expresions are combined using || operator. The result will be true when either of the expressions is true, and the result will be false when all the expressions are false.

expn. 1	expn. 2	result
false	false	false
true	true	true
true	false	true
false	true	true.

Logical AND (&&) : This operator is used to combine two expressions. This will give true when all the expressions are true, but if any of the expression is false then the answer will be false.

Example 1	Example 2	Result
F	F	F
T	T	T
T	F	F
F	T	F

e.g. :

```
public class test
{
        public static void main(String[] args)
        {
```

```
                    int a = 10;
                    int b = 40;
                    boolean R;
                    R = a >= 5 && tb <= 100; // value of R will be true because both conditions are true.
                    System.out.println(R);
                    R = a > 50 && b <= 100; // value of R will be false because first condition is true.
                    System.out.println(R);
                    R = a == 5 || b == 10; value of R will be true because second condition is true.
                    System.out.println(R);
                    R = a == 5 || b > 15; // value of R will be true because second condition is true.
                    System.out.println(R);
                    R = a == 10 || b == 40; // value of R will be false because all conditions are true.
                    System.out.println(R);
            }
    }
```

6. Explain ternary operator. Give syntax with example.

Ans. Ternary operator is very similar to if else conditional statement. This operator checks for the condition, if the condition is true, expression 1 is executed else, expression 2 is executed.

Syntax : condition ? expression 1 : expression 2;

OR

Variable = condition ? expression 1 : expression 2

Example : int a = 5, b = 0;

b = (a > 3 ? a * a : a * a * a);

System.out.println(b);

In the above example if the value of variable a is greater than 3, the square of value of a will be assigned to b else cube of value of a will be assigned to b and b will be printed.

7. Explain the methods print() and println().

Ans. A computer program is written to manipulate a given set of data and to display or print the results. Java supports two output methods that can be used to send the results to the screen.

print() method

println() method

The print() method sends information into a buffer. This buffer is not flushed until a new line (or end-of-line) character is sent. As a result print() method prints output in one line.

The println() method, by contrast, takes the information provided and displays it in a line followed by a line feed.

8. Explain with an example the if-else-if construct.

Ans. if...else...if statement is used to make nested conditions :

When an if statement is placed within another if, it is known as a nested if else if structure.

Syntax :

```
    if (condition 1)
    {
            statements
    }
    else if(condition 2)
    {
            statements
    {
    else if(conditions 3)
```

```
        {
                statements
        }
        else
        {
                statements;
        }
```

e.g. :
```
public void check(int a, int b)
{
if (a > b)
System.out.println("First number is greater");
else if (a == b)
System.out.println("Both numbers are equal");
else
System.out.println("Second numbers is greater");
}
```

9. Explain the function of each of the following with an example :

break;

continue;

Ans. (i)   The break statement is a jump statement used to terminate a switch / for / while / do while statement.

e.g. :
```
class demo
{
        void findsum()
        {
        int i, sum = 0;
                for(i = 1;; i++)
                {
                        sum = sum + i;
                        if(sum > 50)
                        break;
                }
        System.out.println("Sum = " + sum);
        }
}
```

(ii) The continue statement transfers the control to the beginning of the loop and skips the rest of the loop body.
```
class odd
{
        void print()
        {
        int i;
                for(i = 1; i <= 50; i++)
                {
                        if(i % 2 == 0)
                        continue;
                System.out.println(i);
```

```
                    }
                }
        }
```

10. Explain, with the help of an example : The purpose of default in a switch statement.

Ans. In switch if none of the cases match the value of the expression, then the default statement is executed.

Example :

```
switch(choice)
{
        case 1 :
        System.out.print("x");
        break;
        case 2 :
        System.out.print("y");
        break;
        default :
        System.out.print("Invalid choice");
}
```

11. Explain the term for loop with an example.

Ans. For loop is used to repeat a statement block for a required number of times. In the example below, BlueJ will be displayed 10 times in different lines.

Example:

```
for(i = 1; i <= 10; i++)
{
        System.out.println("BlueJ");
}
```

12. Explain the term conditional branching.

Ans. When a program breaks the sequential flow and jumps to another part of the code it is called branching. When the branching is based on a particular condition it is known as conditional branching.

13. Explain how are programs executed sequentially ?

Ans. In a sequence construct, statements are being executed sequentially. Every java program execution begins with the first statement and after that each statement is executed/processed step by step.

14. Explain the method of program execution through selection.

Ans. Selection construct means the execution of statements depending upon condition test.

If the condition is true the statements after the conditions are executed otherwise another set of statements get executed.

15. Explain the concept of iteration.

Ans. Iteration means repeating a set of statements depending upon the condition. The statements inside the loop are executed till the condition is true.

16. Explain the statement if along with syntax ?

Ans. The if statement in java is a conditional branch statement. It can be used to route program execution through different paths.

Syntax : if (test condition)

statements;

e.g.:

```
int a = 15, b = 6;
if(a > b)
System.out.println(a);
```

Output : 15

17. Explain the switch statement with syntax ?

Ans. Java provides a multiple branch selection statement known as switch. This selection statement successively tests the value of an expression against a list of integer or character constants.

When a match is found, the statements associated with that constant are executed.

Syntax :

```
switch(choice variable)
{
case constant 1 :
statements;
break;
case constant 2 :
statements;
break
    .
    .
    .
    .
default :
statements;
}
```

18. Explain while statement with syntax ?

Ans. While loop is one of the java's most fundamental looping statement. This loop is also known as an entry control loop, which means it checks for the condition while entering inside the loop, if the condition is false no statements inside the loop are executed, and if the condition is true the statements inside the loop are executed.

Syntax :

```
while(condition)
{
        statements;
}
e.g. :
int a = 5;
while(a < = 10)
{
        System.out.println(a);
        a++;
}
```

Output :

```
5
6
7
8
9
10
```

19. Explain the do-while statement with syntax.

Ans. do - while statement is also a looping statement but it is not very similar to while statement.

This statement is also known as exit control loop, as it checks for the condition while moving out of the loop.

In this statement, the statement(s) inside the loop get executed at least once even if the condition is false. The loop continues for the number of times as specified by the programmer if the condition is true.

Syntax :

```
do
{
        statements;
}
while(condition);
```

e.g. :

```
int a = 5;
do
{
        System.out.println(a);
}
while(a <= 3);
```

Output : Since in the above statement the condition is false the loop will execute only once with output 5.

20. Explain for statement along with syntax ?

Ans. The for statement is the easiest to understand. In this statement all the elements are gathered in one place. The work of for statement is very similar to while statement.

Syntax :

```
for(initialization expression; test expression; update exp)
{
statements;
}
```

e.g. :

```
int a = 2;
        for(a = 2; a <= 10; a = a + 2)
        {
                System.out.println(a);
        }
```

Output :

2

4

6

8

10

21. Explain the working of break statement.

Ans. By using break statement, the programmer can force immediate termination of a loop. This statement can be used with any Java loop. This statement has 3 uses :

(i)   It terminates a statement sequence in a switch statement.

(ii) It can be used to exit a loop. When break is used inside nested loops, the break statement will only break out from the inner loop.

(iii) It can be used as a 'civilized' form of goto.

22. Explain the term nested loop ?

Ans. Loop within another loop is termed as nested loop. In nested loop the program first checks the outer loop condition, if the condition is true it enters the inner loop and does not return to the outer loop until the inner loop is executed completely. Nested loops can be the combination of for-for, for-while, for-do-while, do-while-while, etc.

Syntax :

```
Outer loop
{
statements;
        inner loop
        {
        statements;
        }
}
```

Chapter 3. User - Defined Methods

1. Explain function overloading with an example.

Ans. Function overloading is the process of using the same name for two or more methods, but with different signatures ,that is, with different number of arguments/type of arguments. Through this process Polymorphism is implemented.

e.g.

```
public class test
{
        public int sum(int a, int b, int c)
        {
                return a + b + c;
        }
        public int sum(int a, int b)
        {
                return a + b;
        }
        public static void main(String[] args)
        {
                test t = new test();
                int x = t.sum(2, 6, 90);
                :

                :

                :

                x = t.sum(4, 9);
        }
}
```

In the above example function sum() is overloaded. By the arguments, compiler will decide which function should be called.

2. Explain the function of a return statement.

Ans. return statement has two forms :

(i) return;

(ii) return value;

The first form is used to return from any method. It passes the program control back to its caller. Second form passes the control back to its caller and passes a value to its caller also.

3. Explain the definition of a function with syntax.

OR

Explain function declaration.

Ans. The general form of a function definition is given below :

Syntax :

[access specifier] [modifier] returntype function-name(parameter list)

```
{
    body of the function
}
```

Access specifier : can be either public or protected or private. These keywords are used to determine the type of access to the function.

Modifier : can be one of final, native, synchronized, transient, volatile. A final method means that the functionality defined inside this very method can never be changed.

Return type : specifies the type of value that the return statement of the function returns. It may be of any valid Java data type.

4. Define function prototype.

OR

Explain function prototype or signature.

Ans. Function prototype is one very useful feature of Java function. A function prototype describe the function interface to the compiler by giving details such as the number and type of arguments and the type of return values.

Thus, the prototype is a declaration of the function that tells the program about the type of the value returned by the function and the number and type of arguments.

Chapter 4. Constructors

1. Explain default constructors.

Ans. A default constructor is a method having same name as that of the class and have no parameter in it. If we do not explicitly define a constructor for a class, then Java creates a default constructor for the class. The default constructor is often sufficient for simple classes but not for sophisticated classes.

e.g.,

```
class distance
{
        int feet;
        int inch;
        public distance()
        {
                feet = 0;
                inch = 0;
        }
        void showdata()
        {
                System.out.println(feet + "feet and " + inch + "inches");
        }
}
public class testclass
{
        public static void main(String [] args)
        {
                distance d = new distance();
                d.showdata();
        }
```

}

In the above example, the statement distance d = new distance(); creates a new object and calls the default constructor.

2. Explain the concept of constructor overloading with an example.

Ans. Defining more than one constructor having the same name but different signatures is called constructor overloading.

e.g :

class Rectangle

{

       int l, b;

       public Rectangle()

       {

            l = b = 0;

       }

       public Rectangle(int x)

       {

            l = b = x;

       }

       public Rectangle(int l1, int b1)

       {

            l = l1;

            b = b1;

       }

}

Chapter 5. Library Classes

1. Explain the method to convert a string to lowercase().

Ans. This method converts all the characters in a string from upper case to lower case.

Syntax : String toLowerCase().

e.g. : String S = "HELLO HOW ARE YOU";

String low = S.toLowerCase();

Output : hello how are you

2. Explain the method toUpperCase().

Ans. This method converts all the characters in a string from lower case to upper case.

Syntax : String toUpperCase().

e.g. : String S = "hello how are you";

String up = S.toUpperCase();

Output : HELLO HOW ARE YOU

3. What are the benefits of organizing classes into packages ?

Ans. In packages, classes can be unique compared to other programs and can easily be reused. It logically combines (group) the similar classes under one name.

4. Mention the steps involved in creating our own package.

Ans. (i) Declare the package at the beginning of a file using the form package packagename.

(ii) Define the class that is to be put in the package and declare it in public.

(iii) Create a subdirectory under the directory where the main source files are stored.

(iv) Store the listing as the classname.class file in the subdirectory.

5. Explain the method of importing a package member.

Ans. To import a member of a package into the current file, put an import statement at the beginning of the file before any class definitions but after the package statement, if there is any.

Syntax : Import java.package name.class_name;

6. Describe the method to import an entire package.

Ans. To import all the classes contained in a particular package, use the import statement with an asterisk(*) wild card character.

e.g. :

import java.packagename.*;

Chapter 7. Arrays

1. How can arrays be initialized ?

Ans. Arrays can be initialized by providing the value list at the time of declaration.

For example :

char[] vowel = new char[] = {'a', 'e', 'i', 'o', 'u'};

Chapter 8. String Handling

1. Explain the term String classes in Java.

Ans. In Java, a string is a sequence of characters. But Java implements strings as object of class String. Implementing strings as built-in objects allows java to provide a full complement of features that make string handling convenient.

2. Define an Exception.

Ans. Exception in general refers to some contradictory or unusual situation which can be encountered at run time.

3. Explain the function of the following :

   (i)   String length;

   (ii) String concatination;

   (iii) String comparison;

Ans. (i)   String length() : The length of a string is the number of characters that it contains. To obtain this value, call the length() method shown below :

   int length();

   char a[] = {'a', 'b', 'c'};

   String s = new String(a);

   System.out.println(s.length());

   Output : 3

   (ii) String concatenation : concate() function concatenates two strings in java.

   e.g. :

   String years = "I am 5";

   String name = years.concat(" years old");

   System.out.println(name);

   Output : I am 5 years old.

   (iii) String Comparison : The string class included compareTo() function that compares strings or sub strings within strings.

   To compare two strings for equality we use compareTo() function.

   e.g. :

   int equals(object str);

Where str is the string object being compared with the invoking string objects. It returns 0 if the string contains same character, else return negative or positive integer.

4. Explain the method replace().

Ans. Method replace() is used to replace all occurrances of one character in the invoking string with another character.

It has the following general form :

String replace(char original, char replacement);

e.g. :

string P = "engineer"

replace('e', 'k');

The result string will be : knginkkr

5. Explain the method trim().

Ans. Method trim() returns a copy of the invoking string from which any leading and trailing white spaces has been removed.

Syntax : String trim();

e.g. : String S = " Hello world ".trim();

The above statement puts the string "Hello World" in S by removing leading and trailing spaces.

6. Explain the use of the following functions :

(a) charAt()   (b) indexof()   (c) concat()

Ans. (a) charAt() : This fucntion returns the character present at the specified index.

Syntax : String.charAt(index);

e.g. : char a;

a = "computer".charAt(2);

value of a will be m.

(b) indexof() : This function searches the specified character in the string, if it is found then return its index, otherwise gives –1.

Syntax : String.indexOf(character);

e.g. : int i;

i = "computer".indexOf('P');

value of i will be 3.

(c) Concat : This function is used to concatenate Strings.

Syntax : String.concat(String 2)

e.g. : String A = "Hello";

String B = A.concat(" Friends");

Value of B will be "Hello Friends"

●●

ICSE Solved Paper 2020

(THEORY)

(Two Hours)

Answers to this Paper must be written on the paper provided separately.

*You will **not** be allowed to write during the first **15** minutes.*

This time is to be spent in reading the question paper.

The time given at the head of this Paper is the time allowed for writing the answers.

This paper is divided into two Sections.

*Attempt **all** questions from **Section A** and **any four** questions from **Section B**.*

The intended marks for questions or parts of questions are given in brackets [].

SECTION-A (40 Marks)

*Attempt **all** questions*

Question 1.

(a) *Define Java byte code.* [2]

(b) *Write a difference between class and an object.* [2]

(c) *Name the following:* [2]

    (i) *The keyword which converts variable into constant.*

    (ii) *The method which terminates the entire program from any stage.*

(d) *Which of the following are primitive data types?* [2]

    (i) *double*   **(ii)** *String*

    (iii) *Char*   **(iv)** *Integer*

(e) *What is an operator? Name any two types of operators used in Java.* [2]

Answer 1.

(a) It is a machine instruction for java processor chip called JVM.

(b) Class is a set of objects that shares common characteristics and behaviour whereas object is an instance of a class.

(c) **(i)** final

    (ii) System.exit(0)

(d) (i) double , char are primitive datatypes.

(e) Operator is a symbol which specifies the type of operation to be performed on the operands.

    Ex: Arithmetic Operator (+,-,*,/,%) or Relational operator(>,<,>=,<=, ==, !=) etc.

Question 2.

(a) *What is autoboxing in Java? Give an example.* [2]

(b) *State the difference between length and length() in Java.* [2]

(c) *What is constructor overloading?* [2]

(d) *What is the use of import statement in Java?* [2]

(e) *What is an infinite loop? Give an example.* [2]

Answer 2.

(a) Converting primitive types to corresponding wrapper class object is called Autoboxing.

    For eg: int to Integer, double to Double type etc.

(b) Length is a variable used with arrays to find its size whereas length() is a function used with Strings to determine the no. of characters present in it.

    If arr[] = {1,2,3,4,5} then arr.length will return 5.

    If s="JAVA" the s.length() will return 4.

(c) Defining more than one constructors having same name but different signature is called constructor overloading.

```
class Overload
{
    String s;
    public Overload()
    {
        s="DPC Jhansi";
    }
    public Overload( String s1)
    {
        s=s1;
    }
}
```

(d) Import keyword is used to include predefined classes and functions in our program which are available in java.

    import java.util.*; will include all the classes of util package in our program.

(e) Non terminating loop whose test condition is always true is called infinite loop.

```
for(i=1 ; i > 0 ; i++)
{
    System.out.println("This is Infinite Loop");
}
```

Question 3.

(a) *Write a Java expression for the following:* [2]

$$\sqrt{b^2 - 4ac}$$

(b) *Evaluate the following if the value of x = 7, y = 5* **[2]**

$x += x++ + x+ ++ y$

(c) *Write the output for the following:*

String s1 = ''Life is Beautiful'';

System.out.println (''Earth'' + s1.substring(4));

System.out.println(s1.endsWith(''L'')); **[2]**

(d) *Write the output of the following statement:*

System.out.println(''A picture is worth \t \''A thousand words.\'' ''); **[2]**

(e) *Give the output of the following program segment and mention how many times the loop will execute:* **[2]**

int k;

for (k = 5 ; k < = 20; k += 7)

if (k% 6==0)

continue;

System.out.println (k);

(f) *What is the data type returned by the following library methods?* **[2]**

(i) *isWhitespace()*

(ii) *compareToIgnoreCase()*

(g) *Rewrite the following program segment using logical operators:* **[2]**

if (x > 5)

if (x > y)

System.out.println (x+y);

(h) *Convert the following **if else if** construct into **switch case:*** **[2]**

if (ch== 'c' || ch=='C')

System.out.print(''COMPUTER'');

else if (ch== 'h' || ch=='H')

System.out.print(''HINDI'');

else

System.out.print(''PHYSICAL EDUCATION'');

(i) *Give the output of the following:* **[2]**

(i) *Math.pow (36,0.5) + Math.cbrt (125)*

(ii) *Math.ceil (4.2) + Math.floor (7.9)*

(j) *Rewrite the following using ternary operator:* **[2]**

if(n1>n2)

r = true;

else

r = false;

Answer 3.

(a) Math.sqrt(b*b – 4*a*c)

(b) x = 28 , y = 6

(c) Earth is Beautiful

false

(d) A picture is worth   " A thousand words."

(e) Loop will execute 3 times output 19.

(f) **(i)** boolean

(ii) int

(g) if(x > 5 && x > y)

System.out.println(x + y) ;

(h) switch(ch)

{

case 'c' :

case 'C' : System.out.print(" COMPUTER ") ;

break;

case 'h' :

case 'H' : System.out.print(" HINDI") ;

break;

default: System.out.print

("PHYSICAL EDUCATION") ;

}

(i) **(i)** 6.0 + 5.0 = 11.0

(ii) 5.0 + 7.0 = 12.0

(j) r = n1 > n2 ? true : false ;

SECTION-B (60 Marks)

*Attempt **any four** questions from this Section.*

The answers in this Section should consist of the

Programs in either

Blue J environment or any program environment with Java as the base.

Each program should be written using

Variable descriptions/Mnemonic Codes

so that the logic of the program is clearly depicted.

*Flow-Charts and Algorithms **are not required**.*

Question 4.

A private Cab service company provides service within the city at the following rates: **[15]**

	AC CAR	NON AC CAR
Up to 5 Km	₹150/-	₹120/-
Beyond 5 Km	₹ 10/- Per Km	₹ 08/- Per Km

*Design a class **CabService** with the following description:*

Member variables /data members:

String Car-type   :   To store the type of car (AC or NON AC)

double km   :   To store the kilometer travelled

double bill   :   To calculate and store the bill amount

Member methods :

CabService()   –   Default constructor to initialize data members.

String data members to '' '' and double data members to 0.0.

void accept() – To accept *car_type* and *km* (using Scanner class only).

void calculate() – To calculate the bill as per the rules given above.

void display() – To display the bill as per the following format

CAR TYPE:

KILOMETER   TRAVELLED:

TOTAL BILL:

Create an object of the class in the main method and invoke the member methods.

Answer 4.

```
import java.util.*;
class CabServices
{
    String car_type;
    double km,bill;
    public CabServices()
    {
        car_type="";
        km=bill=0.0;
    }
    void accept()
    {
        Scanner sc = new Scanner(System.in);
        System.out.println("Enter Car Type and
                               no. of Km");
        car_type=sc.nextLine();
        km=sc.nextDouble();
    }
    void calculate()
    {
        if(car_type.equalsIgnoreCase("AC"))
        {
            if(km<=5)
            {
                bill=150;
            }
            else
            {
            bill=150 + (km – 5) * 10;
            }
        }
        else if(car_type.equalsIgnoreCase("NON
                               AC"))
        {
            if(km<=5)
            {
                bill=120
            }
            else
            {
                bill=120 + (Km – 5) * 8;
            }
        }
        else
        {
            System.out.println("Wrong Type");
        }
    }
    void display()
    {
        System.out.println("CAR TYPE :
                               " + car_type);
        System.out.println("KILOMETER
                       TRAVELLED : " + km);
        System.out.println("TOTAL BILL :
                               " + bill);
    }
}
```

Question 5.

Write a program to search for an integer value input by the user in the sorted list given below using **binary** *search technique. If found display ''Search Successful'' and print the element, otherwise display ''Search Unsuccessful''* **[15]**

{31, 36, 45, 50, 60, 75, 86, 90}

Answer 5.

```
import java.util.*;
class Search
{
    int A[]={31,36,45,50,60,75,86,90};
    int n,low,high,mid,flag=0;
    void display()
    {
        low=0;
        high=A.length-1;
        Scanner sc=new Scanner(System.in);
        System.out.println("Enter a no.");
        n=sc.nextInt();
        while(low<=high)
        {
            mid=(low+high)/2;
            if(n>A[mid])
```

```
        {
            low=mid+1;
        }
        else if(n<A[mid])
        {
            high=mid-1;
        }
        else
        {
            flag=1;
            break;
        }
    }
    if(flag==1)
    {
        System.out.println("Search
                Successful"+n+"Found");
    }
    else
    {
        System.out.println("Search
                Unsuccessful ");
    }
  }
}
```

Question 6.

*Write a program to input a **sentence** and convert it into uppercase and display each word in a separate line.* **[15]**

Example: Input : India is my country
Output : INDIA
IS
MY
COUNTRY

Answer 6.

```
import java.util.*;
class Sentence
{
    String s,w;
    int i,l;
    public Sentence()
    {
        s="Destination Point Computers";
    }
    void display()
    {
    Scanner sc=new Scanner(System.in);
    System.out.println("Enter a Sentence");
    s=sc.nextLine();
    s=s.toUpperCase();
    s=s+" ";
    l=s.length();
    for(i=0;i<l;i++)
    {
```

```
        w="";
        while(s.charAt(i)!=' ')
        {
            w=w+s.charAt(i);
            i++;
        }
        System.out.println(w);
    }
  }
}
```

Answer 7.

```
class Overload
{
  void Number(int num,int d)
  {
    int c=0,d1;
    while(num>0)
    {
        d1=num%10;
        if(d1==d)
        {
            c++;
        }
        num=num/10;
    }
    System.out.println("Frequency of digit " + d
                + " = " + c);
  }
void Number(int n1)
{
int d,s=0;
while(n1>0)
{
    d=n1%10;
    if(d%2==0)
    {
        s=s+d;
    }
    n1=n1/10;
}
System.out.println("Sum of Even Digits = " + s);
}
}
```

Question 7.

Design a class to overload a method number( ) as follows : **[15]**

(i) *void Number (int num,*   – *To count and*
    int d)   *display the frequency of a digit in a number.*

Example:
num = 2565685
d = 5
Frequency of digit 5 = 3

(ii) void Number — To find and
(int n1) display the sum
of even digits of
a number.

Example:
n1 = 29865
Sum of even digits = 16

Write a main method to create an object and invoke the above methods.

Question 8.

Write a menu driven program to perform the following operations as per user's choice: **[15]**

(i) *To print the value of $c = a^2 + 2ab$, where **a** varies from **1.0** to **20.0** with increment of **2.0** and b = **3.0** is a constant.*

(ii) *To display the following pattern using **for** loop:*

A
AB
ABC
ABCD
ABCDE

Display proper message for an invalid choice.

Answer 8.

```java
import java.util.*;
class Menu
{
    int ch;
    double a,b=3.0,c;
    char :i,j;
    void display()
    {
        Scanner sc=new Scanner(System.in);
        System.out.println("1. Value of c");
        System.out.println("2. Pattern");
        System.out.println("Enter Your Choice");
        ch=sc.nextInt();
        if(ch==1)
        {
            for(a=1.0;a<=20.0;a=a+2)
            {
                c=a*a + 2*a*b;
                System.out.println(c);
            }
        }
        else if(ch==2)
        {
            for(i='A';i<='E';i++)
            {
                for(j='A';j<=i;j++)
                {
                    System.out.print(j);
                }
                System.out.println();
            }
        }
        else
        {
            System.out.println("Wrong Choice");
        }
    }
}
```

Question 9.

*Write a program to input and store integer elements in a double dimensional array of size **3 × 3** and find the **sum** of elements in the left diagonal.*   **[15]**

Example :

1	3	5
4	6	8
9	2	4

Output: Sum of the left diagonal elements = (1 + 6 + 4) = 11

Answer 9.

```java
import java.util.*;
class Matrix
{
    int A[][]=new int[3][3];
    int i,j,s=0;
    void display()
    {
        Scanner sc=new Scanner(System.in);
        for(i=0;i<3;i++)
        {
            for(j=0;j<3;j++)
            {
                System.out.println("Enter a no.");
                A[i][j]=sc.nextInt();
            }
        }
        for(i=0;i<3;i++)
        {
            for(j=0;j<3;j++)
            {
                if(i == j)
                {
                    s=s + A[i][j];
                }
            }
        }
        System.out.println("Sum of the left diagonal
                           elements = " + s);
    }
}
```

●●